Mosquito Pathfinder

Mosquito Pathfinder

The Combat and Operations, Loss and Excavation of a WW2 Low-Level Target Marker

Steve Crump

AIR WORLD

First published in Great Britain in 2025 by
Pen & Sword Military
An imprint of
Pen & Sword Books Ltd
Yorkshire - Philadelphia

Copyright © Steve Crump, 2025

ISBN 978 1 03613 433 4

The right of Steve Crump to be identified as the Author of this work has been asserted by him in accordance with the Copyright, Designs and Patents Act 1988.

A CIP catalogue record for this book is available from the British Library.

All rights reserved. No part of this book may be reproduced, transmitted, downloaded, decompiled or reverse engineered in any form or by any means, electronic or mechanical including photocopying, recording or by any information storage and retrieval system, without permission from the Publisher in writing. No part of this book may be used or reproduced in any manner for the purpose of training artificial intelligence technologies or systems.

Typeset in INDIA by IMPEC eSolutions
Printed and bound in the England by CPI Group (UK) Ltd, Croydon, CRO 4YY

The Publisher's authorised representative in the EU for product safety is Authorised Rep Compliance Ltd., Ground Floor, 71 Lower Baggot Street, Dublin D02 P593, Ireland.
www.arccompliance.com

For a complete list of Pen & Sword titles please contact

PEN & SWORD BOOKS LIMITED
47 Church Street, Barnsley, South Yorkshire, S70 2AS, England
E-mail: enquiries@pen-and-sword.co.uk
Website: www.pen-and-sword.co.uk

or

PEN AND SWORD BOOKS
1950 Lawrence Rd, Havertown, PA 19083, USA
E-mail: uspen-and-sword@casematepublishers.com
Website: www.penandswordbooks.com

Dedication

This book could not have been written were it not for my wife Claire, who allowed me to shirk my duties in the kitchen and more often than not my opting out of walking our Cockapoo Tilly. Interest and support from our son James, daughter Rhiannon and some of our closest friends kept me going through a period of unexpected poor health, which has now thankfully been resolved; it would have been very easy to give up.

I dedicate this work with love, respect and thanks to them and the 'many' in Bomber Command.

Contents

Foreword ix

Acknowledgements xi

Chapter 1	'It Came Down at Night'	1
Chapter 2	Aerial Bombing – A Brief History	5
Chapter 3	The Structure of Bomber Command Operational Units	8
Chapter 4	Bomber Command – The Commanders	11
Chapter 5	The Bomber Command Offensive Against Nazi Germany 1939–45	13
Chapter 6	The Pathfinder Man	34
Chapter 7	The Pathfinders	39
Chapter 8	Training Civilians for War	47
Chapter 9	The Pathfinder Mosquitos	52
Chapter 10	The Battle of the Beams	56
Chapter 11	Bombs and Target Indicators	61
Chapter 12	The Defence of Germany	66
Chapter 13	Germany Under the Bombs	71
Chapter 14	Mosquito Mk IV DZ477 with 139 'Jamaica' Squadron – February to March 1943	73
Chapter 15	DZ477 – War Diary 1943	79

Chapter 16	DZ477 AZ:K with 627 Squadron – January to April 1944	86
Chapter 17	DZ477 – War Diary 1944	106
Chapter 18	RAF Woodhall Spa	145
Chapter 19	Mosquito Crew Trainer	199
Chapter 20	The Men of Mosquito DZ477	201
Chapter 21	Why Did DZ477 'Come Down at Night'?	260
Bibliography		265
Index		268

Foreword

Certain aircraft, for those of us so minded, occupy a special place in history, not to mention hearts, minds, and popular culture. One such is the twin-engined de Havilland Mosquito – the renowned 'Wooden Wonder'.

Surely, no schoolboy growing up in the 1960s could have failed to be both inspired by Director Walter Grauman's 1964 cinematic epic *633 Squadron*, in which surviving Mosquitos flashed by our screens during high-speed, low-level, attacks, or Boris Segal's 1969 offering, *Mosquito Squadron*, echoing Operation *Jericho*, when French resistance prisoners were freed after Mossies broke open Amiens jail. Exciting stuff! More than this, though, for the wartime generations the Mosquito was not just an aviation icon of popular culture.

Largely built of wood and powered by twin Rolls-Royce Merlin engines, the Mosquito forged a legend in war-torn skies all over the world. The fast and high-flying Mosquito performed outstandingly as a night fighter, reconnaissance aircraft and low-level bomber. It struck at enemy shipping and more besides, including the famed 'Pathfinder' role. Flying in the van of Bomber Command's heavy bomber formations, the nimble Mosquitos would mark the target with various coloured flares, guiding the bomber stream to unleash maximum destruction. This was both specialised and dangerous work, the stories of the Pathfinder Force enough to quicken the pulse getting on for a century later.

Like that other wartime icon, the Supermarine Spitfire, countless words have been written about the Wooden Wonder and those who went to war in this very special aircraft. In this new book, Steve Crump takes a refreshing look at the big picture – context being all – walking us through, in simple language, the chronology and rationale of the bombing war, the story of Bomber Command, and, Pathfinder Force. Then, the author focusses upon one particular Mosquito: DZ477, exploring the history of this particular machine and the men who flew her. The reader may ask 'Why DZ477?'.

Ultimately, DZ477 perished in a training accident close to the author's one-time Herefordshire home. Knowledge of this incident sparked a lifelong interest, and Steve, interested in 'aviation archaeology' investigated the crash site and recovered certain items from the wreck. These tangible links to the violent past signposted Steve on a life-changing journey, to research the aircraft's story and trace the surviving aircrew connected with the story. Forty years ago, therefore, Steve then a young man, had the foresight to invest his own time and resources in finding survivors and recording their memories – this providing the rich tapestry of human experiences punctuating this book. The cold facts and figures, the operational records, are all readily accessible to all – but sadly very few wartime Mosquito men now survive, making the accounts Steve collated unique. Having known Steve since his journey began, I know that his heart and soul have been invested in this project – now set before you, esteemed reader, as a Pen & Sword book.

Suffice it to say, I commend both this book and the author to you – and hope to see more from Steve Crump's pen in the future …

Dilip Sarkar MBE, FRHistS, FRAeS, BA(Hons), 2024

Acknowledgements

It is difficult to thank the kind individuals, sadly no longer with us but during our many conversations and items of correspondence they knew how grateful I was. So many letters from Bomber Command veterans including Bill Horsman, Jack 'Benny' Goodman, Jim Marshallsay, Bill De Boos and Ron Eels proved to be a goldmine of personal memories and reflections prompted by retirement. One man in particular was incredibly productive but could not control his printer so in frustration he would simply cram the bundle of A4 sheets into an envelope and send them to me. I looked forward to receiving the bulging envelopes and I was happy and grateful to sort the reams of paper into order. In every case, his letters and documents were full of experiences and insights into the world of Bomber Command, and in particular his world.

Benny Goodman was truly inspirational, not only identifying why DZ477 crashed but also providing many wonderful examples of life and death in Mosquitos. Benny was patient, generous and always ready to help; it is not surprising that he became much in demand as a Mosquito 'expert' for all sorts of events and publications. Jim Marshallsay and Bill De Boos were also incredibly friendly, supportive and fascinating. It was not always a one way flow of information as I was delighted to help some of these men regain contact with their former colleagues by providing addresses and so on; not so easy these days … I know that a forwarded address prompted Bill and Sheila to come to the UK specifically to visit a reunion with former comrades.

My wife Claire and I were delighted to spend a few days with them in Hereford.

I will always be grateful to my old friend Dilip Sarkar MBE for his inspiration, advice and foreword. Dilip started my aviation history interest when he located former Polish Spitfire pilot Kaz Budzik in the mid-1980s during research for his book *The Invisible Thread*. Kaz and I met several times and I continue to remember him with respect and fondness.

I would like to express sincere gratitude to my Pen & Sword adviser John Grehan for his patience and advice; he has been invaluable to the whole process; thank you John.

In conclusion, this account is a small part of a much bigger picture but nevertheless it's a story of heroism and dedication and without these men and women this story could not have been written and memories of this pivotal period of the war lost forever. Thanks, admiration and sincere respect to all of you.

Steve Crump, October 2024

Chapter 1

'It Came Down at Night'

On the evening of Monday, 15 August 1944, Warrant Officer Claud Evered Cook and his navigator, Sergeant John Hartley, took off in Mosquito Mk IV DZ477 from RAF Warboys in Cambridgeshire to conduct a night cross-country exercise as part of the training syllabus with 1655 Mosquito Training Unit. The unit provided pilots and navigators with the skills, training and experience prior to facing the challenge and responsibility of taking the Mosquito over occupied Europe.

Having left Warboys, Cook and Hartley had been airborne for nearly three and a half hours and conducted a change of course heading above the countryside of south-west Hereford at one minute to midnight but the manoeuvre caused the pilot to become disorientated. Having lost control of the aircraft, the crew bailed out and landed by parachute in a field close to RAF Madley. They were detained at the station sick quarters with minor injuries but were later transferred to the RAF Hospital Credenhill, north-west of Hereford.

The pilotless aircraft continued its course over the countryside and gradually descended, passing trees and the farm buildings of Leys Farm in Grafton Lane, Hereford. Local farmer James (Jim) Morgan had decided to retire to his bed and was about to close his bedroom curtains when, unbelievably an aircraft streaked past the window. Jim clearly saw flames flashing from the side of the aircraft as it continued beyond the farmhouse. The aircraft crossed several fields and crashed to earth when its starboard wing struck a tree on the perimeter of the field alongside the A49 Hereford to Ross-on-Wye road. The impact caused the aircraft to slew to the right and immediately dive into the ground. It exploded and started a large conflagration that spread rapidly to a nearby orchard. Despite the late hour, and without the knowledge of his parents, a local resident, a young boy of about 9 years' old cycled to the location to investigate the explosion. He recalled in 1990 that he saw a sea of flames but was prevented from progressing further by uniformed servicemen, possibly United States Military Policemen that were stationed nearby and often referred to as 'Snowdrops' owing to their use of white helmets.

The premature grounding of the aircraft may well have prevented a disaster as a short distance from the impact point and on the aircraft's flight path was the Royal Ordnance Factory at Rotherwas, employing hundreds of men and women filling bomb cases with explosive materials on a twenty-four-hour shift system. It is possible that a greater altitude of the aircraft could have caused utter devastation and considerable loss of life had it impacted within the vast complex. Apparently, the crash was not reported by local newspapers and remained forgotten for over forty years; the Morgan farming family, however, continued to turn up wreckage during crop preparations.

The incident first came to my notice in 1990 when I browsed through a copy of the de Havilland Mosquito Crash Log compiled by David J. Smith, where, to my surprise at the bottom of page 21 I discovered the entry for the loss of DZ477. A week or so later my enquiry for information was printed in the *Hereford Times* and later that Thursday evening I received a telephone call from Colin Morgan, the owner of Leys Farm. He explained the circumstances as he understood it and asked if I was interested in digging up the remains. However, I asked him to wait until I had received a licence to excavate the site. Excavation was granted and we planned the dig to coincide when Colin next harvested his crops. On 29 August 1990 a mechanical digger was on site and our small team began to lift the soil in the close proximity to the tree struck by DZ477; it was flourishing but still bore the scars of the impact. We did not expect to discover anything of substantial size as I was certain that the inferno had cremated the wooden airframe; we did, however, find fragments of molten aluminium and glass. We discovered one piece of wood that revealed the aircraft fuselage paint schemes of layers of grey, green and black. One decent piece of Merlin engine was recovered, which was later preserved for me by the RAF Museum restoration experts at Cardington. The recovered items were enough to fill three shoe boxes, and these had to be photographed and listed in a report for the Ministry of Defence. On 9 October I received a reply stating that title of the items and property was transferred from the Crown to me and I could therefore consider the items to be my property! Was I now the proud owner of a Mosquito?

Following the dig, my wife Claire and I took several days' annual leave to visit the Public Record Office, now the National Archive, at Kew armed only with pencils and pieces of paper in order to copy longhand the Operational Record Books entries for the aircraft and squadrons. The additional experience of holding Guy Gibson's logbook without the use of gloves raised the hairs on the back of my neck. With the full list obtained, I decided to explore one raid in particular, the attack of 4–5 July 1944 on the V-1 storage caves at Saint-Leu-d'Esserent, north-west of Paris, so we recorded the details of the entire bomber force sent that night.

My request for information published in *FlyPast* magazine started a steady stream of letters from squadron association members, which included information, anecdotes, photographs and some one-off signed mementoes from former Dambusters. Former 627 Squadron personnel Benny Goodman, Jim Marshallsay and Bill De Boos sent me photographs, photocopies and reams of paper describing their experiences. A telephone conversation with former 627 Squadron crew chief Doug Garton was fascinating as we chatted for over an hour discussing his memories and in particular the night Guy Gibson was killed; I will keep the nature of our conversation private!

In hindsight, it was fortuitous that the arrival of our children, James and Rhiannon, in 1989 and 1993 and the changes in my working career caused the box files and photographs to be closed for thirty years before being reopened in March 2023, when retirement prompted another look.

Chapter 2

Aerial Bombing – A Brief History

The desire of people to fight with one another led to the development of aerial warfare, with the ancient Chinese using kites as a method to gather military intelligence. By the third century, warfare had progressed to the use of balloons. After the Wright Brothers' first powered flight on 17 December 1903, influential leaders took opportunities to develop the value of using aircraft for reconnaissance purposes, with the first military aircraft being introduced in 1909. Two years later the French Army found that aeroplanes could accurately find enemy positions up to 37 miles away and could even be used for aerial combat to shoot down opposing reconnaissance planes.

Born in 1869, the Italian Giulio Douhet was an air power theorist and a proponent of strategic bombing. When the First World War began in 1914, he urged Italy to begin a military aircraft build-up in order to gain command of the air to render an enemy harmless. The Italian government ignored Douhet's proposals and when Italy entered the war in 1915 he sent a memorandum to the cabinet outlining his shock at how incompetent and unprepared the Italian military were. Subsequently, Douhet was court-martialled and imprisoned for one year for criticising Italian military leaders. However, he remained unbowed and continued to write about air power from within his cell. Having been exonerated in 1920 and promoted to general in 1921, he completed his influential treatise on strategic bombing called *The Command of the Air*. The principle later called 'The bomber will always get through', was based on the belief that bombers would deliver a knockout blow, destroying the enemy's war production, and the targeting of civilians would reduce morale, prompting them to rise up against their own government for failing to defend them.

Early military airmen had used revolvers to shoot at one another and also took the opportunity to drop grenades on enemy positions, which was ineffective. However, improved aircraft design and the addition of weapon systems required trained pilots and a second airman to shoot down enemy aircraft. This reduced the manoeuvrability and speed of the aircraft, but although First World War aircraft were slow, they were stable in flight. This facilitated the new technology of photography in order to map fixed enemy positions such as trenches, gun emplacements, munitions dumps, and communications hubs. Designs were developed to include the placement of a gun immediately in front of the pilot, who could now manage both jobs and simply aim the plane directly towards the target and fire the gun. Aircraft technology of 1918 consisted of wooden biplanes with canvas skins, wire rigging and air-cooled engines, and it was not until the late 1930s that the introduction of metal-framed monoplanes with stressed skins and liquid-cooled engines became common. The capacity for vastly increased speeds and altitudes and, more importantly, longer ranges and increased bomb payloads, began to dictate the use of aircraft for strategic bombing during the Second World War. Some theorists thought that a war would be won entirely by the destruction of the enemy's military and industrial capability from the air.

The Luftwaffe air attacks against British cities after the German air forces failed to gain air superiority over Fighter Command during the Battle of Britain prompted the British to start a strategic bombing campaign in 1940 that was to last for the rest of the war. Military aviation development accelerated, with Nazi Germany ultimately developing the first short-range ballistic missiles, prompting the RAF to strike development, storage and launch sites of these 'weapons of terror'. After the war, ballistic missiles became of key importance during the Cold War when the superpowers of the United States and the Soviet Union stockpiled missiles armed with nuclear warheads, forcing a state of checkmate with each deterring the other from using them. Twenty-first-century technology and changes to the physical battlefront has almost brought air warfare to a full circle, with modern, unmanned drones used as reconnaissance and weapons delivery platforms often operated by 'pilots' situated thousands of miles from the battlefront in an almost computer game scenario. The real-time data and video links providing high-definition images has transformed the bombing capability together with the capacity to gather live 'intel' on enemy movements; something the ancient Chinese did thousands of years ago using kites.

Chapter 3

The Structure of Bomber Command Operational Units

The Second World War began with Bomber Command operations divided into groups:

1 Group. Reforming on 22 June 1940, it was sent to France and then returned to Bomber Command control after the evacuation of France.

2 Group. Consisted of light and medium bombers operating by day and night and remained part of Bomber Command until 1943. It was reallocated to the control of Second Tactical Air Force to form its light bomber component.

3 Group. Reformed on 1 May 1936 as 3 (Bomber) Group.

4 Group. Reformed on 1 April 1937 as 4 (Bomber) Group but was transferred to Transport Command on 7 May 1945, and disbanded on 2 February 1948.

5 Group. Reformed on 1 September 1937 as 5 (Bomber) Group based at RAF Grantham for most of the war but was disbanded on 15 December 1945.

6 Group. Transferred as 1 (Air Defence Group) on 14 July 1936 and renamed 6 (Bomber) Group on 1 January 1939. Reformed as part of the Royal Canadian Air Force on 25 October 1942, it was unique among Bomber Command groups as it was not an RAF unit; it was a Canadian unit attached to Bomber Command. It was disbanded on 31 August 1945.

7 Group. Reformed on 15 July 1940 as 7 (Operational Training) Group, Bomber Command, it was renamed 92 Group on 11 May 1942 and reformed on 1 November 1944 to control Heavy Conversion Units until disbanded on 21 December 1945.

8 Group. Reformed as 8 (Bomber) Group on 1 September 1941, it was disbanded on 28 January 1942 but returned as 8 Pathfinder Force on 13 January 1943 and became a critical part of solving the navigational and aiming problems experienced at the time by Bomber Command. New electronic navigation aids such as Oboe, GEE and H2S were used by the Pathfinders, helping them to become an elite, specially trained and experienced force that flew ahead of the main force to mark the routes and targets with flares and special marker bombs. It was disbanded on 15 December 1945.

Bomber Command Headquarters oversaw a highly centralised and controlled bombing offensive using Groups to ensure the squadron crews were briefed in raid technicalities according to Bomber Command instructions. The stations provided the ongoing support to keep the squadron operational and the squadrons provided the administration and aircraft maintenance. The rapid expansion of Bomber Command during 1942 and 1943 increased the strain on the organisation and administration, so it was reorganised into the Bomber Operational Base System in March 1943 to add another level between Group Headquarters and the stations. Several small bases became the responsibility of one group captain station commander on a larger station, allowing a centralised administration and maintenance service and reducing the smaller base squadrons to flying and basic servicing capabilities only. Each station usually hosted two flying squadrons under a wing commander and normally comprised two or three flights, each equipped with approximately eight aircraft, with a squadron leader in charge.

Chapter 4

Bomber Command – The Commanders

Bomber Command was formed on 14 July 1936 with headquarters in Hillingdon House at RAF Uxbridge under the command of the Air Officer Commanding-in-Chief of Bomber Command, Sir Edgar Ludlow-Hewitt.

In April 1940, Air Marshal Sir Charles Portal replaced Ludlow-Hewitt and, at 46 years of age, the quiet but likeable man was relatively young when he was appointed as Commander in Chief, Bomber Command. Portal became committed to using Bomber Command to its full capacity in order to destroy Nazi Germany but the disastrous daylight operation against the German Fleet at Kristiansand in April saw him wisely restrict Hampdens and Wellingtons to night operations along with the Whitleys. Portal took office as Chief of the Air Staff in October 1940 with the temporary rank of Air Chief Marshal (made permanent in April 1942). He remained at his post for the duration of the war and in January 1944 he was advanced to the highest rank of Marshal of the RAF.

Portal's successor was Air Marshal Sir Richard E.C. Peirse, appointed in October 1940, and during his fourteen months at High Wycombe, Peirse presided over the expansion of the bomber force and the introduction of the Stirling, Manchester and Halifax bombers, which despite their promise, failed to live up to expectations. It was a difficult transition from a poorly equipped force into the heavy bomber force that his successor Sir Arthur Harris would take to victory. Towards the end of 1941, and alarmed at the growing losses suffered by the Command, Portal became increasingly dissatisfied with Peirse's performance as Commander in Chief, so he posted him to command the Allied Air Forces in South East Asia. Following the exit of Peirse, Air Vice Marshal 'Jack' Baldwin, the commander of 3 Group, acted as caretaker until the new leader took over.

Air Chief Marshal Sir Arthur Harris became the driving force of Bomber Command, known as 'Bomber' to some and 'Butcher' to others. Harris was the architect of Britain's strategic air offensive and for three years sought the systematic destruction of Germany with a single-minded dedication that bordered on obsession. Harris was and continues to be the most controversial of all the Allied wartime commanders concerning his policy of area bombing. It was a theory that was not his idea but it was one he exploited completely and applied himself to demonstrate the importance of strategic air power and the decisive role it could play in the Allied war effort.

Harris could express himself clearly and possessed a clear sense of purpose. He was regarded with affection by his bomber crews and with awe by his many staff at Bomber Command Headquarters. On the other hand, some considered him to be an unrefined, rude man who lacked sensitivity and patience and was completely inflexible. The reality remains that when Harris was appointed in 1942, the bomber war was in its very early stages. The statistics show that in the thirty-month period before he took command, Bomber Command had dropped about 90,000 tons of bombs and lost about 7,000 aircrew killed on operations. In the period of his command from 1942 to 1945, more than 850,000 tons of bombs were dropped on raids that claimed the lives of more than 40,000 aircrew.

Chapter 5

The Bomber Command Offensive Against Nazi Germany 1939–45

The bombing offensive against Nazi Germany was one of the longest and most expensive Allied campaigns of the Second World War, and with Douhet's theory that 'the bomber will always get through' it was the aim to destroy the Germans' desire and capability to fight. It was central to the Allies' strategy for winning the war. Bomber Command was initially equipped with light and heavy bomber squadrons but as the war developed the limited and relatively ineffective force was transformed into a weapon of immense destructive power. This required huge economic and technological resources and the dedication of the brightest and best minds. As war broke out in Europe, Bomber Command faced at least four major problems:

1. It was not large enough to operate effectively as an independent strategic bombing force.
2. The scope of targets allocated to Bomber Command was not wide enough.
3. There was a lack of navigational aids to allow accurate target location at night or through cloud.
4. There was limited accuracy of bombing, especially from high level, even when the target was visible to the bomb aimer.

1939 The Second World War began on 1 September 1939 when Germany invaded Poland and with it began the Luftwaffe bombing of Polish cities and the civilian population. Following the unsuccessful intervention of the British Government, the United Kingdom would be at war with Germany.

RAF Bomber Command had 280 aircraft operating within twenty-three operational bomber squadrons, giving Britain the means to immediately strike military targets in Nazi Germany. However, over the coming months, with the war expanding, there were limited bombing campaigns by the Axis or the Allied air forces. Allied aircraft on daylight offensives against warships, docks, airfields and military targets in Germany were easy targets for enemy fighters and losses were heavy, so night operations over Germany were restricted to the dropping of propaganda leaflets. RAF commanders and strategists believed that bombers such as the Vickers Wellington could defend themselves in daylight if they flew in close formation. This theory was soon proved to be wrong.

1940 Hitler's forces invaded France, prompting the RAF to begin a night-time bombing campaign against German industrial centres, with synthetic oil production top of the list. The RAF began targeting Berlin in August 1940 and in September the Luftwaffe began the attack on British cities now known as the 'Blitz'. The early principal twin-engine bomber, the Bristol Blenheim, was vulnerable to fighter attack, so Bomber Command turned to a policy of area bombing at night in order to satisfy its requirement to inflict heavy damage. This failed dismally owing to bomber crews failing to identify and find individual factories and refineries in the darkness. Despite the disappointing results of scattered bombing and limited damage being inflicted on its targets, low-level daylight operations with a variety of aircraft continued until May 1943.

1941 As Bomber Command's strength grew and the offensive gathered intensity, so did the German defences, with night fighter capability and anti-aircraft guns becoming more effective. This inflicted heavy

RAF losses, causing a drop in the morale and frustration of crews as navigation over a blacked-out Europe was a major concern. German warships and U-boats during the Battle of the Atlantic also caused setbacks and required a major effort to combat the threat. The Stirling was the first of the RAF's four-engine bombers to enter service but its low maximum service height made it vulnerable to anti-aircraft fire. They were withdrawn from bomber operations in November 1943. The publication of the Butt Report in August 1941 was of major concern to bomber commanders when it stated that only 5 per cent of aircraft were dropping their bombs within 5 miles of the target. This concern was compounded when main force bombers suffered a mauling by German night fighters on 13 November 1941, so orders were given to conserve forces. Things had to change.

1942 Things did change when the British Government's Air Ministry Area Bombing Directive was given to the RAF on 14 February 1942. Having accepted that precision bombing was proving impossible, it sanctioned the targeting of whole cities known as 'area bombing' in order to destroy Germany's industrial workforce and with it the morale of the German population. The order 'You are accordingly authorised to employ your forces without restriction' coincided with the introduction of the Avro Lancaster and a new leader of Bomber Command, Arthur Harris, who promptly sent 1,000 bombers to destroy Cologne.

Essen, the target on the night of 8–9 March, was followed by repeated incendiary attacks and on other targets listed in the Ruhr, including the use of experimental incendiaries to assess their effectiveness. Squadrons were instructed to bomb Frankfurt, Bremen, Stuttgart and Kassel 'to reduce the output of enemy aircraft, especially fighters, to assist Russia and projected Combined Operations'.

By June 1942, seven squadrons were equipped with the new Lancaster and it was to become the most important and numerous of the Allied 'heavies'. The formation of the Pathfinder Force in August 1942 saw some improvements in bombing performance, and primary targets listed in the directive of industrial areas in the Ruhr were within the range of the navigation aid GEE. Also within GEE range were the German cities of Essen, Duisburg, Düsseldorf and Cologne and these were listed for attack using high explosive. Industrial areas beyond the reach of GEE such as Berlin were to be bombed when the weather was more suitable for bombing than that over the primary GEE targets. Bomber Command was also expected to undertake periodic bombardment of targets of immediate strategic importance such as naval units, but only if good opportunities to attack primary targets were not missed. At this point, however, the Germans had discovered how to jam the GEE sets, so with no target indicators to mark the aiming point, the task varied from thankless to impossible.

German industrial targets up to this point had only covered one plant in France but the emphasis was changed so that targets there should only be bombed by experienced crews and only in weather conditions that prevented stray bombs falling on adjacent civilian properties. Targets that were further afield were added later, particularly when the British discovered that the synthetic oil plant at Pölitz, believed to be the largest in the world, was supplying the majority of the German requirements for their offensive on the Eastern Front.

1943 The 'Casablanca' Conference held in January 1943 was to plan the Allied European strategy for the next phase of the war.

US President Franklin D. Roosevelt and British Prime Minister Winston Churchill, along with support teams, formalised the plan. Stalin did not attend, citing the ongoing Battle of Stalingrad that required his presence in Moscow, but Generals de Gaulle and Giraud, representing the Free French forces, were forced to attend, although no French representatives were allowed at the military planning sessions. The commitment to demand the Axis powers' unconditional surrender was the resulting directive's primary goal and came to represent the determination that the Axis powers would be fought to their ultimate defeat. The directive set out a series of priorities for the strategic bombing of Germany by the RAF and US Eighth Air Force.

The instructions to the heads of the Allied bombing forces stated:

> Your primary object will be the progressive destruction and dislocation of the German military, industrial and economic system and the undermining of the moral of the German people to the point where their capacity for armed resistance is fatally weakened. Every opportunity is to be taken to attack Germany by day to destroy objectives that are unsuitable for night attack, to sustain continuous pressure on German morale, to impose heavy losses on the German day fighter force and to contain German fighter strength away from the Russian and Mediterranean theatres of war.

Harris did not like the directive as it halted his intention to go all out for German industry by stating that submarines, aircraft, transportation and oil would take precedence over industrial targets; his objective since being appointed as Bomber Command leader in 1942 was to 'ruin Berlin and break the morale of its people'. Harris reinterpreted the two important strategic issues, rewording the directive: 'Your primary object will be the progressive destruction and dislocation of the German military, industrial and economic system aimed at undermining of the morale of the German people to the point where their capacity for armed resistance is fatally weakened.' Harris's deliberate misreading and reinterpretation implies that undermining the German people's morale would be a consequence of attacks on German industry, with attacks on industry and attacks on morale being regarded as two separate issues so it would give him the freedom to assault the German industrial centres. Bomber commanders had received monthly directives from the government air staffs since the beginning of the war to ensure that the strategies implemented were within the general structure of Allied concerns.

At this point Churchill thought the Americans were capable of night attacks, with daylight bombing receiving less importance and only mentioned briefly in the directive ruling. The oversight allowed Harris to mount operations independently of the USAAF, which would concentrate on precision bombing. However, Harris famously predicted that the Allies could wreck Berlin from end to end if the Americans would come in on it.

Churchill had been lobbying the Air Ministry for attacks on Berlin since Operation *Barbarossa* in 1941, when the Soviet Union joined the Grand Alliance. In early 1943 he requested attacks on the 'Big City' to take the pressure off Russia and he repeated this in August by approving the Hamburg attack and the American attack on Regensburg. Churchill was informed that Harris would commence attacks on the German capital at the beginning of the next moonless period but it became clear that the USAAF would not attack Berlin owing to the high casualties associated with long-distance, unescorted daylight operations. Berlin would be out of bounds until the introduction of the P-51 Mustang escort fighter.

Harris informed Portal in December 1943 that Lancaster production should be given priority as the force should be sufficient, but only just sufficient, to produce in Germany by early April 1944 a state of devastation in which surrender would be inevitable. In August and September, when the Stirlings were withdrawn from the front line, Harris's statement proved to be more than optimistic and it appears resistance actually increased because of the bombing.

The Casablanca directive was approved on 21 January 1943 and issued to the RAF and USAAF commanders on 4 February.

It remained in force until 17 April 1944, when the Allied strategic bomber commands based in Britain were directed to prepare for Operation *Overlord*. In the air, improved tactics and new technology began to enable crews to find and hit their targets with increasing precision and was developed further within the Pathfinder Force use of coloured marker flares and electronic navigation aids.

A modification to Casablanca in June known as the Pointblank Directive was issued as a response to an expansion of the German fighter force. American bombers were suffering unsustainable losses in their daylight 'precision attacks' on German industry, so German fighters and their production facilities became the primary goal of the RAF and USAAF. A round-the-clock bombing offensive known as Operation *Pointblank* or the Combined Bomber Offensive began with the night area bombing of certain cities running in tandem with the raids on the Atlantic coast U-boat bases during May 1943.

Harris continued to believe that the destruction of large industrial centres like Essen would bring the Germans to their knees, and he disagreed with two aspects of Pointblank. He regarding the bombing of selected industrial targets as a waste of resources and also argued that targets that were beyond Oboe range were outside the RAF's capability. Harris won both points, so Pointblank was revised to allow German industry to remain the RAF's main priority. Hence, the British continued their night attacks, with the Americans targeting German aircraft production by day.

The invasion of Europe depended on the Allies having total air supremacy and to help achieve this the destruction of the German fighter force became the priority by attacking the industrial and economic system, particularly the aircraft manufacturing and associated production centres. The eradication German fighter force became a priority that had to be completed before the beginning of April 1944, so the Americans targeted the Regensburg Messerschmitt factory, the Schweinfurt ball-bearing factory and the facility producing

Bf 109 fighters. Their attack in August 1943 was catastrophic as they lost 195 aircraft.

The Americans had repeatedly asked the RAF to provide daytime fighter escorts but it was argued that the need to carry additional fuel would reduce their performance and the long flight times would fatigue the pilots. Fighter Command had always thought of their assets purely for defensive purposes and prior to Pointblank this policy had never been reconsidered. Previous requests by both Bomber Command and Coastal Command for escorts led Fighter Command to deny help on the grounds that the Supermarine Spitfire could not be converted for such a role. This was a curious statement considering the unarmed photo-reconnaissance version of the Spitfire was available from 1940 and offered the required range and performance.

The issue was taken up by USAAF General Henry H. Arnold, who requested that RAF allocations of the P-51 Mustang fighter be directed to provide escort for daytime raids under the control of the Eighth Air Force. Chief of the Air Staff Charles Portal responded to Arnold with the offer to provide four squadrons. The offer upset Arnold, who considered it was not enough as it appeared that thousands of fighters were not making use of their full capabilities. He maintained that the Allies' transition from the defensive to the offensive should carry with it the application of the large fighter force offensively. The addition of long-range fuel tanks to the P-47 Thunderbolt permitted offensive action several hundred miles from England despite the basic design having a shorter range than the Spitfire.

Experience proved that the high-performance and heavily armed P-51 Mustang was more than capable of defending daytime US bomber streams from their base all the way to target and back again. US bomber crews regarded the P-51s as 'Guardian Angels' and they were made to feel invincible in the presence of their 'Little Friends'.

The Battle of the Ruhr – 5–6 March to 24 July 1943

Bomber Command had attacked Ruhr targets from as early as 1940 but bombing efforts were hampered by industrial pollution, which produced a semi-permanent smog. The spring of 1943 to the spring of 1944 was the period that Harris referred to as his 'main offensive' and, having negotiated Bomber Command through the recent winter with great skill, Harris had recognised that the time was not right for an all-out offensive. He chose to conserve and build up his force and to experiment with new tactics and devices to improve bombing methods and accuracy. In early March 1943, Harris saw the Battle of the Ruhr as the beginning of a sustained and major effort against Germany which would provide the potential to devastate more German cities.

The Ruhr and Wupper rivers in valleys 40 miles across and 25 miles long enclosed the widespread industrial region of about 1,200 square miles and fourteen towns with a population of just over 4 million. It was the most industrialised area in Germany and was the centre of the production of heavy industry, coke plants, steelworks, armaments factories and synthetic oil plants. Earlier successes depended on favourable weather conditions but when it became within the range of the new blind-marking device Oboe and with the shorter nights of spring and summer, the Ruhr was the logical place for Bomber Command to strike. The Germans had recognised the importance of the Krupps works and built a decoy site in 1941 to deceive and lure the British bombers by deliberately illuminating the site and railway goods yards, which proved successful until the British used night navigation and blind-bombing devices from late in 1942.

At the beginning of the battle, Bomber Command had nearly 600 bombers available, growing to 800 towards the end of May and with the ability of the Pathfinder Force to find the Ruhr targets using Oboe beams vital to allow the Mosquito Pathfinders to release their target indicators with pinpoint precision.

The Ruhr offensive lasted for five months but Bomber Command battles would not concentrate exclusively on one target area as this would have allowed the Germans to concentrate their night fighter and flak defences appropriately to defend their cities. The Ruhr had the most powerful flak and searchlight defences in Germany and the bomber routes between the coast of Europe and the Ruhr were manned by the most experienced and best-equipped night fighter units in the Luftwaffe. Of the forty-three major raids carried out over thirty-nine nights, twenty-six were against Ruhr targets. The remainder were scattered across Europe, the Baltic, Bavaria, Italy and Czechoslovakia. Attacks on Berlin, Hamburg, Munich, Stuttgart and Nuremberg during March through to late June never allowed the Germans to concentrate all their defences in the Ruhr.

One operation during this time would become one of the most famous of the Second World War. On the night of 16–17 May 1943, nineteen Lancasters left their base at RAF Scampton in Lincolnshire to attack the source of the Ruhr water and hydroelectric power. Operation *Chastise* was carried out by the newly formed 617 Squadron using specially designed bombs. Six bombers did not reach the dams, one turned back after losing its bomb and five were shot down. Five Lancasters bombed the Möhne dam, three the Eder, two the Sorpe and one the Schwelme. The Möhne dam was breached, releasing its water into the Ruhr valley and causing extensive flooding and much damage to road, rail and canals. This led to electricity and water shortages, with rationing becoming necessary until the autumn rains. The breach of the larger Eder dam, 60 miles away from the Ruhr, had more effect on the Kassel area. The Sorpe dam was only slightly damaged and continued to keep the Ruhr operating while repairs to the Möhne were undertaken. The human cost was considerable: 1,294 civilian casualties, including Ukrainian slave labourers, were drowned; another fifty-eight bodies were found around the Eder dam. Three aircraft were lost on the return flight and a total of fifty-three airmen were killed and three taken prisoner.

Bomber Command's five-month-long campaign caused shortages of parts, castings and forgings all over Germany; Ruhr steel production was cut by 200,000 tons, at a time when Albert Speer, the head of the Reich Ministry of Armaments and War Production, was expecting output to increase to 2,800,000 tons. A total of 18,500 bomber sorties were dispatched for a loss of 872 aircraft, nearly 5 per cent, while another 2,126 aircraft were damaged, some beyond recovery. However, aircraft production exceeded losses by just over 100 aircraft per month from March to July.

The British now turned their attention to another area of interest, Hamburg. More than any other German city, this was a centre of Germany's shipbuilding industry, and included U-boat pens, oil refineries and additional industrial targets.

The Battle of Hamburg (Operation *Gomorrah*)

Gomorrah – one of the two Canaanite cities, Sodom and Gomorrah, whose destruction is recorded in the Bible: 'Then the Lord rained brimstone and fire on Sodom and Gomorrah from the Lord out of the heavens.' (Genesis 19:24)

The ancient city of Hamburg, Germany's second largest, was constructed predominantly of wood and in the summer of 1943 had experienced unusually warm weather and with no recent rain everything was very dry. The British, having learned from the experiences of the Blitz earlier in the war, felt that Hamburg was susceptible to an attack with incendiaries and this was likely to inflict more damage than high-explosive bombs. Hamburg contained a number of high-value targets that supported the German war effort, and aside from the military objectives these factors led to the port being chosen as a priority target for a firebombing raid.

Hamburg's reasonably close proximity to the bomber bases in Britain offered a shorter flight with less exposure to anti-aircraft fire and night fighters, and its position close to the coast and on a prominent river made the target easy to find for RAF navigators. New navigation technologies like H2S and Window that were used for the first time during the initial attack on Hamburg confused German radar, allowing the Pathfinders to identify and mark the target and keeping aircraft losses to a minimum. Breaking radio silence, the Pathfinders reported the winds they encountered and this information was processed and relayed to the bomber force navigators. No. 35 Squadron led the target marking in clear weather using H2S radar navigation, resulting in high accuracy with markers falling close to the aiming point. On 24 July, at approximately 0057hrs, the hour-long bombing started and then combined raids by the RAF and USAAF continued for eight days and seven nights, causing one of the largest firestorms of the war.

The offensive continued with Mosquitos of the Light Night Striking Force sweeping over the city, carrying out nuisance raids that kept the defences on a state of alert. To ramp up the terror, delayed-action bombs from the raid the previous night exploded at intervals. On the ground, 40,000 firemen were available to tackle fires but their telephone exchange caught fire and rubble blocked the passage of fire engines through the city streets. Firefighters from other cities including Hanover were brought in, but when the American bombers attacked that city in daylight their firemen were in Hamburg. Hanover was still burning three days later and was virtually destroyed. The USAAF conducted a daylight raid on Hamburg at 1640hrs but only ninety of the 300 B-17 Flying Fortresses reached the target owing to problems with assembling the force in the air.

Severe thunderstorms and high winds over the North Sea hampered the RAF night attack of 26 July, forcing some crews to jettison their bombs although they did retain their incendiaries.

Just before midnight, the following night 787 aircraft bombed the dense housing in a number of the working-class districts such as Hamm, Hammerbrook and Rothenburgsort. Owing to the dry and warm weather, the concentration of the bombing caused severe firefighting limitations and the recall of Hanover's fire crews to their own city culminated in a firestorm. The raging inferno created a vortex of super-heated winds of up to 150mph with temperatures reaching 800°C and whirling updrafts reaching altitudes in excess of 1,000ft. More than 8 square miles of the city were incinerated and the phosphor from the fire bombs caused the streets to combust. In addition, fuel oil from ships, barges and damaged storage tanks spilled into the canals and the harbour and ignited.

The damage to Hamburg prompted the Germans to change their air defence systems, with priority given to fighter production and research into more effective radar. Aircraft and guns were taken from the front line to defend German cities and were increased by 25 per cent and by August 1943 nearly half of all German fighters were defending the home front with additional units in northern France, causing the fighting fronts to suffer from the lack of air support.

The total numbers of the lives lost during the raids on Hamburg will never be known but it is estimated to be 37,000. Many of the dead were unidentified and in some cases people who had perished could only be estimated from the quantity of ash left on the floor. Hamburg was subjected to a further sixty-nine air raids before the end of the war, being hit with a total of 22,580 tons of bombs. At the time the destruction of Hamburg became a major news story and caused controversy owing to the extent of the damage and loss of life. No subsequent city raids shook German officials as did those on Hamburg and recovered documents and later Allied interrogations of Nazi officials revealed that Hitler stated that further raids of similar weight would force Germany out of the war. The industrial losses were severe and Hamburg never recovered to full industrial production, having lost 183 large factories out of the 524 in the city. Some 4,118 smaller factories out of 9,068 were destroyed and the local transport systems were completely disrupted and did not return to normal for some time. The number of homes that were destroyed amounted to 214,350 out of 414,500.

The Battle of Berlin – the 'Big City'

During the good weather of August 1943, Bomber Command continued to assault German defences along with raids against Italian cities in an attempt to remove Italy from the war; Italy surrendered to the Allies on 8 September 1943. The moon period in the third week of August gave some respite for the bomber squadrons but at the end of the month Harris launched what he intended to be the opening of his offensive against Berlin, for which he was prepared to devote several months.

Berlin, the 'Big City', was the heart of Hitler's Reich and as home to Göring, Goebbels, Himmler and Speer, it was the seat of government, the administrative and political centre. At nearly 14 miles across, it was the third largest conurbation in the world, with many parks, open spaces and solid blocks of flats that would not burn as Hamburg had. For Bomber Command and Harris in particular, Berlin was a morale and propaganda target as well as a strategic one, with the centre of twelve strategic railway complexes and the second largest port in Europe connected to the German canal system. Firms such as Siemens, Daimler-Benz, Heinkel, Dornier, Focke-Wulf and AEG produced tanks and radar aides.

Berlin was the most heavily defended city in Germany, with massive air defences in a searchlight belt 60 miles deep containing rings of 700 flak guns 40 miles across, the core of which had twenty-four enormous 128mm guns mounted in pairs on three gigantic, almost impregnable, concrete flak towers. A heavy bomber attack on Berlin involved a 1,200-mile round trip taking about eight hours. This would need the cover of darkness, so given the distance, it was only possible when the nights were longer. The aircrews flying throughout the winter months sat in the brutal conditions of freezing, vibrating aircraft in the limited protection of layers of heavy clothing knowing that death would come in minutes in the event of oxygen failure. It would be a physically and psychologically demanding experience, intensified by the presence of night fighters. These were just reaching a peak in both numbers and experience as the night fighter crews would defend the heart of the Reich to the death. It is important to remember that the serviceability of the aircraft was down to the dedication and hard work of the ground crews back in Britain servicing the aircraft in what would prove to be one of the bitterest winters in recent years. The dependable and much-loved pre-war aircraft, the Wellington, was withdrawn from the main force but some were retained into 1944 for minelaying sorties. The production rate of the Lancaster was such that the RAF struggled to increase the numbers of the front-line squadrons as there was a need to replace battle casualties and worn-out aircraft.

Berlin, beyond Oboe range and offering poor H2S characteristics, produced disappointing results on the raids between 23 August and 4 September that were not comparable with the results from Hamburg. The heavy bomber losses of more than 7 per cent indicated that German defences were recovering from the setback of Window. Bomber Command now began its greatest test of the war, the all-out assault on Berlin from November 1943 to March 1944, beginning with the first of sixteen major raids on the night of 18–19 November and sixteen on other large cities. It was soon apparent that the Stirlings were suffering heavy casualties owing to their poor performance preventing them from achieving the altitude attained by the other bombers. The Lancasters and Halifaxes were ordered to descend to share the dangerous lower altitudes to offer the Stirlings some protection but when the night fighters struck they quickly climbed again, leaving the Stirlings to get on with it. Harris's 3 Group were forced to withdraw around 250 aircraft from front-line operations, which amounted to about one third of his total strength of heavy bombers and at least 20 per cent of his bomb-carrying capacity. A similar fate was to befall the Halifax bombers of 4 and 6 Groups, which were equipped with inferior engines and saw their casualties rise after the Stirlings left. From the beginning of December to the middle of February, no fewer than almost 10 per cent of Halifax Mk. II and Mk. V aircraft sent on offensive operations crashed or were shot down. The old Stirlings and Halifaxes withdrawn from operations were now joined by training groups and these would carry out minelaying operations and drop Window over the North Sea to simulate the approach of a large force, then turn away before they reached the German coast.

The German defences were now forcing the main bomber stream to fly by indirect routes with frequent course changes and at times the neutrality of Swedish airspace was ignored in wide sweeps to the north on the route to Berlin. This was a disappointing period for Bomber Command as the recent introduction of Window only caused setbacks to the German night defence for a few weeks, so efforts were made to cut the time to allow 800 aircraft to pass over the target in less than twenty minutes and reduce the length of the stream from 300 miles to 70.

The Pathfinders allowed Harris to maintain the momentum of his bombing offensive but as the Battle of Berlin moved into 1944, he started to turn the screw by ordering his Lancasters to carry more bombs. There were some crews who did not comply fully with orders, jettisoning the extra bombs over the North Sea in order to make their aircraft more manoeuvrable. On the approach to the target some crews were referred to as 'fringe merchants' as they dropped their loads a little early, causing the aiming point to creep back for many miles. Such accusations must be kept in perspective as most crews did not abort unnecessarily, did not drop bombs in the sea and did their utmost to reach the centre of the target. The familiar trips to Berlin became known to crews as the 'Berlin Express' and the 'Milk Round' but the loss of efficiency caused by adverse weather and the longer routes forced the use of heavier fuel loads at the expense of bomb tonnage. It is possible that rising casualties were also attributed to an increasing reliance on inexperienced crews in both Pathfinder and main force squadrons and the limitations of the electronic aids such as Oboe, which had proved so successful in the Battle of the Ruhr but were not available over Berlin.

Mosquitos terrorised Berlin, sometimes twice in one night, swapping crews in between operations while the aircraft were refuelled and rearmed on the tarmac; they would sometimes attack four different cities in one night. Despite the limited damage they caused, the fast, nimble Mosquito had a considerable psychological impact on both civilians and the military. Berlin was almost thirty times the size of Hamburg, yet Harris wanted to destroy it with just four times the volume of raids. It was not a realistic option with the resources available but during the Battle of Berlin 25 per cent was destroyed by 33,000 tons of bombs and many factories were temporarily out of action. The destruction of Berlin's railways and canals, which were so vital for transporting war materials, was more decisive but in defending the capital with guns and personnel the Luftwaffe used valuable military hardware that could otherwise have been deployed elsewhere.

About 10,300 German people died, while the 2,700 airmen killed, and almost 1,000 more captured, indicated a steady deterioration in the effectiveness of the bomber force at increasing cost. Despite it all, Berlin remained standing and industrial production continued, while the morale of its people remained intact. The material and psychological damage was still considerable as with every German shell fired, every window smashed and every military person killed, they had to be replaced, adding to the burden on the German war machine. Above all, Bomber Command proved it could strike hard at the heart of Hitler's Third Reich. With the nights of March 1944 becoming shorter, operations to Berlin were reduced and Harris's dream of crushing the German capital was over. All attention was now turning to the second front: D-Day, the Allied invasion of France.

1944 By the spring, the combined Allied bomber and fighter force began to overwhelm the Germans and gained air superiority, allowing Bomber Command to operate in daylight, attacking coastal defences on a daily basis and hitting railways to block German reinforcements. Bombers flew in support of the D-Day landings and carpet bombed enemy troops in advance of major Allied ground offensives. Germany's vulnerable fuel supplies were heavily damaged but Harris continued his city attacks, still convinced they would prove decisive.

The Transportation Plan – the support of the Allied Invasion of Europe March–August 1944

In January 1944, Supreme Headquarters Allied Expeditionary Force began to plan for the greatest seaborne invasion in history, Operation *Overlord*. There were major concerns about the extent of French civilian casualties, which might alienate the French as allies, but Eisenhower discussed these concerns with the commander of French forces in Britain, French Major General Pierre Koening. He understood that casualties were a reality in the fight to liberate France. Eisenhower was confident that during the first critical days of the invasion the Allies could land sufficient forces to establish a bridgehead along the Normandy coast. However, he was not confident the force could sustain itself without the protection of Allied air superiority over the landing beaches and the prevention of German forces from receiving reinforcements. The plan was adapted to include strategic bombing to limit the German military response to the invasion by disrupting or destroying the entire network of supply routes such as bridges, rail centres, marshalling yards and repair shops.

Harris had reservations about the ability of his force to hit small targets without killing too many friendly civilians but his fears were put to rest when on the night of 5–6 April 144 Lancasters of 5 Group attacked and destroyed an aircraft factory in Toulouse. The raid was not marked by Pathfinders but was carried out with unusual accuracy by 617 Squadron in the first low-level marking flight of the war when the commanding officer, Wing Commander Leonard Cheshire, dropped his markers on the target with outstanding results. Harris was now convinced to divert his bombers away from their strategic campaign against German industry and direct his loyal men in a far more precise manner against targets on the invasion coast by immediately changing the way they operated. Harris informed Air Vice Marshal Cochrane that 5 Group could now operate as an independent force with the addition of two 8 Group Lancaster Pathfinder units, 83 Squadron and 97 Squadron, along with more Mosquitos for 617 Squadron. Some of 8 Group's 139 Squadron Mosquitos were also transferred to 5 Group to form 627 Squadron.

Hitler's desire for 15,000 emplacements to be manned by 300,000 troops was vastly restricted by shortages of concrete and manpower but strongpoints were concentrated in the expected invasion area of the Pas-de-Calais with the best fortifications at the port facilities at Cherbourg and Saint-Malo. Concrete gun structures at strategic coastal points and wooden stakes, barbed wire, metal tripods and mines placed on the high tide line of beaches would delay the approach of landing craft and impede the movement of tanks.

For three months leading up to D-Day thousands of RAF and USAAF bombers and fighters conducted intensive air campaigns, dropping more than 75,000 tons of bombs on French and Belgian rail centres, major road junctions, bridges and tunnels. The Germans were forced to continuously seek alternative routes, which delayed and reduced their movements in and to the Normandy area and prevented them from pinpointing the planned landing sites in Normandy. By D-Day Allied air supremacy over Western Europe had crippled the Luftwaffe, so Rommel knew he could not expect effective air support and this rendered daylight movement virtually impossible. On 13 June 1944 the German Air Ministry had accepted that the raids had caused the breakdown of all main lines, which had effectively cut off the coast defences from the supply bases. The intensity of Allied attacks had prevented large-scale strategic movement of German troops by rail and by August 1944 German military daylight movements had stopped completely and most of the Luftwaffe had been driven out of France.

The Invasion of Europe – 5–6 June to 16 August 1944

Bad weather delayed the invasion for twenty-four hours and any further postponements would delay the operation for at least two weeks owing to the requirements for the correct phase of the moon, tides and the time of day. The invasion started shortly after midnight with American, British, and Canadian airborne troops parachuting inland accompanied by an extensive aerial and naval bombardment in preparation for the amphibious landings. At 0630hrs on Tuesday, 6 June 1944 the Allied armed forces landed on the 50-mile stretch of the Normandy coast divided into five sectors: Utah, Omaha, Gold, Juno, and Sword. Further up the Channel, in Operation *Taxable*, 617 Squadron were dropping bundles of Window to suggest to the German radars that a naval convoy was approaching near Le Havre. This extremely precise and complicated operation was bolstered by a group of small vessels towing barrage balloons.

The exploits and heroism of men landing on the Normandy beaches is legendary and Allied forces would battle with a determined German defence for ten weeks, but the men of Bomber Command played their part during those historic weeks. For the bomber crews it was a time of almost unbelievable intensity with crews flying more than 5,000 sorties in direct support of the invasion forces. However, with the Allies in France, they were now well placed to break out and sweep further into Europe and on towards the Reich heartland.

1945 With 108 squadrons and more than 1,500 aircraft, the bomber offensive reached the peak of its destruction with effective raids against oil and communications disrupting enemy production. Almost starved of fuel, the German military machine ground to a halt. Industrial cities were pulverised and Dresden, previously untouched, was razed to the ground. This provoked public and political criticism and left Bomber Command clouded in controversy to the present day despite its major contribution to the Allied victory and the death of more than 55,000 aircrew.

Chapter 6

The Pathfinder Man

Air Vice Marshal Donald Bennett, CB, CBE, DSO

Born on 14 September 1910 in Toowoomba, Queensland, Donald Bennett joined the Royal Australian Air Force in 1930 and transferred to the Royal Air Force. He was a true Australian aviation pioneer with a passion for accurate flying and precise navigation that would dictate the path of his future. After a period as an instructor on flying boats, he left the service but retained a reserve commission and spent the next five years specialising in long-distance flights with Imperial Airways, breaking a number of records and pioneering techniques such as air-to-air refuelling. In 1936 Bennett wrote the first edition of *The Complete Air Navigator*, which covered the syllabus for the flight navigator's licence. In July 1938 he was awarded the Oswald Watt Gold Medal for piloting a Short Mayo Composite flying boat across the Atlantic. During 1940 RAF aircraft were also produced in the United States and Canada, so to aid transatlantic delivery to the UK, Bennett helped to set up the successful Atlantic Ferry Organisation, which demonstrated that inexperienced pilots with suitable training could safely deliver new aircraft across the North Atlantic.

In 1941 Bennett was recommissioned into the RAF Volunteer Reserve as a squadron leader to oversee the formation of the Elementary Air Navigation School at Eastbourne to provide initial training for observers, later called navigators. Bennett was soon promoted to wing commander with 77 Squadron in 4 Group, flying Whitleys from RAF Leeming. In April 1942, this unit was transferred to Coastal Command and Bennett was given command of 10 Squadron equipped with Handley Page Halifaxes. He led a raid on the German battleship *Tirpitz* but was shot down and evaded capture, escaping to Sweden before returning to Britain. Bennett and his co-pilot were awarded the DSO on 16 June 1942.

Bomber Command had started night-time raids deep into Germany that delivered poor results, prompting the Air Ministry's Directorate of Bomber Operations to establish an elite precision bombing force. 'Bomber' Harris opposed the idea, suggesting that it would lower the morale of the other squadrons, but he was overruled so he selected Bennett as his obvious choice as force commander without considering other candidates. Harris knew that Bennett was an efficient man that possessed excellent navigational skills and had the ability to instruct others; he was the obvious choice for the role. Bennett was appointed to command the new Pathfinder Force with effect from 5 July 1942, with a promotion to group captain. The elite 'Pathfinders' would lead the bomber stream accurately towards the target areas by dropping pinpoint route flares and then drop markers directly on the target for the main force to aim at.

With the upgrading of the Pathfinder Force in 1943, Bennett was promoted to group status with the rank of air commodore and then in December to acting air vice marshal, the youngest officer to hold that rank. He remained in command of the Pathfinder Force until the end of the war, having seen it grow to nineteen squadrons, a training flight and a meteorological flight. He continued to work to improve its standards and campaigned for better equipment, particularly for more Mosquitos and Lancasters to replace obsolete aircraft, and he faced problems with the supply of new crews. No. 8 Group had seen a marked improvement during the period from the Battle of the Ruhr through to the end of 1943 but the Battle of Berlin had inflicted heavy losses that included very experienced pilots and navigators, some of which were about to finish a third and in some cases the fourth tour. Experienced main force crews had moved to training units, with many showing little enthusiasm for the Pathfinder work. This resulted in a general impression that the 'bottom of the barrel' was being reached.

In the spring and summer of 1944, Bennett asked Hamish Mahaddie to increase his 'horse thieving' to identify and recruit the best crews to join the Pathfinders but this difficult task was made harder as he did not have the support of Harris, despite pleading with him to let his crews have some breathing space. Post-war, Bennett felt that he had replaced his entire crew strength one-and-a-half times owing to his limited influence at higher command levels.

Bennett's deteriorating professional relationship with Harris was tested further following a raid over Hanover when inaccurate Pathfinder marking caused a poor bombing attack. An annoyed Harris criticised Bennett, saying that the attack had been a complete flop and was the worst failure yet. He told Bennett to ensure that his crews were not simply blindly joining in with inaccurate marking, confounding the confusion even more. Bennett was to ensure that the Hanover raid was a lesson and make sure that careless action could not lead the entire force astray in future.

Bennett replied to Harris, agreeing that the results had been extremely bad but added that operations were generally very successful compared to the farcical raids before the arrival of the Pathfinders. In addition, Bennett set out details of a Pathfinder Force review and the ways he felt his force was being let down by aspects beyond his control. For instance, when the Pathfinder Force was set up he was promised the best crews yet one third came straight from training units with no operational experience and the average experience of Pathfinder captains now stood at twenty sorties, some twelve fewer than the previous winter. For the Pathfinder Force to work efficiently they needed the best crews, and ideally those that had completed at least one main force tour, but Bennett thought they were often sent the dregs. Bennett reminded Harris that the smaller 'spoof' raids used to draw night fighters away from the main raid meant his squadrons sometimes had to be briefed on two or even three different operations per night. The Pathfinder Force briefings were longer and more complex and could only start once Bennett had received the target from Harris earlier in the day. Harris dismissed or ignored a number of Bennett's points but did promise to remind main force group commanders to send Bennett their best crews.

Bennett was a hands-on commander and kept in close contact with the men and stations under his command. He strived to understand what his crews were facing, so he requested the opportunity to fly on operations. Harris replied to Bennett with a stinging letter reminding him that this was forbidden for good reasons. However, Harris was not aware that Bennett had already made unofficial and highly secretive flights over Germany in a high-flying Mosquito in a bid to witness the challenges his crews faced. Bennett had navigated to the target and took notes as the pilot circled the aircraft over the raid. After once being spotted by a Mosquito squadron commander from another group, Bennett warned him to keep his mouth shut.

Bennett earned a great deal of respect from his crews but he could be coldly ruthless to those not achieving the high standards he demanded. However, he was not a hard man and he became emotionally affected by the loss of his crews. To Bennett, these weren't just any crews, they were the most successful and experienced men that he got to know and regard as friends, and their loss was a personal blow. At one point Bennett thought that the Pathfinder Force had been broken and after debriefing returning crews in the early hours of the morning he would drive home and find it difficult to avoid breaking down and shedding a few tears as the constant strain over such a long period of time, night after night and month after month, had its wearing effect. Every morning after breakfast, Bennett would anxiously call Bomber Command Headquarters to find out how many planes were lost from the previous night's operation; he would then personally speak to the wives of the missing airmen if they lived nearby.

Harris considered Bennett to be a difficult and naturally aloof man who would not suffer fools gladly, and therefore owing to the high standards Bennett set, there were many fools. Bennett did not get on well with the other group commanders, especially Air Vice Marshal Ralph Cochrane of 5 Group with his specialist 617 Squadron, which also pursued Bennett's high levels of accuracy. The two men were always at odds but the decisive factor was that Cochrane had the ear of a certain 'Bomber' Harris.

As the war drew to a close, the considerable achievements of the Pathfinders may have been overshadowed by Cochrane's 5 Group and their 'Dambusters'. Bennett was the only bomber group commander not to be knighted, and having resigned his RAF commission, he returned to private life. He became a Member of Parliament as Liberal MP for Middlesbrough West but was defeated in the 1945 general election. Bennett became a director of British South American Airways and took up designing cars and light aircraft. However, following a disagreement with the board members in February 1948, Bennett was dismissed from BSAA. He then started his own airline, Airflight, based at Langley Airfield, Berkshire; also the base of BSAA. It operated two Avro Tudor airliners carrying fuel during the Berlin Airlift. However, tragedy stuck on 12 March 1950 when one of his charter flight aircraft crashed at Llandow in Wales, killing eighty of its eighty-three occupants. Bennett's technical knowledge and his operational ability was exceptional and his moral and physical courage was outstanding; as a technician he was unrivalled. He was described as one of the most brilliant technical airmen of his generation, an outstanding pilot and a superb navigator who was also capable of stripping a wireless set or overhauling an engine. Donald Bennett, the Pathfinder leader, died aged 76 on 15 September 1986, 'Battle of Britain Day'.

Chapter 7

The Pathfinders

The August 1941 Butt Report prompted the Government and the Air Ministry to develop a specialised force of aircraft with appropriately trained crews. This was the initial proposal by Group Captain S. Bufton but was met with opposition from Harris. Harris disliked Bufton and argued that an elite force would have an adverse effect on morale by breeding envy and rivalry within the groups. However, Sir Henry Tizard, adviser and one of the chief scientists supporting the war effort, thought that a formation of a first XV rugby union team would not cause little boys to play any less enthusiastically. R. V. Jones, the British genius who studied German theories and solved scientific and technical problems in the defence of Britain, particularly by the use of deception to confuse the Germans, was appointed to the Intelligence Section of the Air Ministry. Jones concluded that the technique was sound, so Harris had his objections overruled but forced the matter further by suggesting the lead crews be distributed among the squadrons. Again, his objections were dismissed as it was thought unlikely to produce the desired result. The Pathfinder Force would be responsible for navigating the entire bomber stream by dropping coloured marker flares for the main force to follow and as the bombing run began, flares of different colours would indicate the target itself. The Pathfinders began using volunteer crews from five squadrons, one from each of the operational bomber groups, and these were stepped up in rank and had an increase in pay. Their usual tour of thirty trips was increased to sixty, later reduced to forty-five to encourage more volunteers.

The Pathfinders first operated on the night of 18–19 August 1942 when thirty-one of them led 118 bombers to Flensburg on an inlet of the Baltic. It was expected to be an easy target but the wind direction changed, sending the bombers north of the target to Denmark. Sixteen Pathfinder crews claimed to have marked the target area and seventy-eight main force crews claimed to have bombed but in reality they had scattered their ordnance around the Danish towns of Sønderborg and Abenra, 25 miles north. Fortunately, only four Danish people were injured in this dismal failure, which was the source of much delight to Harris. The next raid to Frankfurt on 24–25 once again found the crews having difficulty in identifying a target covered by thick cloud, causing most of the bombs to fall in open country north of Frankfurt. Six Lancasters, five Wellingtons, four Stirlings and one Halifax were lost, 7 per cent of the force, with five Pathfinder aircraft lost including that of the commanding officer of 7 Squadron.

The Pathfinders succeeded on the night of 27–28 August when they were able to illuminate Kassel with little cloud over the city and the bombers caused considerable damage. Nuremberg was then attacked at low altitude by 159 aircraft, with the Pathfinders accurately placing new target illuminators adapted from 250lb bomb casings. The crews claimed to have carried out a good attack but raid reports from Nuremberg recorded only fifty aircraft had hit the town, with some bombs striking the town of Erlangen, nearly 10 miles to the north.

As the Pathfinder Force gained experience it encountered new problems, such as target illuminators going out before the raid was complete. Arriving aircraft would either turn for home or bomb randomly on any visible fires on the near side of the flames, which caused 'creep back'; the bomb track moving backward along the attack line and away from the target. To prevent future occurrences, the Pathfinders were split into three groups for each raid: 'illuminators', 'markers' and 'backers up'. The 'illuminators' dropped white flares from 9,000ft at points over long distances along the bombing route for aircraft to follow and as they approached the target, located 'blind' using H2S ground-mapping radar, at about six minutes before H-Hour they would illuminate the target with sticks of white 'hooded' flares, code-named 'Newhaven'. Then the 'marker' crews would pick out the exact aiming point and mark it with up to ten red target indicators, then drop incendiaries on to the target indicators. The red target indicators burned out seven minutes after H-Hour, so with the main force attack lasting about twenty minutes or longer, the bombing was halted to allow additional marking. The target indicators, sometimes called 'spot fires', produced a single spot of red or green light of moderate intensity on the designated aiming point under the illuminations and this was visible under cloud cover.

Primary blind marking required less than seven-tenths cloud cover (ten-tenths is complete cover) and if conditions appeared favourable for visual marking they would mark the aiming point blindly with green target indicators and also drop bundles of hooded white flares. For cloud cover greater than seven-tenths, they were to drop green target indicators and red release point flares with green stars. Visual Markers were to mark aiming points with red target indicators after definite visual identification; otherwise they would retain their target indicators. This blind marking method, code-named 'Parramatta', was used if conditions prevented visual identification of the aiming point and was very similar to the 'blind' part of 'Newhaven' marking; primary markers, usually red or yellow target indicators, dropped by H2S aircraft at the beginning of the attack with the 'backers up' ready with green target indicators for the benefit of the main force. It was prefixed 'Musical Paramatta' if used in combination with Oboe Mosquitos, often from 105 and 109 Squadrons.

Early range limitations of Oboe permitted only one Mosquito every five minutes, with Lancasters and Halifaxes used as backer-up aircraft. If the target area was covered by thick cloud that obscured the target indicators, sky marking was used called 'Wanganui', or 'Musical Wanganui' if used with Oboe. Flares dropped with a small parachute produced an incredibly intense light capable of turning night into day, and with an allowance for wind drift, the sky markers were placed so that the aircraft at the same height and airspeed as the other attacking aircraft dropped their bombs directly over the markers, which would naturally fall into the target area. This was not as accurate as visual bombing but it did allow attacks to be made on nights when cloud cover rendered visual bombing impossible. However, if these variables differed, very large errors could occur. The same principles also applied to 'Wanganui' sky markers. The 'backers up' carrying green secondary target indicators aimed at the primary red target indicators on the aiming point, although the green target indicators were usually less accurately placed and only successful in good weather. If the target was covered with haze or cloud the visual markers would not be able to identify the aiming point, so the target indicators were not used.

The code names of the methods derived from the home towns of three members of Donald Bennett's Pathfinder staff: one was from Newhaven, England, one from Parramatta, New South Wales, and one from Wanganui, New Zealand.

The Germans copied the flare principle and used them to lure the bombers away from their intended target. However, German decoys were shot up from the ground, which produced fewer cascades of weaker-coloured candles that burned for a shorter duration. The British started to add star flares of a contrasting colour to complicate the German effort of duplicating the flares.

In January 1943 the Pathfinder Force was upgraded to become 8 Group and Bennett would continue to bring it into the electronic age of new target-marking techniques, enabling the Force to literally light the way across Europe to achieve the accuracy that had previously eluded it. By mid-1943 raids were controlled by a highly experienced senior officer called 'master bomber' or 'master of ceremonies', who would circle the target and broadcast instructions and any corrections to both Pathfinders and main force aircraft.

Bennett specifically wanted the Mosquito for Pathfinder Force target-marking duties and managed to obtain some surplus to requirement Oboe-fitted 105 Squadron Mk BIX bombers, which were used to conduct diversionary 'spoofs' on other targets to attract enemy night fighters away from the main attack force. A Mosquito 'spoof' would take place about four hours before the main raid and caused carnage on the ground. From April 1943, 'nuisance' raiding was so successful that by the summer a Light Night Striking Force of Mosquitos was established using the aircraft of 139 Squadron. Ultimately, eleven Mosquito squadrons operated in 8 Group along with eight Lancaster squadrons.

Harris disliked the name Mosquito, despite the type's undoubted performance. The aircraft could carry a bomb load to Berlin equivalent to the USAAF B-17 Flying Fortress with its ten-man crew but Harris considered the word 'mosquito' to be symbolic of the insect, which produced an irritating but not particularly effective sting. Harris also disliked the title Light Night Striking Force as he considered it discredited the weight of attack that these aircraft could impose on the enemy. Nevertheless, Headquarters endeavoured to impress upon the public that Mosquito raids were a most serious matter for the enemy.

From the spring of 1943 Bennett would send up to 120 Mosquitos to Berlin and beyond, each carrying a 4,000lb cookie bomb, also known as blockbuster, and these nuisance or 'Siren' raids became a major headache for the German people and their defences. Mosquitos barrelling through the Third Reich airspace every night heaped destruction on the people of Germany and their industry. Berlin was not a safe place with the Light Night Striking Force visiting the capital on at least 170 occasions. In one three-minute early morning raid on Berlin, Light Night Striking Force Mosquitos dropped more than thirty 4,000lb bombs on the city despite heavy cloud. It was apparent to some aircrew that the defences had been caught napping but the flak then became severe. The bombs fell on the markers in the heavy attack and it was all over very quickly. The sustained effort was a feat that even prompted a rare signal of congratulations from Harris to Bennett.

The Nazi Propaganda Minister, Joseph Goebbels, became obsessed with the regular visits from the Light Night Striking Force in February and March 1945 as these 'cursed' Englishmen in their Mosquitos flew over Berlin night after night and deprived despondent people of sleep by driving them into air-raid shelters. Goebbels felt impotent against it and recognised that millions in the Reich capital were gradually becoming somewhat nervous and hysterical; he could not see a way out of the dilemma. Goebbels' irritation was intensified as the Wooden Wonder bombed his offices. Goebbels knew the Germans were completely defenceless against the raids as he considered the Mosquito almost impossible to shoot down. Nevertheless, the Luftwaffe, under increasing pressure from Hitler directly, sought new ways to stop the Mosquito menace. Manfred Meurer, a Junkers Ju 88 pilot, ordered the removal of on-board equipment to reduce weight and increased the power of his engines with the addition of nitrous oxide for high-altitude flight. Alas, interceptions were still very rare but Meurer did shoot down a 139 Squadron Mosquito as it returned from Germany one night. Hitler believed the answer to the Mosquito problem was the Messerschmitt Me 262, a jet-powered fighter-bomber that could reach speeds of 500mph or more. In 1944 Luftwaffe ace Alfred Schreiber made history as he claimed a damaged Mosquito; the first aerial victory by a jet fighter. In late 1944 the British press published a story that Luftwaffe pilots shooting down a Mosquito could claim it as two aircraft. Again, these German countermeasures came too late and Goebbels' prediction of the Reich being gradually turned into a desert was becoming very apparent.

By the beginning of 1944, targets were bombed within 3 miles of the Pathfinder Force indicators but the success depended on accurate marker placement and often required additional corrections. The rivalry between Bennett and Air Vice Marshal Ralph Cochrane was intensified as Cochrane was an advocate of low-level precision marking and strived for the opportunity to prove the theory. Both men thought they knew best but Bennett believed he had already proven his point by turning a wasteful and ineffective force into a mighty and successful one using properly trained, fully equipped squadrons, even in the most challenging conditions. Cochrane, on the other hand, believed that the only way a target could be marked accurately was at extremely low level, particularly as the offensive moved into France and it was, after all, a technique that 8 Group would not attempt. Cochrane's famous leader of 617 Squadron, Wing Commander Leonard Cheshire, had started to develop the practice, first with a Lancaster then with a Mosquito before finally settling on the single-seat P-51 Mustang to mark the target. No. 617 Squadron started to achieve high levels of accuracy using the Stabilising Automatic Bomb Sight. Ironically, Cheshire nearly became a Pathfinder but Bennett insisted that he be tested like everyone else, which rather annoyed Cheshire as he had successfully completed three tours and so decided it wasn't for him. Possibly this was a costly error in judgement by Bennett and his loss was 5 Group's gain.

Cochrane had the 'ear' of Harris and had persuaded a sceptical Harris to permit the dam raid, so as Bennett was pleading with Harris for better crews, Harris told Cochrane to make sure that any tour-expired crews who would like to join 617 Squadron were given the opportunity to do so. Bennett and Cochrane were competing for the same crews and Harris had made it clear where his loyalties lay.

On 15 April 1944, Harris forced Bennett to relinquish three of his squadrons, 83, 97 and 627, to Cochrane's 5 Group, which Bennett viewed as a betrayal. It gave Bennett the impression that those under his command believed that Harris thought the Pathfinders had failed. Bennett also believed the 'Battle of Berlin' had decimated his Pathfinders during January 1944, with three squadrons – 156, 83 and 97 – suffering 227 men killed between them; the equivalent of thirty-two complete crews. In addition, the heaviest-hit squadrons were 7 and 156, both from the Pathfinder Force.

Bomber losses were at 5 per cent, with the average bomber crew expecting to be dead after twenty operations. However, during the Berlin campaign the Pathfinder Force loss rate reached over 13 per cent and included a high number of experienced crews and senior squadron commanders. These men were difficult to replace and the situation was strained by the recruitment and training of fifty new crews each month to the required standards. As Bennett's force focused on tactical air support for the ground armies advancing through Europe and the area-bombing of cities, his Mosquitos continued to harass the Germans. On the night of 20–21 February 1945 they attacked Berlin from in excess of 35,000ft and at high speed on thirty-six consecutive nights, with Mosquitos losses down to 1 per cent per 2,000 sorties, a Bomber Command record. No. 8 Group Pathfinders flew a total of 50,490 individual sorties against some 3,440 targets but the cost in human lives was awful, with at least 3,727 men killed. There can be no doubt that with the sacrifices of these men combined with advances in navigation, bomb-aiming equipment and the increased capability of their aircraft, Bomber Command evolved from a force of very limited capability into a formidable war-winning one.

Chapter 8

Training Civilians for War

The aircrews of Bomber Command operated a variety of aircraft to carry out strategic bombing operations from September 1939 to May 1945 in 126 squadrons from the United Kingdom, Canada, Australia, New Zealand, Poland, France and Czechoslovakia. In addition, other foreign volunteers joined to support the Allied campaigns. The age of aircrew ranged between nineteen and twenty-five, although there were rare exceptions with some as young as sixteen and at least one in his sixties.

The 1939 Air Training Agreement outlined that squadrons of the Royal Canadian Air Force, Royal Australian Air Force, and Royal New Zealand Air Force should be formed, equipped and financed by the Royal Air Force for service in Europe and that their personnel would serve only with their respective squadrons. There were, however, many personnel that were posted to units of the Royal Air Force or other air forces and vice versa.

The outbreak of war saw a huge influx of aircrew volunteers that needed to be trained and that presented a major task for Bomber Command. Some older volunteers had flying experience with pre-war University Air Squadrons or the Volunteer Reserve but the vast majority had never flown before. Aircrew Reception Centres were set up to process recruits and post them on to an Initial Training Wing for further specialist training. From August 1939 thirteen operational training squadrons became known as the Group Pool Squadrons but were renamed Operational Training Units from April 1940. The six-week courses formed individuals into crews with fifty-five hours flying for heavy bombers. Additional Operational Training Units were formed to facilitate the increase in demand for operational training.

Before acceptance, volunteers had to undergo basic theoretical and flying training where drill and physical training were combined with classroom work to prepare them for what was to come. Successful completion of examinations and various psychological and aptitude tests saw the graduates shipped overseas for flying training, with the Empire Air Training Agreement carried out at Service Flying Training Schools in the safer and less-congested skies of the USA, Canada, Australia, South Africa and South Rhodesia. The exception were flight engineers, who were trained in the UK. As the aircrews left training they were posted to Operational Training Units for the final stage, which prepared them for operations on particular types of aircraft or specific roles before being assigned to an operational squadron.

The Operational Training Units 'crewing up' process was a haphazard affair with hundreds of newly trained young men brought into hangars and told to sort themselves into crews. In some cases this was very successful as many men already knew each other from training schools and decided to fly together. They would then seek members from different trades to team up with and once formed and trained as a crew they quickly bonded into tightly knit units as they shared experiences and mutual danger and would often remain together until separated by death, injury, illness or re-posting at a time when only about 17 per cent of RAF crews could expect to finish a thirty-operation tour. Operational Training Unit instructors were usually experienced aircrew being 'rested' having completed an operational tour. They found themselves responsible for leading new airmen through a six- to ten-week course covering the essentials of night flying, navigation and bombing in all weathers.

Operational Training Units would have approximately fifty well-worn Wellington and Stirling bombers available, which were often kept flying longer than they should have been. These aircraft were considered to be death traps and when combined with inexperienced crews it led to a high number of fatal OTU accidents. This hazardous business claimed the lives of as many as 25 per cent of their strength within three or four months, including instructors. Some instructors preferred instead to fly on 'ops' as they felt more in control of their own destiny. It was common for crews fresh from an OTU to be transferred directly to an operational squadron and these 'Freshmen' or 'Sprogs' would begin their operational tour making up the numbers of the lost crews.

By early 1943, the increasing number of four-engine aircraft in the main force squadrons forced the forming of one Heavy Conversion Unit per bomber group and one Conversion Flight of four aircraft per squadron equipped with Halifaxes or Stirlings. During the additional five-week course, a flight engineer joined each crew and together they covered a variety of skills combined with twenty hours of flying instruction to complete a minimum of 350 hours before joining a heavy bomber squadron.

In April 1990, Bill Horsman described to me his experiences and ever-present challenges on a Stirling Heavy Conversion Unit:

> We flew a clapped-out Stirling from a Heavy Conversion Unit at RAF Winthorpe to convert crews trained on two-engine Wellingtons to the complexities of four engines. We used to say that Stirlings were the best three-engine bombers we had as ours were ex-operational, clapped out and suffering from oil cooling problems called 'coring' in which oil pressures and temperature 'yo-yoed' before the engine quit. With wheels and flaps up we could fly on three engines but with them down you could only come down.
>
> There was enough data at the Heavy Conversion Unit to confirm this and our replacement pilot had written off his first crew and it must have been hell for him. He was nervous and

we were equally unhappy. We had carried out 2 and 3 engine rehearsals with and without an instructor and were on our final exercise before going to Lancaster Finishing School and then back on to operations. We were on a night cross-country exercise and we flew over Northern Ireland and then over to Inverness when we lost an engine but managed to restart it. As we turned back toward base we lost an engine, then another – we were not happy. 'We call Darkie' I said firmly.

'Darky' was a position-finding procedure using radio telephony for an aircraft over England lost or in distress to speak to a ground station for a position check or course to steer to find his base airfield.

Eddy, our pilot, wasn't sure and our navigator wasn't keen, [saying] 'They will think I'm lost'. 'But we've only got two engines,' I repeated, so Eddy called, 'Hello Darkie, hello Darkie' along with our call sign. At once a 'drome lit up ahead of us and we got permission for a priority pancake landing. The lost engine powered the undercarriage, so it took me ten minutes of hard work to wind it down by hand and with the wheels down we could not go round again. Eddy took us into the landing approach and you can guess how relieved we were to hear the tyres screech as they hit the ground. Bloody good show Eddy! There was nothing wrong with Tom's navigation, we had landed at RAF Swinderby about 20 miles from base. Later, we refused to take off and returned to Winthorpe by transport and requested to be sent back on Ops, so off we went back again to East Kirkby, this time to 630 Squadron, sharing the same airfield with 57 Squadron. It took us quite a while to shake down with Eddy, he wasn't confident. It was a forced and arranged marriage but slowly we forged ourselves into a competent, professional crew. Our first trip was a shambles, but we survived.

When the Lancaster came into service in 1942, conversion became more complicated and Bomber Command was reluctant to release its precious aircraft to conversion training, so some Heavy Conversion Units used equal amounts of Halifax and Lancaster aircraft. This was abandoned during 1943. Pre-squadron Lancaster Finishing Schools provided a further twelve hours of flying but ceased in 1944 when Lancaster numbers increased to allow Heavy Conversion Units to be equipped.

Trained aircrew were to fly a 'tour' of thirty operations, after which they were 'screened' and 'rested' with a posting to an Operational Training Unit or Heavy Conversion Unit to help prepare the next groups of crews. When they completed an instructional tour some airmen returned to operations, often at their own request or by routine postings, and they would join a newly trained crew and start another operational tour. Some experienced airmen repeatedly returned to operations at their own request, with several brave airmen having recorded over 100 operations.

Chapter 9

The Pathfinder Mosquitos

The twin-engine de Havilland DH.98 Mosquito was the first true multi-role combat aircraft and was the forerunner to the Cold War workhorse the Panavia Tornado and, more recently, the Eurofighter Typhoon.

Nicknamed the 'Mossie' or the 'Wooden Wonder' owing to its wooden construction, its design concept was not favoured by the Minister of Aircraft Production, Lord Beaverbrook. The chief designer, Geoffrey de Havilland, almost saw his pride and joy being written off in 1941 but fortunately, Air Chief Marshal Sir Wilfrid Freeman defended de Havilland and his design concept, prompting some to unkindly tag the aircraft as 'Freeman's Folly'.

Originally conceived as an unarmed bomber, the Mosquito evolved into one of the fastest operational aircraft in the world and was used as a low- to medium-altitude daytime tactical bomber, high-altitude night bomber, pathfinder, day or night fighter, fighter-bomber, intruder, maritime strike and photo-reconnaissance aircraft. It was also used by the British Overseas Airways Corporation to carry small, high-value cargo to and from neutral countries through enemy-controlled airspace. The crew, a pilot and navigator sat side by side, although a single passenger could ride in the aircraft's empty bomb bay when necessary. De Havilland were highly experienced in wooden aircraft construction and with wood plentiful, cheap and easy to work by employing skilled woodworkers, it avoided putting additional demands upon metal supplies and metal workers. The sandwiched balsa wood and plywood was later covered with a dense-weave fabric that would absorb liquids such as ink and paint and was stiffened with dope to produce a smooth surface and part-stressed skin. Owing to the split fuselage, 60 per cent of the installation work could be completed with relative ease before the half-shell sections were joined and the whole assembly fitted with a cockpit canopy. The entire structure would then be lowered and attached to the two-spar stressed skin wing, which carried the pair of Rolls-Royce engines, nacelles, radiators, fuel tanks and undercarriage.

Engine runs and taxiing trials were carried out by Geoffrey de Havilland Jr and the prototype aircraft (later number W4050) made its maiden flight on 25 November 1940.

Nine early production bombers were derived from the first PP Mk I aircraft and were known as Mosquito B Mk IV Series 1s with a modest bomb load of 1,000lb when using standard production British bombs. Tests revealed that it was possible to double the bomb load to 2,000lb if the standard 500lb bombs had their tail fins shortened. Mosquito crews discovered that the Mosquito could outpace an Fw 190 by a small margin, and further tests revealed that improved exhaust systems gave the Mosquito 10 to 12mph more speed.

Famously, in September 1939 Hermann Göring, head of the German Air Force, announced in a radio speech that if as much as a single enemy aircraft was to fly over German soil his name would be changed to Meir! On 30 January 1943 a flight of three Mosquito B Mk IVs from 105 Squadron, the first squadron to receive the type, bombed the main Berlin broadcasting station where Göring was due to address a parade commemorating the tenth anniversary of the Nazis being voted into power. Göring was off the air for more than an hour and later that afternoon a second flight of Mosquitos from 139 Squadron interrupted a speech by Joseph Goebbels, the Third Reich's Propaganda Minister, at the Sports Palace with a perfectly timed attack. However, Berlin's anti-aircraft defences were on the alert and a Mosquito flown by Squadron Leader D. Darling

DFC was shot down, killing him and his navigator. Göring was enraged and was to rage to his aircraft manufacturers that he could 'go berserk' when faced with the Mosquito, which made him 'green and yellow with envy'.

Some pilots and navigators who had completed tours on heavy bombers often dreamt of flying the exhilarating 450mph Mosquito and the prospect of bombing Berlin or tossing bombs into railway tunnels from 60ft was a tempting proposition. The agile Mossie gave the Pathfinder pilot a feeling of immunity but with it came the huge responsibility of dropping target markers on time and on target. The first Mosquito on the scene as the pilot took the aircraft into a dive after giving the 'Tally-ho' was guaranteed to receive the undivided attention of the ground defences. The anti-aircraft guns would send hot projectiles streaking past the cockpit and at times crews would hear and smell the flak, so in an effort to see their instruments, experienced pilots would lower their seats to counter the glare of searchlights. Sometimes the flak bursting under the wings was close enough to knock an aircraft off its run but the pilot had to recover control and carry on. The Mosquitos flew through extreme hazards and most crews had done their stint in the main force and knew full well that their colleagues up high were getting a pasting too.

The Mosquito was a rare commodity and new aircraft were sent directly to front-line squadrons, which presented the problem of how to train new crews as the only comparable aircraft was another Mosquito. The solution was to form 1655 Mosquito Training Unit, which accepted volunteer pilots and navigators with previous operational experience or airmen that had shown exceptional capabilities at a training unit.

The elite Pathfinder crews in their Lancasters and Halifaxes operated with a seven-man crew: pilot, flight engineer, navigator, wireless operator, bomb aimer and two gunners. A Mosquito crew consisted of just the pilot and navigator, but like the 'heavies' they had to perform effectively and they had to rely upon one another and work as a team. The objective was the same: get to the target, drop the ordnance and then get home safely. In the unarmed Mosquito bomber, the navigator was responsible for bomb release, although later developments with 627 Squadron transferred the role to the pilot. The navigator also had the responsibility of navigating the aircraft using 'dead reckoning' to estimate the position by calculating wind, airspeed and course, which although a seemingly simple technique was subject to accumulative errors. The navigator kept a log of the whole flight. The introduction of Window, Oboe, GEE and H2S saw the skill level and operational intensity increase for the navigator.

Mosquito pilot 'Benny' Goodman on navigation:

Flying the Mosquito was a pleasure but navigating it was a completely different kettle of fish. Most navigators had come from Wellingtons but the Mosquito flew twice as fast so the poor old navigator had to work very much more quickly than before. However it seemed to come right in the end for everyone and I am sure that by the time Bill and I rolled to a standstill for the last time in our squadron Mosquito he had become almost blasé about navigating it to and from remote parts of the Third and last Reich.

Chapter 10

The Battle of the Beams

The navigation equipment of the 1930s was limited to a blind-landing aid and as the war developed a technological battle began between Britain and Germany that would become known as the 'Battle of the Beams'. The Germans had used accurate radio navigation during the Blitz bombing of the UK, which used huge antennas to provide greater accuracy at long range. However, British scientists developed a variety of increasingly effective systems for jamming and deception. The sending of their own Morse code signals could convince enemy aircraft that they were always properly centred on German beams but the reality was they were, in fact, wildly off course. The Germans were convinced that the British could bend radio signals. From 1942 a new generation of navigational and radar aids played an increasingly crucial part in Bomber Command's ability to find and then hit the target at night, beginning with Oboe.

GEE

GEE was a navigation and blind-bombing guidance system using synchronised pulses transmitted from separate towers in Britain that were received by the aircraft fitted with a GEE receiver that measured the arrival time difference between the pulses, allowing it to calculate the distance between the two stations. The navigator would instruct the pilot to adjust his course so as to place the aircraft along a line of constant difference in distance between the two stations.

The hyperbola from the two lines was shown as a 'lattice line' on a special chart used by the navigator, who also took occasional fixes to check and correct his dead reckoning navigation. When the two traces overlapped it indicated that the bomber was flying a precise distance from the station. With the aircraft flying along the curve it would take it over the aiming point and when both signals overlapped at the pre-set range the bombs were dropped. The main advantage of GEE allowed position fixing at any time without the need for radio communication. It was, however, limited to a range of 350 miles from the ground stations.

Although used against Essen on the night of 8–9 March, the raid on Cologne on the night of 13–14 March 1942 was the first successful GEE-led attack when the target was successfully illuminated with flares and incendiaries and the bombing was accurate. It was calculated that the attack was five times more effective than the earlier raid on the city and bombing policy was changed as a result. The success of GEE led to the selecting of sixty German cities within GEE range for mass bombing, using up to 1,800 tons of bombs per city.

GEE-H greatly reduced the navigator's workload but kept his attention focused on keeping the blips on the upper trace aligned on the display and keeping an intermittent eye on the lower blips for timing. A bomber could be guided to within 120 yards over Germany, which was an improvement of GEE's performance of one-mile accuracy at the same distance. The alignment process took about fifteen seconds with a sea-level accuracy of 25ft and an accurate fix to a range of 400 miles at an altitude of 10,000ft.

Oboe

The Oboe navigation aid was developed in 1942 by collaboration between 109 Squadron RAF and the Telecommunications Research Establishment. It combined radar tracking with radio transponder technology, which allowed aircraft to bomb targets accurately in any weather, day or night.

Two Oboe stations situated far apart and as far to the east as possible on the English coast used radio transmissions that would be received by aircraft in enemy airspace to fix the aircraft's location. As the aircraft progressed along its route, its transponder picked up radar pulses from one tracking station called the 'Cat' and adjusted its flight path accordingly. After a short delay it sent the signals back to the stations, where the signal time was calculated to determine the distance between the station and the aircraft. The other station, the 'Mouse', would determine the exact bomb release point, therefore establishing a ground-controlled, blind bombing system. Where the two arcs intersected it indicated the location of the target.

Oboe radar did not follow the curvature of the earth, so it was difficult to determine the altitude, but an aircraft flying at 28,000ft could receive Oboe transmissions at about 270 miles, within the range for the targets in the Ruhr. The Mosquito was the only aircraft that had the performance to receive Oboe signals further into Germany and made Oboe accurate to within a few hundred yards after a run in to the target from about 10 miles.

Oboe was used for the first time in March 1943 to mark the Krupp Works in Essen and continued for several months with great success against the industrial centre of the Ruhr and Cologne. In November 1943 Oboe became vulnerable to jamming signals and even suffered interference from the Lancaster device called Monica. Oboe stations could only operate one aircraft at a time and with a marking run taking up to ten minutes and six bomb or marker runs per hour and target indicator illumination lasting for six minutes, it produced a four-minute gap in marking; a failed marking run increased the gap to fourteen minutes. The introduction of multi-channel control and more ground stations eventually increased the concentration of Oboe marking but developments of H2S and

GEE-H systems could provide the accuracy of Oboe for making precision bombings of high-value targets. However, Oboe was by far the most accurate bombing system used during the war and made 9,624 sorties on 1,797 raids.

H2S

H2S was the first airborne, ground-scanning radar system used for navigation and blind bombing by Bomber Command and enabled ground targets to be identified at night and in all weathers. It increased the range of use beyond GEE and Oboe but proved to be inferior to Oboe for blind bombing purposes except on coastal targets. Tests in 1941 revealed that objects such as water, open land, cities and towns produced different distinct radar returns and it was established that the radar scanning and display equipment could map the area below.

The radar scanner displayed the echoes detected on a cathode-ray tube, presenting a visible contrast between different land features and allowing a navigator to determine the aircraft's position even in cloud cover and identify a landmark from which the navigator could begin a timed bombing run. H2S accuracy depended on the skill and experience of the operator as the shape and appearance of a town could vary considerably with the angle and direction from which it was viewed and did not always bear any resemblance to the shape that would be seen by the naked eye. Coastal features and water were easier to distinguish as the presentation between land and sea was more uniform.

Early 1943 saw H2S going into service but it was restricted by slow delivery and the limited number of sets available. As the programme accelerated, six Pathfinder and twelve main force squadrons were equipped and appreciated its value as track keeping could be maintained with an accuracy of about 4 miles.

On the night of 2–3 February 1943, its second operational mission, the Germans captured an almost intact H2S unit from a downed aircraft, followed by a second a week later. They were able to establish how H2S worked and were dismayed to find an image of Berlin displayed on the parts they pieced together! The Germans introduced the 'FuG 350 Naxos' radar detector in late 1943, which enabled Luftwaffe night fighters to home on the H2S transmissions. Pathfinder Mosquitos continued to use H2S Mk II from February 1944 until the end of the war.

Window

Albert Rowe, head of the Telecommunications Research Establishment, coined the code name Window, which became the single most important radar countermeasures used by RAF heavy bombers. In 1937 scientists developed Window, which were clusters of aluminium strips dropped from aircraft in order to generate a cloud of false echoes on enemy radar systems.

Early use of notebook-size sheets were printed to also serve as propaganda leaflets but it was found that the most effective size was strips of black paper backed with aluminium foil cut precisely to 10.63in by 0.79in that were packed into bundles each weighing 1lb.

Official permission to use Window was delayed owing to the limited supply of aluminium and the shortage of suitable manufacturing plants. There were also concerns that the Germans would turn the jamming method back on to the UK radar defences but it is now known that they were influenced by this same fear of radar jamming system and it was proved to be well founded.

Eventually, Window was used for the first time over Hamburg on the night of 24–25 July 1943 and continued to confuse German radar for the rest of the war. Possibly the most ambitious and successful use of Window was during Operation *Taxable*, the false D-Day 'amphibious' assault, carried out by 617 Squadron.

Chapter 11

Bombs and Target Indicators

The Second World War saw dramatic changes in the technologies, tactics and design that influenced strategic bombing with high-explosive ordnance.

The light and medium bombers of 1939 to 1941 with limited performance and load capacity had a good supply of pre-war 250lb and 500lb General Purpose bombs but this restricted their offensive capabilities. Within three years, new aircraft design had revolutionised the design of offensive ordnance, culminating in the 22,000lb earthquake monster called 'Grand Slam'. Pre-Second World War bombs were of bulbous appearance but changed to the cylindrical body with a tapered nose and tail fin. However, a 1942 study discovered that only 70 per cent of bombs dropped actually exploded, the remainder failing owing to the arming and detonation mechanism freezing in the storage conditions on RAF airfields. The problem was solved by the squadron armourers fusing the bombs after they had been loaded into the aircraft bomb bay just before the aircraft took off. General Purpose casings were satisfactory when used against German built-up areas, especially with a quarter-second delayed tail fuse or a nose fuse delay of one tenth of a second. In 1943, a new set of standardised General Purpose bombs were produced with weights of 250lb, 500lb, 1,000lb and 2,000lb and these accounted for the vast majority of the bombs dropped until the end of the war.

The 500lb Medium Capacity bomb contained almost twice the high-explosive content of the General Purpose bombs, with approximately 50 per cent explosive and the rest made up of the fragmentation casing. Along with its 1,000lb partner, they were very effective weapons, although during some of 1944 they were in short supply, prompting careful rationing. At this time, the high-explosive material varied but most used Amatol, RDX or Torpex. The 4,000lb 'cookie' or 'blockbuster' high capacity had a thin wall casing that collapsed on impact and allowed 75 per cent of its weight to consist of explosives. The 8,000lb variant was similar in shape and resembled two oil drums bolted end to end. To aid stability, a tail fin was added. The thin wall and lightweight body would collapse on impact, so the cookie was fitted with instantaneous fuses. Some armourers considered the 4,000lb cookie dangerous to transport and load as the detonating pistols were sensitive to the flow of air, occasionally causing some to explode when dropped even when they were considered 'safe' and unarmed. This cookie was the largest carried by Mosquitos with a modified bomb bay and some crews were surprised by the concussive force it generated as aircraft dropping the device from lower than 6,000ft risked being damaged by the explosion's shock wave.

Bomb Fusing

Bombs were fused with a pistol detonator or fuses operated by barometric, clockwork, pyrotechnic or hydrostatic processes usually detonated in an air burst. Targets requiring ground penetration such as building foundations or underground facilities used tail time-delay fuses, which could be set to detonate at fractions of a second or up to minutes or hours. Instantaneous-detonation fuses were fitted in the nose of the bomb but had a back-up fuse in the tail should the nose fuse fail.

Bomb Handling

Bomber stations stored up to 200 tons of bombs sited in dumps located around airfield perimeters as a precaution against the ever-present threat of accidents. Depending on the operational requirements, the bombs were selected and loaded on to bomb trolleys, which were then towed by David Brown or Fordson tractors to the aircraft dispersal. Nearly all bomb trolleys had a low rectangular chassis with small pneumatic tyres at each corner and were made to accommodate the different weights. They had adjustable chocks on the bed to prevent the bombs rolling. It was vitally important for the bombs to be loaded in the correct sequence; one small miscalculation in handling a bomb could be deadly and one misplaced coloured flare could threaten the success of a raid over enemy territory. The 'chop rate' for armourers on bomber squadrons was second only to that of the aircrew and the rate increased with the pressure of operations with more aircraft, more bombs and more fuel needed to be loaded in less time.

Incendiary bombs

Incendiary bombs were constructed of light casings filled with pyrotechnic substances that were detonated by a mildly sensitive explosive built in the nose and/or tail or a mechanical striker pistol. Detonation could be delayed if required and some were fitted with anti-handling devices to prevent the enemy bomb from rendering the weapon safe.

Up to 236 4lb magnesium incendiary bombs could be carried in open aluminium boxes called Small Bomb Containers inside the aircraft bomb bay. The containers were fitted upside down and stacked in five rows, six rows deep, held in place by hinged bars that had an electrical release mechanism at the other end that would release the entire contents. In a Lancaster, twelve Small Bomb Containers were often used in conjunction with a 4,000lb cookie bomb, the blast from which would blow the rooftops off the building, allowing the incendiaries to drop into the building before igniting. The empty Small Bomb Containers remained in the aircraft bomb bay until the aircraft had landed so armourers would check that they were empty before they were unloaded and refilled. The one disadvantage of incendiary bombs was that once dropped they were susceptible to drifting in the wind and would become widely dispersed. Bombers at lower altitudes were at risk of being showered over the target area. As a regular feature of the bombing campaigns, in excess of 8 million 4lb incendiary bombs were dropped during the course of the war.

The RAF dropped more than 400,000 J-Type incendiary bombs, which produced an intense glare made by a spectacular jet of flame similar to that of a flame thrower to a distance of 15ft and burned for one minute. They were developed for target marking, illumination and identification.

To assist with proving that bomber crews had hit their intended target, photographic flares were developed to illuminate the area to record exactly where the bombs fell. The crews were required to fly straight and level after bomb release and with the flash igniting at a predetermined height it allowed a clear photograph to be taken without displaying the flash bomb in the picture.

Target Indicators

The target indicator bomb was a 250lb bomb case with good ballistic properties filled with red, green, yellow, or white coloured 'candles'. When dropped over the target, it burst at a predetermined height controlled by a barometric fuse that ignited the contents of the bomb and ejected the pyrotechnic candles that would descend to the ground. This produced a brilliant, luminous cascade of about 100 yards in diameter that lasted for about three minutes.

The raid over Nuremburg on 28–29 August 1942 saw a basic target marker used for the first time. Known as a 'red blob', a 250lb bomb casing was filled with a mixture of Benzol, rubber and phosphorus that burst at a predetermined height, ejecting a parachute that floated to the ground and burned red for up to twenty minutes. A month later, against Düsseldorf, a converted 4,000lb cookie bomb casing was filled with the same substances and was the largest of all markers, actually weighing 2,800lb. It continued to be used throughout the remainder of the war but a change in the colour made the device burn bright pink on impact, which warranted the nicknamed 'pink pansy'. Generally, crews referred to the ground markers as 'spot fires'.

Ideally, target markers were to burn for as long as possible and the Germans became desperate to extinguish them as soon as possible, so the British introduced explosive candles into the bombs designed to detonate at different times. Although losing some of its intensity, the marker would burn for a longer period of time. Later techniques saw the use of a yellow ground marker, called a long stop, which marked the edge of the bombing area to prevent the bombing from straying further. Once dropped, it cancelled out all stray target indicators and was used along with bracketing flares dropped on either side of the aiming point.

Chapter 12

The Defence of Germany

The Luftwaffe was responsible for German anti-aircraft defences for the entire war and prompted massive expansion of personnel, guns and searchlights.

'Light' flak guns of 2cm and 3.7cm guns were suited for engaging low-flying and fast aircraft and could produce a curtain of fire from the automatic weapons at twenty rounds per minute with their 30kg shell travelling at nearly 3,000ft per second and capable of destroying a bomber flying at 30,000ft.

'Heavy' flak of 8.8cm and 10cm were single-shot guns operated by a ten-man team with a four-gun battery controlled by a predictor providing the gun with azimuth, elevation and fuse settings. These could discharge projectiles at about fifteen or twenty rounds per minute up to between 26,000 and 35,000ft, right into a bomber stream. Predicted flak was feared by crews during the bombing run to the target and it is believed that nearly 700 Pathfinder bombers fell to 'heavy' flak. The closing stages of the war saw 'heavy' flak guns relocated to the east in an attempt to counter the Soviet advances, which stripped large German areas of their defences and rendered them almost defenceless to aerial attacks.

When Berlin was bombed on 25 August 1940, Hitler immediately ordered the construction of flak towers to protect the centre of his Reich. Eight enormous flak towers were constructed to defend major cities against air attack from bombers, with three in Berlin, two in Hamburg and three in Vienna; other cities had towers but they were not on the same scale.

The Berlin towers were constructed in two sections, a gun tower and a fire control and command tower. Standing at over 100ft and over 200ft square supported by 11ft-thick walls, they provided dual-level gun platforms. The upper level was equipped with eight pairs of 12.8cm Flak 40 guns to deal with higher-flying aircraft, while the lower platforms dealt with lower-flying aircraft with their smaller guns. The towers were also used as public air-raid shelters with capacity for up to 10,000 civilians and even had their own medical facilities. One sixteen-year-old Flakhilfer in the Berlin Zoo tower in 1943 recalled:

> The people were crammed in every room and in every section, right up to the fourth floor, where the military section began. They crowded into the passages so that we had to step over them as they slept on the floor. I think we had up to 20,000 people on the worst night (of the Battle of Berlin). In the morning, when the raid was over, it took hours to get everyone out.

In 1941, Hitler decided that high school students born between 1926 and 1927 should be conscripted into the Luftwaffe Air Force Auxiliaries, where they were called Luftwaffenhelfers. The young men, often delighted to be free of school and proud to serve their Fatherland, were taken straight from school to operate anti-aircraft units of the Reich. Many soon found themselves on the receiving end of fair share of incendiaries and bombs. An anonymous individual who was conscripted remembers:

> I remember being afraid with a sick feeling of anticipating the inevitable but this was only before the raids. When the female voice on our special radio frequency gave the position of approaching bomber streams we waited for data to come in for the gun controls. After that, training took over, and along

with the din of the guns and the exploding bombs, I forgot my fear and even experienced a kind of devil may care high. We graduated to battle-hardened gunners constantly tired and on edge and we could only relax if the weather was bad. Our alarm periods lasted from four to six hours depending on the weather and the moon. Quite often a lone Mosquito, aptly called a 'Schlafzerstorer' or 'sleep destroyer', arrived after the raids had ended and catapult us out of bed once again to run to the guns. When the American daylight raids began on Berlin in 1943, all Luftwaffenhelfer leave was cancelled. Only 88mm guns were able to reach the heights that the USAAF B-17 Flying Fortresses achieved and we were forced to stand by and observe as they bombed the city to ruins. Fire and smoke spread across the horizon and high up into the sky, while the thunder made the ground shake under our feet. At night it was quite similar but in full colour with the Christmas trees descending in slow motion from the sky.

It is estimated that between 70,000 to 80,000 students served in this unit.

In 1941 Germany provided an enormous 'belt' of searchlights up to 20 miles in depth and without the support of flak they were used to direct the German night fighters towards the enemy bombers. In May 1942 this poor system was changed to be used in conjunction with flak defences, providing circular groups of between ten and forty lights in fighter-protected areas on the approach routes to important targets controlled by master lights. As the bomber force crossed the enemy coast, they often ran the gauntlet of searchlight corridors right through to the target area. When an aircraft was picked out, other lights would concentrate their beams, producing a 'cone' that followed the path of a silhouetted bomber by intense light, which was easily seen by night fighters. The 'cones' offered excellent illumination to heights up to 18,000ft and it was common for bomber crews to become dazzled, preventing them from seeing night fighters or even the target area itself.

Following the fall of France in July 1940, and concerned about Allied bombing, the Germans built a belt of radar stations called Freya to act as an enemy aircraft early warning system. Known to the Allies as the Kammhuber Line, it consisted of a series of overlapping radar stations known as a Himmelbett (four-poster bed) zone, layered three deep from Denmark to near the Swiss border. Each was subdivided into a series of three-dimensional night fighter boxes or a 'Raum' in which three circular control zones of two giant Würzburgs and a single Freya radar set lay side by side with a radius corresponding to the range of about 60 miles. The Würzburg radar beam was too narrow to detect a bomber, so required the assistance of an additional Freya system with its broader beam to acquire the target and inform the Würzburg crew where to look in the sky. One night fighter could be guided towards a single bomber by the radar and once the night fighter crew detected the bomber on their on-board radar the crew took over the tracking and made their attack on the bomber. However, it was not capable of identifying friend from foe.

The Allied introduction of GEE from May 1942 forced the Germans to increase the depth of the Himmelbett system in front of and behind the original belt but it was limited to the tracking of two bombers and two night fighters simultaneously. By June 1943 the Germans had increased its night fighter force to eighteen Gruppen, five more than at the start of the year, but the Himmelbett system limited the number of night fighters over the Ruhr to thirty-six. The dropping of Window by mid-1943 paralysed the 'Kammhuber Line' and the Würzburg network, leaving only a limited number of fighters able to attack the bombers. The British were funnelling large numbers of bombers through a narrow channel in a short space of time, which provided an element of safety in numbers as they passed over the target in under twenty minutes. In response, 400 flak batteries, including the recalled equipment from Italy and the Eastern Front, were assembled at important targets to counter the shorter time the bombers were over the area. Later in July, attention would be focused on Hamburg but Bomber Command continued to raid the Ruhr in an effort to keep the German defences dispersed.

The Germans changed their tactics by deploying all its single-seat night fighters along the bomber routes both to and from the target. Messerschmitt Bf 109s and Focke-Wulf Fw 190s, referred to as Wilde Sau (Wild Boar), were instructed to roam freely above the flak barrage to search for bombers. The formidable Fw 190A was diverted from daylight duties against the USAAF 8th Air Force and was expected to deal with the increasing number of Mosquitos, which easily outpaced their twin-engine counterparts. German fighter controllers depended on early detection to direct their Wilde Sau crews but the British continued to frustrate them by keeping them guessing for as long as possible helped by flying 'spoof' raids that took the Wilde Saus in the opposite direction of the actual main force.

The British frequently jammed German signals and also transmitted 'spoof' orders by German-speaking RAF controllers but bombers would continue to be mauled by the night fighters. Fw 190s employing the Wilde Sau tactics was only a short-term solution until May 1944. By spring 1945 the night fighter force was still an effective adversary but it suffered from a lack of aviation fuel and the collapse of the ground control systems kept many aircraft grounded. It is fair to say that by the end of the war the night fighter force remained undefeated in battle.

Chapter 13

Germany Under the Bombs

The Blitz of 1940 prompted Harris to say that German civilians would 'reap the whirlwind' and experience the effects of bombing first hand on a nightly basis for many months. Melita Maschmann was a twenty-six year-old civilian Berliner and a convinced National Socialist who, on the night of 9 August 1944, was in the town of Darmstadt, 32 miles south of Frankfurt. At twenty minutes to midnight the sirens sounded, so everyone went down to the cellar and sat shivering on wooden benches as the first wave passed over. She wrote in her 1954 memoir *Account Rendered*:

> The hum of the approaching engines became a roaring hurricane. The crashes of the first explosions could already be heard. The light went out. Folding our arms over our heads in an instinctive gesture of self-defence, we cowered in the darkness and listened as the bombers came over in waves. Their infernal roar drew them near then moved away, approached again and withdrew. But they returned yet again and a few seconds of frantic hammering of the heart shut out all other sensations. Then came a longer pause as the explosions receded to the edge of town and the humming of the engines became distant.

The cellar turned into a prison and as Melita's mother cried to God for help, a fresh wave of bombers passed overhead. Escape was impossible as the building was an inferno, so climbing out of a small window and running through a sea of fire, the girl dipped her shoes in the nearest water tank and ran back but the window could only be opened from the inside.

'The human in me collapsed,' she said, 'and the animal took over. I ran to save my life; desperately summoning every scrap of energy. There was not a house anywhere in the street which had not turned into a burning firebrand. Above the sea of flames a glowing cyclone raged over the town and whenever it caught the bodies of people in flight it shrivelled them in a second to the size of a child. The next day they lay all over the streets, hardly burned like mummified children.'

That night 15,000 people died and nearly 80 per cent of Darmstadt was destroyed. Of those in that particular cellar, the only one to escape was Melita Maschmann.

Chapter 14

Mosquito Mk IV DZ477 with 139 'Jamaica' Squadron – February to March 1943

No. 139 Squadron was formed on 3 July 1918 at Villaveria in Italy using a flight previously attached to 34 Squadron for reconnaissance and fighter patrols over the Piave front until the end of the First World War.

No. 139 was reformed on 3 September 1936 at RAF Wyton with Hawker Hinds, converting to Bristol Blenheims in July 1939. As war broke out a Blenheim IV, N6215 piloted by Flying Officer Andrew McPherson, was the first British aircraft to cross the German coast to provide photographic information of the German Fleet in the northern ports of Germany, for which he was awarded the DFC. The results of the reconnaissance prompted the first air raid of the war the following day, when 107 and 139 Squadrons attacked German shipping near Wilhelmshaven. The squadron was posted to northern France from December 1939 but lost most of its aircraft during the German invasion, so returned to the UK to re-equip with Blenheim IVs. No. 139 started to carry out day and night bombing attacks on enemy-occupied ports and airfields until the end of May 1941.

The general public and private companies raised money for the purchase of much-needed aircraft and a Jamaican newspaper, the *Daily Gleaner*, raised enough money to buy twelve Blenheims by 1941. In recognition, Lord Beaverbrook, the Minister of Aircraft Production, declared that Jamaica's name shall evermore be linked to the 139 Squadron of the RAF, so it became 139 (Jamaica) Squadron.

After a brief period in Luga, Burma, 139 was absorbed into 62 Squadron and operated against the Japanese invasion, but by June 1942 the unit had returned to Horsham St Faith in Norwich, England. Although re-equipped with the Blenheim V, they were not flown operationally and were replaced by de Havilland Mosquitos borrowed from 105 Squadron.

On 3 March 1943, 139 Squadron attacked a molybdenum processing plant at Knaben in Norway, with a number of crews awarded decorations following this daring raid. Sadly, some of the men were lost on 20 March, just before their decorations were officially announced. The raid is believed to have inspired the fictional book and film *633 Squadron*. From 4 June 1943, 139 ceased daylight operations and joined 8 Group Pathfinder Force in July, based at RAF Wyton then RAF Upwood. It remained at Upwood for the remainder of the war, receiving new aircrews from 1655 Mosquito Training Unit, the specialist Pathfinder Mosquito training unit.

After 109 Squadron had pioneered the use of Oboe, 105 Squadron became the second Oboe squadron operating with the 'heavies' against special targets while 139 conducted high-level nuisance raids flying B.IX Mosquitos. No. 139 Squadron Mosquitos fitted with GEE-H and later H2S would lead the Light Night Striking Force on night-time 'siren tours' as part of Operation *Ploughman* designed to disrupt night-time factory production or to bring loss of sleep to the general public by attacking several targets within a single sortie. Careful and creative planning would cause the air raid sirens to wail throughout Germany on successive nights by bombing several targets on one sortie. This started on 20–21 April 1943, when nine 105 Squadron Mosquitos and two from 139 delivered a special birthday present for Hitler in Berlin. Tragically, Mosquito DZ386, piloted by Wing Commander Peter Shand, the leader of so many daylight operations, was shot down over the Dutch coast by a German fighter, a shattering blow to his squadron.

Berlin was relatively easy to locate in good weather but limited navigation equipment in the Mosquito prevented accurate bombing in poor weather conditions. However, by the end of May, Berlin had been bombed five times. An estimated 27,000 sorties were flown by the Light Night Striking Force for the loss of fewer than 200 aircraft, with as many as 685 operations flown when the heavy bombers were not operating, a stunning achievement for an unarmed, wooden, two-man aeroplane.

During take-off, the 139 Squadron Mosquitos lined up on the aerodrome almost wingtip to wingtip and as the leader started to move forward on the left side of the formation each aircraft accelerated gradually and the whole formation took off in a tight echelon to starboard. Often, the entire station personnel would turn out to watch the formidable striking force take off. As the Mosquitos rolled along the bumpy grass airstrip and gathered speed they would occasionally find themselves in each other's slipstream, which made the fully loaded aircraft difficult to control. Following a number of close calls they adopted the safer but less spectacular policy of each aircraft taking off several seconds after the previous one. When airborne they would close up into a tight formation, make a couple of circuits of the aerodrome, then set course for the coast.

By the end of June 1943 GEE navigation fixes became more frequent and on 29 November 139 Squadron began a regular task of dropping Window on the route to Berlin ahead of the main force to confuse German radars. Canadian-built, new-version Mosquitos supplemented the supply of new aircraft, which allowed sufficient Mk IVs to form 627 Squadron at RAF Oakington.

Post-war, the squadron replaced their Mosquitos with Canberras in November 1953 and in the following February the Victor B2 Intensive Trials Unit became 139 Squadron at RAF Wittering, forming part of the V-Bomber Force until it was disbanded on 21 December 1968.

In December 1938 King George VI authorised the squadron badge, which depicts a 'fasces', an axe head inserted and tied into a bundle of sticks. Used as a symbol of authority and power, it can be traced back to ancient Roman leaders. The motto 'Si placet necamus' translates to 'We Destroy at Will'.

RAF Marham

RAF Marham in Norfolk occupied an 80-acre site within the boundary of the present-day station situated near the village of Marham. It opened in August 1916 as RAF Narborough with the Royal Flying Corps' 51 Squadron based there focused on defending Norfolk from Zeppelin raids.

The airfield was not used for most of the inter-war years but was held in reserve until the expansion of the RAF in early 1935. Considerable work was required to make the airfield active and on 1 April 1937 it operated with 3 Group Bomber Command. Marham's future lay with heavy bombers as a succession of squadrons moved in. No. 38 Squadron, with its ungainly Fairey Hendons, was commanded by a certain Captain A.T. Harris, later to become 'Bomber' Harris.

During the 'Phoney War' of winter 1939, 115 Squadron mounted operations against German shipping along the Norwegian coast and the new Vickers Wellington dropped thousands of propaganda leaflets over enemy territory on night sorties lasting many hours. In November 1941 105 Squadron arrived and was the first to receive de Havilland Mosquitos. It worked hard to perfect the new Oboe-led Pathfinder techniques to become fully operational in May 1942 as an important part of the Pathfinder Force.

In 1942, every bomber and training station in eastern England began to prepare to provide all available aircraft for special operations called 'maximum efforts'. Weekend passes and crew leaves were cancelled and crews on leave received immediate recall telegrams, with ground crews told to make every aircraft available. Eventually, and following much speculation, Group Headquarters announced on the morning of 30 May that Cologne would be the target that night. The crews were relieved that the objective was not the 'Big City', Berlin, and that it was a night operation. The first bomber left Marham at 2230hrs and joined the massive bomber stream of 1,047 aircraft forming over East Anglia and heading towards Germany. A total of 868 aircraft bombed the target, setting the city ablaze with many fires still burning several days later. The majority of the forty-one aircraft that were lost came from the Wellington squadrons. Marham crews were to be involved in other '1,000-bomber' raids to Bremen and Essen.

On 25 September 1942, 105 Squadron delivered a low-level daylight attack on the Gestapo headquarters in Oslo, Norway. Intended to boost the morale of the Norwegian resistance, this daring attack was to coincide with a Nazi rally in the city that day but en route one of the four Mosquitos despatched was intercepted and shot down by Fw 190s. Four bombs hit the building but three passed right through the walls and failed to explode. The fourth, which remained inside the building, also failed to explode. Nevertheless, this was the first low-level Mosquito attack of the war and set the trend for many other attacks of 1943–44 in unarmed aircraft, which relied on high speed to escape the attentions of enemy fighters. They targeted enemy infrastructure including engine sheds, small industrial works, oil storage and river and canal traffic. Nos 105 and 139 Squadrons mounted spectacularly successful daylight raids over the next few months, which was noticed by the chiefs at Bomber Command and a change in operational emphasis was now imminent; that of target marking for the heavy bombers of Bomber Command.

On 4 July, 139 Squadron relocated to RAF Wyton, allowing 109 Squadron to move in. Having completed considerable training, 105 Squadron were ready to mount their first Oboe attack on the Krupps factory on 25 July with 750 main force bombers following them. Using Oboe, Marham's two Mosquito squadrons continued to carry out spectacular low-level missions with very low losses of less than 1 per cent.

Wartime operations at RAF Marham halted in March 1944 for the construction of three new concrete runways of the familiar wartime triangular pattern with new perimeter tracks and dispersal areas, making Marham, along with nearby RAF Sculthorpe, the only airfields built for heavy bombers.

Post-war years at Marham saw operations as a Cold War Air Force base, hosting many types including the English Electric Canberra and later the V-bomber force and Vickers Valiant and Handley Page Victor tankers. The station was one of the few large enough for the operation of the USAF's huge Boeing B-52 Stratofortress, which operated from Marham on exercises in the 1970s and 1980s.

The arrival of the Panavia Tornado was the beginning of a success story similar to that of the Mosquito. As a true multi-role combat aircraft with variable-sweep wings and two engines, the Tornado was designed as a primary strike aircraft with the capability to deliver conventional and nuclear ordnance in all weathers. The Tornado made its combat debut as part of Operation *Granby*, the British contribution to the Gulf War in 1991, with Marham-based crews from 617 Squadron, who also flew Storm Shadow attacks during Operation *Ellamy* over Libya and later in Operation *Shader*, the military intervention against the Islamic State of Iraq and the Levant. The much-loved Tornado (or 'the fin' or 'Tonka') was updated over the years and was a potent, capable aircraft that served with distinction until it was withdrawn in April 2019. RAF Marham is now the home of the F-35B Lightning, a fifth-generation, multi-role, fighter operated, appropriately enough, by 617 Squadron.

Chapter 15

DZ477 – War Diary 1943

Sunday, 14 February
Target: Tours engine sheds
Crew: Squadron Leader R. B. Bagguley and Flight Lieutenant K. Hayden
Time: Up: 1630hrs, down: 1915hrs

The Tours raids of 14 and 18 February 1943 became known as the 'Great Tours Derby'. Both trips in driving rain and low cloud were led by Wing Commander Shand and Squadron Leader Bagguley and proved to be a nerve-racking 'follow my leader' trip into France. Ten Mosquitos from 139 Squadron were split into two formations. The first six set a course at 1640hrs and crossed Selsey Bill but lost each other in the bumpy condition and thick clouds on several occasions. However, by flying a straight and level course they regrouped on breaking through the cloud. Sergeant G. Cummings and Sergeant B. C. Kemp in DZ423 abandoned the mission 50 miles inside the French coast when they were cut off from the other aircraft by extremely bad visibility and heavy rain, so they dumped their bombs in the sea. Flying Officer W. E. Rennie and Flying Officer Embrey in DZ476 also lost formation but carried on to find clearer visibility. They climbed to 1,000ft and bombed a goods train near Mayenne, dropping all four bombs in one salvo. On turning back, there was a scene of devastation with clouds of steam and a lot of rubble.

As the remaining aircraft approached, the clouds cleared slightly so the formation climbed to 2,500ft and Wing Commander Shand led the first formation of six Mosquitos into a shallow diving attack from 1,000ft at 1750hrs. There was still low-level cloud, which prevented complete success but the formation succeeded in bombing their primary target of the engine repair shops on the north side of the town from 50ft through the flak and tracer over the target.

Squadron Leader Bob Bagguley in DZ477 led the second formation of four aircraft but lost the first group in the low cloud and rain, so he had no alternative but to turn back without dropping his bombs when 60 miles inland. Three aircraft turned back but Flying Officer C. V. Pereira and Flying Officer G. H. Gilbert in DZ470 climbed away through thick cloud and carried on alone for ten minutes before descending through a break in the cloud, finding five other aircraft below him. They re-joined the formation at 1751hrs and made a shallow dive attack on the engine round house to the east of the town, scoring two direct bomb hits, one of which hit the turntable in the middle.

On 17 February, Flying Officer Mike Wayman and his navigator, Flying Officer O. 'Pops' Clear, took off at 1250hrs in DZ465 for a photographic reconnaissance and followed a similar low-level route to that taken by the attack formation. Five photographic runs were made over the target at 4,000ft with no opposition met. They landed at 1725hrs, delivering photographs that showed that the western end of the repair shops had been severely damaged with the round house without its roof.

Thursday, 18 February
Target: Tours engine sheds and railway yards
Crew: Sergeant E. G. Matta and Sergeant G. J. Sleeman
Time: Up: 1630hrs, down: 2045hrs

The twenty-six Mosquitos from 139 and 105 Squadron was the largest formation yet an they were sent to finish the job started on the 14th. The aircraft formed up over the aerodrome and flew to the south coast at 1,000ft at 1640hrs, taking the same route as the previous raid. Soon after take-off, Flying Officer J. H. Brown and Flying Officer G. Pounder in DZ418 were forced back to base with an electrical failure and took the reserve aircraft. However, they were unable to re-join the formation before reaching the south coast so they returned to base.

In fine weather the formation split up when they dived to 50ft to cross the sea but Mosquito, DZ464 crewed by Flying Officer W. Sutherland and Flying Officer G. E. Dean, flew into a flock of ducks off the French coast. The bomb aimer's Perspex panel was shattered and the starboard main plane was holed. Later another unfortunate bird was found protruding from the port main plane. The navigator, Flying Officer Dean, received a cut over one eye and a mouthful of feathers but they continued on, with Sutherland having to use increased engine boost to counteract the extra drag. They managed to hold formation and continued on to strike the target but found the remainder of the journey to be extremely draughty! This was not the first occasion a high-speed, low-level Mosquito was intercepted by birds; aircraft were soon to be fitted with bulletproof windscreens to provide the only sensible solution.

On crossing the French coast, the crews encountered ground fire from one machine gun and as the weather closed in down to 300ft then 100ft they descended low to the deck about 30 miles inside France.

Flying Officer W. Talbot and Sergeant J. Der-Stepanian in DZ422 lost the formation and decided to return to base but the others continued and remained in cloud for another ten minutes until they emerged into bright sunlight with the formation almost intact. Oddly, the wing commander found himself at the back of the formation instead of leading it from the front. As the River Loire was seen, the weather started to clear again so the formation climbed to prepare for a shallow dive attack from 1,000ft on the round house in the centre of the town, encountering some light flak as they went as low as 100ft. DZ477 bombed successfully.

The attack on the engine sheds and round house, which caused thick smoke to rise to about 700ft, was successful and put the facilities out of action for a considerable time. On the return journey some flak was encountered and the occasional balloon but one Mosquito, DZ420 crewed by Flight Sergeant F. A. Budden and Sergeant F. Morris, failed to return after crashing at Vengeons, 4km north-north-east of Sourdeval. Both crew members are buried in Vengeons Cemetery.

Friday, 26 February 1943
Target: Rennes naval stores
Crew: Sergeant Massey DFM and Sergeant Fletcher DFM
Time: Up: 1650hrs, down: 2140hrs

Ten 139 Squadron aircraft and ten from 105 Squadron set out to attack the stores led by Wing Commander G. P. Longfield and Flying Officer R. F. Millns of 105 Squadron. However, as they led the low-level formation into the target, he flew straight into a heavily defended area of the aerodrome Aéroport de Rennes-Saint-Jacques. Undamaged, he banked steeply to avoid the flak but collided with his number 2, Flying Officer S. G. Kimmel and Flying Officer H. N. Kirkland in DZ413. Both aircraft broke up in the air and crashed, killing all four men.

DZ477 and its 139 Squadron colleagues made low-level, shallow dives into the target and bombed successfully without opposition. DZ477 was considered lost over England on the return but in reality the aircraft suffered radio failure and landed at Ridgewell in north-west Essex. The low-level 105 Squadron formation was late to attack the target and had to bomb just after 139 Squadron's bombs had exploded, flying through thick clouds of smoke, steam and descending debris. Flying Officer A. N. Bulpitt and Sergeant K. A. Amond successfully bombed the target but on return to base landed at Bodney in Norfolk in error. DZ481 was lost over this country on its return journey with the loss of the crew, Lieutenant T. D. D. C. Moe and Second Lieutenant O. Smedsaas.

Post-raid photographs show very good precision bombing and it is interesting to note that a hutted detention camp for French native troops immediately adjacent to the target was left untouched.

Monday, 8 March
Target: Auinoye railway repair sheds
Crew: Flying Officer Pereira and Flying Officer Embury
Time: Up: 1745hrs, down: 1935hrs

Ten Mosquitos carried out a dusk raid on railway repair sheds at Auinoye, a second attack by 139 Squadron. All crews reported accurate bombing and seeing dense clouds of smoke from a considerable distance from the target area. The formation of six aircraft was very skilfully led by Wing Commander Shand DFM and F/S Handley DFM, who approached the target in DZ421 in a shallow bombing dive. Squadron Leader Bagguley in DZ496 led the remaining four aircraft in a low-level attack. No apparent flak was encountered over the coast or journey to the target area, although flak was encountered in several areas on the return route. All aircraft returned safely.

Photographs taken after the raid were conclusive proof of its success.

Tuesday 16 March
Target: Paderborn engine sheds and workshops
Crew: Sergeant Massey DFM and Sergeant Fletcher DFM
Time: Up: 1650hrs, down: 2105hrs

At over 200 miles from the coast, the target was deeper into Germany than any previously attacked by a big formation. Ten Mosquitos of 139 Squadron were followed by six from 105 Squadron on a combined, two-wave attack on railway engine sheds at Paderborn, east of the Ruhr. It seemed to be a long way into Germany when crews studied the large-scale map in the briefing room beforehand!

Second Lieutenant H. Wenger and Sergeant M. Gleed in DZ465 returned early owing to wireless trouble and Sergeant G. Cummings and Sergeant B. C. Kemp in DZ423 had to return to base following a collision with a duck near the Dutch coast. The lead duck crashed through the Perspex windscreen and landed in a heap of blood and feathers on the navigator's lap, while others hit the starboard engine nacelle. It was very draughty and messy in the aircraft, so they turned for home.

The formation proceeded smoothly over the flat lands of Holland and into north-west Germany but at low level the pilots would lift a wing to avoid a church steeple from time to time. Visibility was good enough to read a map but between Münster and Osnabrück the country became hilly and the formation became more ragged, although everything was still and quiet. Flying deeper into Germany, at about 25 miles from the target the lead formation climbed to 3,000ft while the other six Mosquitos stayed down to bomb at low level. Aircrews describe the uncomfortable feeling of being up at 3,000ft after a spell of low flying and the sense of vulnerability and of being motionless, which posed a sitting target for ground defence gunners. However, the element of relative safety returned when they dived on the target, bringing the earth closer and with the feeling of high speed returning.

The first section of six aircraft led by Wing Commander Berggen DFC dived down to 1,300ft before bombing at low level, then climbed to allow the section led by Flight Lieutenant W. W. Blessing DFC of 105 Squadron to attack. The remaining ten aircraft in the second wave encountered considerable flak. Timing and a certain amount of luck had to play its part as it was hoped that bombs would begin falling just as the last of the low-level aircraft had got clear of the target. The formation delivered direct hits to the engine workshops and as some crews looked back at the target they saw Mosquitos bucking like broncos among the debris going up into the air around them. Other Mosquitos were desperately trying to avoid the streams of orange balls streaking up at them from all angles.

Following the leader, DZ477 released its bombs over the target but was immediately hit by flak in the port wing root, causing damage and fuel leaks. Sergeant Massey shut down the engine to prevent the risk of fire but failed to restart it, and with the propeller not feathering and flying at low level, the aircraft was silhouetted by searchlight beams over the Dutch coast, where they were hit again in the fuselage. With poorly responding controls and still some 30 miles from the English coast, the remaining engine began to run rough so they radioed an emergency and obtained assistance to land in Norfolk. They were unable to land on the flare path due to the violent swing caused by the throttled-back starboard engine, so with great skill and courage Massey brought the aircraft down, saving his and his navigator's lives. They crashed at 2105hrs at Docking airfield, coming to rest after striking a windsock.

Flight Sergeant P. J. D. McGeehan DFM RNZAF and Flying Officer R. C. Morris DFC in DZ497 attacked the target but were hit by Kriegsmarine flak near the island of Texel; both men lost their lives. The remaining returning aircraft had the cover of the typical Ruhr low-lying mist and industrial haze.

DZ477 was condemned to the scrap heap but somehow it escaped the salvage team and spent many months under repair. It was given a new lease of life with a transfer to the new low-level target marking specialists, 627 Squadron.

Chapter 16

DZ477 AZ:K with 627 Squadron – January to April 1944

RAF Oakington

Six miles from Cambridge, RAF Oakington airfield was built during 1939–40 and was one of the last commissioned under the expansion schemes of the 1930s. It was not complete when the airfield opened on 1 July 1940 as part of 2 Group. The airfield occupied the land between the villages of Oakington, Longstanton and Westwick, and used the village's connecting roads as the perimeter track, which caused a long diversion for the residents of Longstanton who wished to visit Cambridge. The station technical and domestic buildings were situated on the northern side of the runways close to the railway line running from Cambridge to St Ives.

In mid-July 1940, the Bristol Blenheim IVs of 218 (Gold Coast) Squadron moved in after returning from France but the personnel had to be accommodated in tents and marquees until the permanent quarters were completed later that autumn. Initially, they carried out reconnaissance missions and daylight operations against airfields in the Netherlands, but during October some crews took part in attacks on targets of opportunity; an early example of the raids later performed by intruder Mosquitos. On 19 September some Blenheims were practising airfield attacks when an aircraft made an unexpected approach and promptly belly landed on the airfield. Seconds later, two Hurricanes of 17 Squadron streaked overhead. The aircraft, initially mistaken for a Blenheim, was in fact a Luftwaffe Ju88a, 7A + FM, Werk Nr 0362 of 4(F)/121. The pilot and crew were unhurt and taken prisoner. Their aircraft was loaded with cameras, which provided excellent information for the Photographic Reconnaissance Unit. Some specially adapted Spitfires were brought in for daylight flights, which were supplemented by a couple of Wellingtons for experimental night photography using high-powered flash bulbs. The special Spitfires were painted deep blue, known as PR blue, and others were coloured pink in an effort to maximise camouflage.

On 29 October the first of 7 Squadron's Short Stirling bombers arrived from RAF Leeming and they remained at Oakington for the rest of the war. During October some of the crews started to undertake 'roving commissions', which allowed them to attack targets of opportunity as they saw fit. They were the forerunners of the Mosquito intruder raids that were so successful later in the war.

November saw the formation of 3 Photographic Reconnaissance, which was to take high-altitude photographs of targets to assess the bombing accuracy and damage that had been caused. The unit moved to Alconbury in the New Year when the grass runways at Oakington were declared unfit for Spitfires.

For most of January 1942, 7 Squadron Stirlings were withdrawn from operations to allow new Gee sets to be fitted and by August they switched to the role of Pathfinders, backing up primary markers with flares added to their high-explosive bomb loads. Their first operation was to Frankfurt on the night of 24–25 but it was costly with sixteen aircraft lost, five of them Pathfinders.

On 1 April 1943 additional hangars were constructed to prepare for the arrival of eight Mosquitos of the newly formed 1409 Meteorological Flight, which carried out long-distance weather reconnaissance 'Pampas' patrols over targets to be bombed by the Main Bomber Force. During the winter of 1943–44, 7 Squadron suffered the highest losses in the whole of Bomber Command when during nineteen operations, twenty-six aircraft were lost and 185 airmen either lost their lives or were posted as missing in action.

Bomber Command's presence at Oakington came to an abrupt end on 24 July 1945 when RAF Transport Command took over and further changes in residents continued over the years, the base acting as home to more modern aircraft as the years progressed. The British Army occupied Oakington through the 1970s until around 1996, and the Home Office used some of the buildings as an Immigration Reception Centre from 200 until 2010. The airfield has since become a planned housing estate with up to 9,500 houses.

627 Squadron

On 12 November 1943 'C' Flight of 139 Squadron was reformed as the new 627 Mosquito Squadron at Oakington with Wing Commander Roy Elliott DSO, DFC taking charge of the staff and five Mosquito Mk IVs.

Roy Elliott, born in Bristol in April 1917, was granted a short service commission in May 1937, serving on a Vickers Wellesley bomber squadron that became 15 Operational Training Unit in April 1940. Elliott moved to 75 Squadron in October to prepare for delivery of Wellington bombers and had a narrow escape later in the month. Having taken off from Mildenhall with five crew, Wellington IC R3158 collided with a barrage balloon cable, forcing it to crash-land at Manston aerodrome; fortunately no one was hurt. Later, Elliott converted to the high-performance Mk IX photo-reconnaissance Spitfire but his 'Wimpy' experience saw him posted to the Air & Armament Experimental Establishment at Boscombe Down, Wiltshire. Elliott returned to Bomber Command in April 1942 with the Lancasters of 83 Squadron, one of the first in Bennett's Pathfinder Group. Elliott, one of the few bomber pilots to survive two tours, began his third tour of operations and was recognised by being awarded a DSO.

In January 1943 the Pathfinder leader Don Bennett confirmed his confidence in Elliott by giving him command of 83 Squadron and then appointed him to his Group Operations staff, followed by the command the Pathfinders' navigation training wing. In November 1943 Elliott formed 627 Squadron to begin an almost nightly assault on Berlin, however the unit was destined for 5 Group to transform the identification and marking of targets for Bomber Command's bombers.

Elliott became a very popular leader and was known to be friendly, considerate, ultra-efficient and incredibly brave. He would often fly a 627 Mosquito as low as 50ft to mark the targets and always displayed an indomitable spirit that set an example and drew the admiration of all members of his squadron. Elliott's inspiration to his crews and their extraordinary low-level flying would occasionally create unexpected and additional work for ground crews, having to remove pieces of chimney and even an airfield windsock from damaged Mosquitos.

The high-altitude electronic methods the Pathfinders used to locate their targets was in contrast to the more skilful, low-level techniques used by 627 Squadron, who relied on human, visual methods combined with excellent flying. Elliott promoted the continuous practice of dive-bombing to achieve the required accuracy of placing the marker within 50 yards of the target. Practise dives began at 18,000ft down to 12,000ft for the point of release but it was soon found that the aircraft speed was too high so dives were lowered until the optimum was found. Dives from 3,000ft with target indicators released at 1,000ft was ideal but in combat conditions this was entirely dependent on weather conditions as the crew had to identify the target and make a shallow dive ending in a low-level run before releasing the markers from as low as 100ft. The crews made considerable effort to refine the marking techniques and they soon discarded the original red spot fire marker used by Leonard Cheshire in favour of the new target indicators, which burned for a longer time and covered a wider area.

The new target indicators were easier to see by the main force aircraft and were less prone to be obliterated by the bombs of the first aircraft over the target. No. 627 used the vector system of bombing by selecting a marking point a mile or so away from the target so the bomb aimers in the approaching aircraft on their prearranged heading adjusted their bomb release mechanisms to operate a second or two after their aircraft passed over the target indicators. The prolonged life of the target indicators could get 200 main force aircraft over a target within twenty minutes of H-hour. The mid-1944 concern for European civilian safety was minimised by the techniques used by 627.

The squadron contingent was dismayed and shattered to learn that Elliott, their 'beloved' leader, was to be replaced on 3 June 1944 by Wing Commander George Curry DSO DFC and Bar, a stranger from 5 Group and not one of their own flight commanders. Some members of 627 Squadron still had a great deal of loyalty to Don Bennett and 8 Group and were unhappy with this final takeover by 5 Group. Elliott was considered by many on 627 Squadron to be one of the finest squadron commanders in the RAF. Curry would remain in charge until 627 was disbanded on 1 October 1945.

The crews became operational on 24 November 1943 and were sent to Berlin that very night, with three detailed to take off from Oakington between 1907hrs and 1910hrs. These included F/S J. Marshallsay and Sergeant N. F. Ranshaw in DZ353 AZ:T and Flight Sergeant S. Parlato and Sergeant D. Thomas in DZ442 AZ:A. Marshallsay developed complete GEE failure and Parlato's aircraft cabin heating failed, so they both returned early. The third crew, Flying Officer J. R 'Benny' Goodman and navigator Flying Officer

S. T. L. Hickox in DZ615 AZ:Y, continued. 'Benny' Goodman describes that first 627 sortie:

> Early that evening Bill and I boarded DZ615 and set off for the Big City, a trip which turned out to be completely uneventful except that on returning to the airfield we were flying in thick cloud at 500ft in heavy rain and approached and landed very carefully. On reporting to the Ops room for debriefing we were astounded to be told that DZ615 had been the only RAF aircraft out over Germany that night. Ops had been cancelled by Bomber Command at a very late stage but the two of us were already airborne so we were left to get on with the job.

Initially part of 8 Group's Light Night Striking Force, the squadron carried out normal bombing missions and Pathfinder duties involving eleven attacks on Berlin and Cologne. Throughout December, along with 139 Squadron they operated in concerted efforts, occasionally attacking different targets; 627 Squadron concentrating on bombing with 139 Squadron dropping flares and target indicators. They also carried out spoof and window-dropping sorties, and up to mid-April 1944 had carried out 2,250 sorties within the Light Night Striking Force, almost all at night.

In March 1945 King George VI authorised the squadron badge, which depicts a diving hawk holding a firebrand in the beak, symbolising the squadron's wartime functions of both high-level bombing and low-level target marking. The motto 'At First Sight' is significant, referring to the responsibility of the individual air crew calling 'Tally-ho' when the target was first identified.

To sum up 627 Squadron, Chief Doug Garton told me that his wife, WAAF Jo Garton, considered it to be a very happy unit with no bickering or resentment often found on other stations, and to a young leading aircraftwoman the aircrews were like beings from another planet.

627 Squadron – Target for Tonight

627 Squadron comprised a wing commander, an adjutant and two squadron leader flight commanders, with Mosquito crews split equally between two flights, A and B. Each Mosquito had a pilot and navigator, so the aircrew complement was around fifty personnel, all of which were exceptionally well trained and highly motivated. This produced a fellowship and camaraderie that would be vital when the inevitable losses occurred. Sadly, over its short operating period, 627 lost forty-two good men but despite these unhappy occasions, squadron morale never dropped and there was often a drink in the mess with a glass raised to fallen comrades.

The planning of operations was carried out at Bomber Command headquarters in High Wycombe and relied on accurate weather forecasting at bomber bases, the routes used and in target areas, and needed to be detailed enough to allow operations to be planned with confidence. Early in the war aircrews were trained to make and record in-flight weather observations as a source of valuable information to meteorological officers at stations during post-raid debriefings but this proved to be insufficient. No. 1409 (Pampa) Flight was formed in January 1942 at Bircham Newton and became part of the Pathfinder Group in April 1943. It would make flights in every kind of weather and crews who flew these sorties were singled out for the highest praise by Harris.

Accurate wind forecasting was equally important, so in December 1943 a dedicated Upper Air Section was set up and played a vital role in the successful application of PF methods of accurate time keeping for concentrated bombing by aircraft over the target. On deep-penetration operations selected wind-finder crews were tasked with reporting back the values of wind direction and velocity to headquarters every half hour, beginning at a position and time at which radio silence may be broken. These found winds were plotted and examined by the Upper Air Forecasters before they were transmitted back to the aircraft at prearranged intervals so that navigators could amend the forecast winds.

Every morning Harris would arrive at his underground room for 'Morning Prayers', the derisory term he gave to his morning conference with Air Marshal Robert 'Sandy' Saundby, his minions and a USAAF liaison officer. Harris considered the results of the previous night's operations, the consequences of which would affect his decision that morning. Having selected the target, Harris returned to his office at ground level, leaving Saundby and other staff officers remaining underground to plan the operations for later that night. Several 'Pampa' flights over enemy territory were then taken before the first bombers took off to obtain surveys of weather features and cloud distribution along the route to the target. These reports could help the command to accurately forecast the weather for operations.

With the target decided, an effective bombing route was determined based on minimum flying time, minimum fuel use, maximum bomb load and minimum exposure to the German defences. The route had two principal options: a direct flight path straight to the target and straight back with no deviation or a multi-leg, indirect route. The planners had a daunting choice to make and it was a decision upon which the lives of hundreds of men depended. The 25,000 square miles of airspace from the north of Denmark to south of Frankfurt and an area stretching from Hamburg in the north to Stuttgart in the south was defended by twenty-five night fighter stations with more than 2,000 night fighters.

The advantages of the direct route was easier navigation, shorter flying time, less fuel consumption, greater bomb load, lower crew fatigue and less time over enemy territory and exposure to defences. It did, however, give the enemy an excellent chance to intercept the stream. The indirect route could be the safer choice but negated all the advantages of the direct route. A change in direction at the beginning of each leg could deceive the enemy into predicting the target and could provide protection from searchlights and fighters. Often, the weather such as the prevalence of fog or low cloud along the route would influence the decision but whatever route was decided it was normally finalised a matter of hours before the aircraft left the ground. It was now time for the group captains at the bomber bases to take over.

Where inclement weather was expected to cause problems for returning bombers, provisional diversions to airfields outside a particular group or to USAAF bases would be arranged before the aircraft took off. Final decisions on diversion airfields could also be taken after the bombers had departed.

The 627 Squadron crews that were involved in the attack that coming night would have breakfast at around 0900hrs, while those who had not been on operations the previous night would report to their respective flight officer's squadron office situated in a building on the edge of the airfield, a short walking distance from the control tower complex that also housed the operations room and intelligence section. During the next hour, the wing commander waited for a telephone call to establish whether the squadron was on operations that night or if they were to be stood down, in which case the flight commanders would initiate a training programme for that day such as practice bombing at targets on the range at Wainfleet Sands in The Wash, not far from Skegness. Crews welcomed the practice sessions, which gave them the opportunity to maintain excellence in accurate bombing and, almost as important, the prevention of boredom. Additional duties for those who were not on the operation list included air testing the aircraft scheduled to fly that night. Any issues were reported to the ground crews, who would then be very busy preparing the aircraft for take-off later that night. At that point the aircrews were stood down for the remainder of day. No other flying would take place.

If operations were detailed for that night, the wing commander would leave his office and walk to the operations room for a meeting with the station commander, who would inform him about the target selected for that night and then decide the time for the first briefing. The wing commander would then meet with his flight commanders to establish the names of the crews chosen for operations. A and B flights operated alternately and the names of the crew on operations would be written on a blackboard in the flight office. Normally, a marking team was led by the marker leader, which was usually the flight commander or sometimes the wing commander chose to lead with a deputy appointed just in case. The remaining marking crew names were also on the board with the identifying number of the aircraft they would fly alongside each name.

At an agreed time the operations crews attended a briefing in a soundproofed room that had a scrambled link-up with other Bomber Command units to ensure that everyone involved in the operation was fully aware of every detail and had the opportunity to interject should there be any point that required further clarification. The master bomber or controller would be in charge of the raid once the target had been marked.

The main briefing took place in the station briefing room situated alongside the crew locker room and parachute section just inside the main gate on the perimeter road. The entire operation staff were in attendance at the scheduled time; the squadron commander, heads of navigation, signals, intelligence, armaments, weather forecasters and the crews taking part in the operation. The briefing room was laid out with tables and chairs facing an array of maps and blackboards with a curtain covering the large wall map of Europe, which had red and blue patches indicating German defences and the route marked out with coloured tape showing the point on the east coast of Lincolnshire to the target itself. By the target, a collection of coloured pins indicated the colours of the markers that would be dropped and on blackboards either side was a large drawing of the target on one side and on the other a list of crews who were detailed to fly, their take-off times and bomb loads etc. Another blackboard displayed weather and the cloud conditions to be expected on the journey. The squadron commander explained the details of the target, the objectives and the reasons for the attack and then handed over to the heads of the various specialties to discuss the finer details. The details included the number of aircraft taking part and the routes that would be followed, which were rarely the same as on previous raids. The flying control officer announced the engine start-up and marshalling times and the runway to be used, then the exact instructions for the target were given and these would include details of the run-in to the target and types of flare and marking colours to be used based on cloud conditions.

The weather for both the outward journey and return to base was detailed and the areas of enemy defence crews would need to avoid. Crews were also told about the numbers of heavy and light anti-aircraft guns, searchlights and possible enemy night fighter activity. The location of the marking point was given and 'H-Hour', the time at which the bombing would begin. Pathfinder take-off times and those of the main force were given, however, owing to its superior performance, the Mosquitos would leave some time after the heavies. The navigators, particularly those in the 'heavy' squadrons who flew different routes to the Mosquitos, would very carefully and precisely draw the proposed route on their maps with a flight plan of times for the various stages or 'legs' with consideration to the aircraft's drifting caused by the wind. Key additional weather information was given such as cloud heights, freezing levels, icing indexes and the route and the details of any planned spoof raids.

The chief armaments officer would detail the type and weights of the bombs that were to be carried by the various aircraft, for instance Mosquito DZ477 AZ:K could carry 250lb and 500lb bombs, spot fires and target indicators. Some aircraft carried red and yellow target indicators. If the first red markers were not considered as within the acceptable margin of error of about 50 yards, the marker leader would call the same aircraft to drop his yellow TIs alongside the inaccurate red and then the target would be re-marked by the other members of the team. The bomber crews knew to ignore bombing on a red and yellow together and to concentrate on the red ones burning alone.

The signals officer then outlined the procedures for that night, including the various radio channels to be activated at set times and the identification colours and passwords to be used if challenged on returning to their own base. This was important as enemy night fighter intruders would sometimes try and attack the returning aircraft as they were going into land, often silhouetted against the illuminated flare path of their airfield. Complete radio silence was imposed right up to the moment the raid commenced, when crews were then able to communicate with each other to ensure its successful completion.

The considerable detail of the briefing was now complete, so to set the vitally important prerequisite of perfect timing the signals commander called for the synchronisation of watches. A few words of encouragement were given, then everyone was dismissed to their duties. In the meantime, absolute secrecy was demanded and no discussion was allowed outside the ops room, including between the pilot and his navigator! It is then time for the crews to go to the mess for the operational supper of bacon and eggs but some felt this was the worst possible thing to eat before a flight as the fried food tended to create gas and as the aircraft gained altitude stomach bloating occurred.

The ground crew would have checked the barometric pressures to reset altimeters to give a zero reading at ground level, which was essential considering the low levels the high-speed Mosquitos would be flying at during the actual marking in the middle of the night. Completely unarmed and operating at low level over the target and in the daylight conditions caused by hundreds of flares, they were then at their most vulnerable but the crews felt confident that with speed on their side they would be OK. The Mosquitos were, at times hit by lucky bursts of flak as they streaked over the target but the Lancasters were the focus of attention of the night fighters, who chose the slower and less manoeuvrable aircraft as easier prey.

The Mosquito navigators had a separate briefing with the squadron lead navigation officer an hour before the main briefing where they discussed the flight plans for both the outward and return journeys, which were based on the winds that had been forecast. The 627 crews were very experienced, all having completed one or two tours of ops or spent the equivalent time as instructors. The pilots acknowledged their gratitude to 'their other half' for their skills using limited navigational aids in getting their aircraft to the target within sixty seconds of the scheduled time of arrival after a 600-mile flight and then navigate back to base over hostile territory, sometimes in aircraft suffering battle damage. The navigators would keep on track by using dead reckoning with the forecast winds and looking for constant visual fixes that could be observed to maintain course and timing. From the flight plan the navigator could calculate any change in wind speed and direction and amend course accordingly. They would then advise the pilot, who had to translate the information into a high standard of flying in order to keep a very accurate course, constant airspeed and height. This required considerable concentration lasting possibly six hours and without the luxury of an automatic pilot.

At the predetermined time, the crews collected their parachutes and Mae Wests from the stores, then went to the locker room to hand in their valuables and collect escape kits before changing into flying kit. Sandwiches and flasks of coffee for the return journey together with slabs of chocolate and barley sugar sweets were handed to each crew member, who was aware of the luxury of such things; severe rationing was imposed upon the civilian population during these hard times.

Outside the locker room the buses, generally driven by a WAAF, arrived to take the crews to their aircraft dispersal around the perimeter of the airfield, where the ground crews had worked all day preparing their aircraft with great pride and dedication. Once again, the aircrew were aware of the hard work the maintainers put in, often working under extremely difficult conditions in all weathers to ensure that their particular aircraft went to war in the very best order possible. Any adjustments and repairs that were necessary after the air tests that had taken place earlier in the day were now complete and the Mosquito was finally bombed up with the appropriate load required for the op.

Once at the dispersal, each pilot completed the formalities of signing the Form 700 for the ground crew corporal after a careful check of the control surfaces, wheels, tyres and undercarriage. Then, after relieving themselves against the tail wheel, the Mosquito pilot and his navigator climbed the short metal ladder into the cramped cockpit, observing the usual protocol of chucking their parachutes in first. The door was closed and locked by one of the ground crew before the pilot received the signal to start engines for engine run-up. With one last check of the instruments, each pilot in turn began to taxi slowly from the dispersal in line behind the marker leader to the take-off point of the runway in use. The pilot went through his final cockpit check and the navigator outlined the flight plan and climbing instructions and when the green Aldis light flashed from the control van the pilot lined the aircraft for take-off, followed in quick succession by subsequent aircraft. As they climbed away, they set an exact time for the starting point on the east coast, which when crossed would give the navigator his first visual check and, by using the Gee set as far as possible over the North Sea, establish the accuracy of the wind forecast on which the entire operation was planned.

Earlier in the evening the 'heavies' had run up their engines to almost full throttle against the brakes and when released the aircraft began to accelerate down the runway, trying to build as much speed as possible by holding down the nose down. As the aircraft strained to leave the ground and using the full length of the runway if necessary, the pilot eased back on the control column and the bomber continued in a shallow climb until the airspeed increased. The navigator would give the pilot a course to steer towards the assembly point and, with the red and green glow of navigation lights on the other aircraft in the sky all around them, they flew in a climb towards the coast before settling into the bomber stream, having turned off navigation lights and left the shores of England behind. Known as a saturation attack tactic, a typical bomber stream consisted of about 700 aircraft and was approximately 10 miles across and 5,000ft deep. The gunners now requested permission to test-fire their guns over the sea and as they approached and crossed the enemy coast the sky was continually searched for enemy fighters while the navigator gave the pilot a new course to steer them towards the target and an estimated time of arrival. They expected a flying time of thirty to forty minutes from the Dutch coast to the Ruhr, but more distant targets like Berlin would take more than two hours.

The 627 Squadron markers made necessary adjustments to their course and airspeed and time over target, and settled down to what was usually an uneventful trip for the Mosquitos. However, it was still important to keep an eye open for enemy night fighters and ensure they did not stray off course over any defended areas. At intervals along the route the Pathfinders would drop flares to mark the route for main force aircraft to follow and at thirteen minutes before H-Hour, H-13, on the approach to the target, two Lancasters from 83 or 97 Squadron dropped six green target indicators as they passed over the target area at 25,000ft. The Lancasters were selected for this task as they were equipped with navigational aids such as H2S, enabling the Lancasters to be certain of their position over the target area, whereas the Mosquito flew by dead reckoning, which could find their position a few miles either side of the target. The 627 crews could make adjustments to ensure they would be in the vicinity as the green target indicators hit the ground. The crews then began to reduce their altitude of 20,000–23,000ft to 5,000–6,000ft as they arrived in the target area. At H-11 another flight of Pathfinder Lancasters passed over the target area and, also using H2S, dropped a wave of small illuminated candle flares, each attached to a small parachute allowing them to slowly float to the ground, lighting up the whole area. These were followed two minutes later, at H-9, by a second flare wave dropped by a third flight of Lancasters, which turned a night-time environment into daylight conditions.

From H-13 the master bomber could break radio silence to call the marker leader to establish if he could see the green target indicators. However, if he felt the weather conditions warranted it, he did not call before H-9 between the two flare waves. The 627 crews were now fully occupied trying to identify the marking point by recalling the topographical details of the area they had committed to memory earlier that day at the briefing sessions.

The descending green target indicators were the signal for the enemy defences to open up with their heavy flak and powerful searchlights probing the darkness but in reality the flares rendered the searchlights ineffective so posed no further threat to the Lancasters. It was the Mosquitos flying at no more than 4,000ft that became the targets of light flak batteries. Mosquito crews were really concentrating at this point and to see hundreds of fiery-red tracer shells being hosepiped around their aircraft was a disconcerting experience for even the coolest pilots. The pressure on the 627 marking team ramped up significantly as they reached H-9 for they had less than nine minutes to find, identify and accurately mark the target, assess the accuracy and if necessary re-mark it before calling in another four aircraft to back up their target indicators. They then had to get clear of the area before the bombs began to drop from the main force at the predetermined time. The Lancasters were also under fierce attack from anti-aircraft defences and felt they were entitled to assume the Pathfinders had completed their part of the operation successfully. Faced with a small delay on their approach, or even worse having to orbit the target again, would be suicidal for the marking team. Flying around the target at a few hundred feet in near daylight conditions while under constant fire was one thing but being in that situation and also having hundreds of high-explosive bombs dropping and exploding all around them was an experience to be avoided.

The first 627 crew to identify the marking point was the first to break radio silence by shouting the British hunting call 'Tally-ho' and it was the signal for the rest of the team to hold back for within a few seconds other crews would be in the same position and cause chaos unless alerted. The flares lit the area to such an extent that the marking crews were able to see one another circling the marking point and the aircraft making the first marking run in a shallow and ever steepening dive. The target indicator was dropped at about 600ft to allow the barometric fuse to operate and allow the pyrotechnics to drift slowly to the ground. The nearest aircraft in the chain then followed his colleague to assess the accuracy of the first drop, which was reported to the marker leader. A second aircraft was in the perfect position to add his TIs to those already dropped in a way that was developed by the constant bombing practice when not on operations. With the target marked accurately, it was unnecessary to re-mark so the marker leader contacted the master bomber and requested permission for the marking team to leave the area.

The master bomber would take over as H-hour arrived and with the approaching main force crews well within sight of the illuminations and their bomb doors open, the pilot held the bomber on a straight and level course for its bombing run over a target area that was a mass of flames, punctuated by the red and green target markers dropped by the Pathfinders. Dozens of searchlight beams groped the sky and flak batteries hunted for bombers during the most vulnerable phase of the operation. Often, crews heard the dull thud of a shell bursting close by and the clattering of shrapnel pieces hitting the fuselage. The bomb aimer directed the pilot with calm instructions of 'left', 'right', 'steady' or 'hold it' until the signal of 'bombs gone' was given. Then the aircraft lifted as it was relieved of its bombs, however, the pilot would continue to fly straight and level for another thirty seconds to enable the aiming point photograph to be taken; without it the operation would not count towards the crew's tour of thirty operations. Most crews considered this as the longest thirty seconds of their lives. Before they could leave the target area the bomb aimer checked his panel for signs of any bomb hang-ups, which could mean another run over the target, but if all was well the bomb doors were closed and they turned for home. As the marking team left the area at high speed through the darkness, the 627 crews rarely encountered any night fighters but they did suffer attack from ground-based hazards. Usually they returned to base and the greeting from their ground crews, who were keen to know if their aircraft did well and was there any damage?

The 'heavies' needed to remain vigilant for flak, searchlights and night fighters, which often infested the route looking for stray bombers on their long haul back across blacked-out Europe to the enemy coast. Some were shot down by enemy intruders lurking in the circuit at their English bases as they prepared to land. Once past the enemy coast, the 'heavy' navigator picked up his GEE lattice line that would lead them home. With 50 miles to go to the English coast, the pilot used VHF to identify his aircraft and once over England the crew looked for the Pundit beacon that flashed in Morse code the identification letters of their home airfield. A call was then made to the control tower asking for permission to join the circuit and land.

If a crew's home base was covered by poor weather conditions they would be diverted to an airfield with clear visibility, but the common presence of fog over Lincolnshire would see aircraft diverted to airfields fitted with a Fog Investigation and Dispersal Operation or FIDO. The system relied on thousands of gallons of petrol being fed into long lines running along the entire length and either side of the runway and at regular intervals burners blasted jets of flame upwards as the petrol ignited. This generated heat that, when combined with the wind and low cloud, would lift the fog to clear the runway for up to 300ft, allowing aircraft to land safely. When in full operation, a typical FIDO system could consume 90,000 gallons of petrol per hour, equivalent to filling the tanks of forty Lancasters.

Having landed safely, the engines were throttled back for the first time in more than six hours and the white hot exhausts began to crackle as the bomber was marshalled to its dispersal, where the engines were finally shut down. The exhausted crew vacated their aircraft and took a crew bus to the briefing room to be interrogated by the station intelligence staff with lengthy questions about the operation. A mug of tea or coffee often laced with rum and a cigarette would help the crew unwind before they returned their flying kit to the stores and lockers and retired for a well-earned sleep. For the aircrews, the whole process would start again the following evening but for the ground crews responsible for the aircraft servicing, fault rectification and battle damage assessment and repair, their work would begin in a only a few hours.

These day-to-day activities were replicated across the airfields across Lincolnshire, with Lancaster and Halifax bases following the same pattern of briefings, routines and support mechanisms. However, with heavy bombers there were more aircrew to cater for than in the Mosquito squadrons. The whole process was repeated the next day and the day after and the day after ...

Chapter 17

DZ477 – War Diary 1944

RAF Oakington

Thursday, 27 January
Target: Berlin
Crew: Squadron Leader E. F. Nelles and Flying Officer A. E. Richards
Time: Up: 1838hrs, down: 2337hrs
Bomb Load: 1 × blue target indicator, 1 × yellow target indicator and 9 white flares

Bad weather was responsible for a pause of six days in main force operations, which helped to prepare the crews for three Berlin trips in four nights. In what would later be considered as the cleverest tactical plan yet employed on the Berlin raids, the planners decided to confound the enemy by sending out a 'spoof' force of eighty Stirlings and Wellingtons into the German Bight accompanied by twenty-one H2S-equipped Halifaxes, which mined Heligoland. The Luftwaffe dispatched half of its night fighters earlier than usual, sending some 75 miles over the North Sea.

At first the main force of 515 Lancasters followed the route of the 'spoof' raid but then dog-legged south-east flying across northern Holland, suggesting to the enemy that Magdeburg or Leipzig would be the targets. Fifteen Mosquitos were in the air with six target markers dropping dummy route markers and flares to the north-east of the stream, indicating that Hanover or Brunswick were to be the targets; so now there was the prospect of any one of four cities to be attacked. After about 300 miles the main force dog-legged north-east towards the north of Berlin, meanwhile three Mosquitos continued south-east dropping window and dummy fighter flares as another diversion. The dynamics of the moves put great pressure on German night fighter controllers, resulting in less action in the main bomber stream than in recent nights, although thirty-three Lancasters would be lost.

At about 60 miles from Berlin, the bombers headed due east for the final approach led by the nine Mosquitos of 627 Squadron, which had found the target covered by cloud so used accurate Wanganui sky markers. DZ477 dropped flares at 2039hrs and yellow target indicators at 2046hrs from 26,000ft but the strong following wind blew them east along a line of the bomb run, causing the bombing to become widely dispersed. Two fires of considerable size were seen on the return journey but the raid could not be assessed except that the bombing appeared to be well spread up and downwind. Local reports confirmed many bombs falling in the southern part of the city, with sixty-one small towns and villages hit outside the city limits with the loss of twenty-eight lives. It is known that 20,000 people were bombed out of their homes. Fifty industrial installations were hit, suffering severe damage. A total of 567 people were killed, including 132 foreign workers. A total of 1,704 tons of bombs were dropped, thirty-eight aircraft aborted and 172 airmen were killed, fifty-five becoming PoWs.

Friday, 28 January
Target: Berlin
Crew: Squadron Leader E. F. Nelles and Flying Officer A. E. Richards
Time: Up: 1946hrs, down: 0022hrs
Bomb Load: 4 × 500lb General Purpose bombs

This was a 'maximum effort' raid for 432 Lancasters, 241 Halifaxes and nine Mosquitos from 627 Squadron accompanied by extensive and complex diversions like those on previous nights' hoax attacks. Three Mosquitos took off at around 2000hrs on a 'spoof' raid to Berlin with the intention of convincing the enemy that there would not be a major attack on the capital that night. An additional hoax raid by four Oboe Mosquitos on Leeuwarden and Hanover was also carried out at the time that the main force was assembling. The further distraction of a Stirling and Wellington spoof and minelaying attacks over Kiel Bay, Heligoland and the Frisian Islands allowed the bomber stream to cross northern Holland in a south-easterly direction as if to threaten Hanover, Brunswick, Magdeburg and even Leipzig. At a point south of Magdeburg, the bomber stream diverted to the north-east while three Mosquitos continued further, dropping window and fighter flares. At the same time, dummy route markers and night fighter flares would be dropped over two areas much further north as the bombers made a final turn to approach Berlin. For once, the diversions had some effect and many fighters were lured away to the mining operation.

Having taken off at midnight, Heavies from 8 Group's 35 Pathfinder Squadron arrived at 19,000ft over the target at 0347hrs to find ten-tenths cloud cover that concealed the ground markers, so Wanganui flares provided an aiming point. With German fighters drawn away by the earlier diversions and the bombers routed over Denmark, it proved too distant for other German fighters to intercept so the controllers were able to concentrate fighters over the target and shot down twenty Lancasters and twenty-six Halifaxes.

With Berlin under broken cloud cover, some ground marking was possible and Bomber Command went on to claim that this was the most concentrated attack of the period. DZ477 bombed on dead reckoning at 2142hrs from 28,000ft. Some bombs were seen to burst but no fires were observed, with many searchlights seen under the clouds. For some Halifax crews the duration of the operation was about eight hours and heavy, accurate flak was encountered, with some airmen reporting that the noise on the aircraft fuselage created the sensation of the aircraft flying through a wall of steel.

No. 627 Squadron's Pilot Officer Wilmott and Flying Officer Hughes in DK353 AZ:B were forced to abandon the sortie at 2030hrs owing to port engine magneto failure and low brake pressure. Despite navigating to the target by dead reckoning and bang on ETA, Flying Officer D. W. Peck DFC and Flying Officer R. F. Davies DFC in DZ442 AZ:D, also of 627, were prevented from bombing by a technical problem with the bomb release mechanism. Earlier Davies, the navigator, suffered a ten-minute lack of oxygen at 25,000ft due to a kink in the tubing.

The red glow of the clouds over Berlin could be seen by the returning bombers from the enemy coast and this was caused by the administrative and public buildings of western and southern Berlin being set alight. The new Chancellery, four theatres, the 'French Cathedral', six hospitals, five embassies and the State Patent Office were hit, along with industrial sites. Some 180,000 people were bombed out of their homes.

Saturday, 29 January
Target: Duisburg
Crew: Flying Officer H. Steere and Flying Officer K. W. Gale (RAAF 404241)
Time: Up: 1802hrs, down: 2036hrs
Bomb Load: 3 × 500lb General Purpose bombs and 1 × 500lb LD bomb

Twelve Mosquitos, six from 627 Squadron, attacked Duisburg. DZ477 released its bombs and target indicators at 1918hrs from 28,000ft but no results were seen. As Harry Steere pulled out of the bombing to run clear of the area, DZ477 was hit by flak, severing fuel supply pipes and damaging the engine cowlings. One minute later Wing Commander Lockhart and Flying Officer Saunders in DZ518

AZ:F had their bombs hang up directly over the target. Both crews managed to return their aircraft safely to base.

Sunday, 30 January
Target: Berlin
Crew: Squadron Leader E. F. Nelles and Flying Officer A. E. Richards
Time: Up: 1815hrs, down: 2235hrs
Bomb load: 6 × white flares, 3 × red flares and 1 × 500 GPLD Bomb

The Pathfinder Squadron had an early take-off at 1701hrs in fine conditions of clear skies and good visibility but the ominous rising half-moon would help night fighters to find the bomber stream unless the expected thick ice-bearing cloud cover over Germany kept them on the ground.

A total of 440 Lancasters and 82 Halifaxes took a similar route to previous raids, although they crossed the Schleswig-Holstein peninsula on the German side of the border to pass over the northern edge of the Ijsselmeer, then crossed the Dutch coast south of Den Helder. With no preliminary diversion raids planned and the failed attempt by the German night fighter controllers to intercept the bomber stream over the sea, the bombers were about 70 miles from Berlin before meeting any fighters. The Germans harried the bombers all the way to Berlin and then followed the bomber stream well into the return flight.

Pathfinder squadrons dropped flares and bombed through the complete cloud cover between 2012hrs and 2019hrs. Twelve Mosquitos, with eight from 627 Squadron, were over the target in advance of the main force, with Wing Commander Elliott and Squadron Leader De Boos, in DZ418 AZ:L, marking the target with white flares at 2019 hrs from 22,500ft, immediately followed by DZ477. Both crews then dropped red flares at 2023hrs from 26,000ft but no results were seen by either crew. The returning main force crews reported that the ground markers were ineffective in the conditions but the scattered sky marking in the early stages of the attack became well concentrated as the raid progressed.

Many explosions, some described as violent, were seen in the target area and heavy damage was inflicted on the central and western districts of Berlin along with many other areas within and outside the city. The local reports repeated a recent trend of heavy damage in the city with widespread bombing in the country areas. Seventy-nine towns and villages reported various numbers of bombs but most of these fell in open country. Many public buildings, including Goebbels' Propaganda Ministry, were seriously damaged and Berlin transport system suffered at the Kreuzburg depot with nearly 100 U-Bahn carriages being destroyed.

Thirty-two Lancasters and one Halifax were shot down; just over 6 per cent of the force.

The enormous effort and cost of the January Berlin raids had lacked concentrated bombing and was not the success that was hoped for. The sheer weight of bombs killed more than 2,000 Berliners in the last three raids and a further 200,000 were now without homes. Despite this, Berlin was still defiantly functioning as a city and the predicted signs of collapse were nowhere to be seen. With this series of raids about to end, the final concerted effort to destroy Berlin would have to rely on operations in isolation and be spread over the next two months.

Tuesday, 1 February 1944.
Target: Berlin
Crew: Flying Officer J. A. Saint-Smith and Flying Officer G. E. Heath
Time: Up: 1806hrs, down: 2255hrs
Bomb Load: 3 × 500lb GPLD bombs

In an all 627 Squadron affair, ten Mosquitos struck Berlin with mixed results, owing to Flying Officer J. G. Grey and Flying Officer F. W. Boyle in DZ418 AZ:L abandoning the sortie soon after take-off when their GEE set failed and they returned to base. Benny Goodman and Bill Hickox in DZ442 AZ:D bombed at 2011hrs from 28,000ft but although their starboard engine failed on the return near the Dutch coast, Goodman managed to get back, landing at Coltishall. DZ477, however, successfully bombed the target at 2012hrs on dead reckoning from 28,000ft in ten-tenths cloud but no target indicators or results were seen. Mosquito DZ551 AZ:E, crewed by P/O Anthony Willmott and Flying Officer John Hughes, failed to return after being hit by heavy flak at 1934hrs. The crew were killed when they crashed north-west of Pattensen near Hanover.

Saturday, 5 February
Target: Berlin
Crew: Flying Officer P. F. Denny and Flight Sergeant A. Denholm
Time: Up: 1801hrs, down: 2235hrs
Bomb Load: 3 × 500lb GP bombs and 1 × 500lb GPLD bomb

Eighteen Mosquitos, six from 627 Squadron, set off for the capital via the Baltic coast by dead reckoning. DZ477 bombed at 2031hrs. DZ484 AZ:G, flown by P/O P. Yarmea and Flying Officer A. F. Dodds, bombed Berlin but were forced to land at Hardwick airfield near Norwich due to low fuel levels, electrical system problems and an unserviceable GEE set.

Monday, 7 February
Target: Frankfurt
Crew: Flying Officer P. F. Denny and Flight Sergeant A. Denholm
Time: Up: 0235hrs, down: 0555hrs
Bomb Load: 3 × 500lb GP bombs and 1 × 500lb GPLD bomb

Nineteen Mosquitos, seven from 627 Squadron, had an uneventful trip, with DZ477 bombing the target at 0402hrs from 25,000ft with no results seen.

Tuesday, 8 February
Target: Brunswick
Crew: Squadron Leader E. F. Nelles and Flying Officer A. E. Richards
Time: Up: 1847hrs, down: 2211hrs
Bomb Load: 3 × 500lb GP bombs and 1 × 500lb GPLD bomb

Eleven Mosquitos, six from 627 Squadron, attacked the target. DZ477 was first in and bombed on a dead reckoning run at 2030hrs from 25,000ft. They were closely followed by Flight Sergeant J. Marshallsay and Flight Sergeant N. A. Ranshaw in DK313 AZ:A, who identified the green route marker at 2031hrs and also ran into the target by dead reckoning. No red target indicators or results seen.

Thursday, 10 February
Target: Berlin
Crew: Flying Officer P. F. Denny and Flight Sergeant A. Denholm
Time: Up: 0056hrs, down: 0452hrs
Bomb Load: 3 × 500lb GP bombs and 1 × 500lb GPLD bomb

Twenty-one Mosquitos took part, with seven 627 aircraft taking off within a twelve-minute time span. The primary target was abandoned owing to strong winds, so only three aircraft actually attacked Berlin and three went to Kiel. DZ477 attacked Sylt airfield on North Frisian Island off north Germany at 0345hrs from 25,000ft with no results seen.

Friday, 11 February
Target: Brunswick
Crew: Squadron Leader E. F. Nelles and Flying Officer A. E. Richards
Time: up: 1845hrs, down: 2252hrs
Bomb Load: 3 × 500lb GP bombs and 1 × 500lb GPLD bomb

Eleven Mosquitos, of which six were from 627 Squadron, carried out an uneventful sortie. DZ477 bombed at 2118hrs from 25,000ft on red target indicators. No results seen.

Tuesday, 15 February
Target: Berlin
Crew: Squadron Leader E. F. Nelles and Flying Officer A. E. Richards
Time: Up: 1843hrs, down: 2317hrs
Bomb Load: 1 × 500lb GP bomb and 9 white flares

After a rest of more than two weeks for the regular main force bomber squadrons, 561 Lancasters, 314 Halifaxes and sixteen Mosquitos, six from 627 Squadron, were dispatched to Berlin, the largest non-1,000 bomber force sent to any target since 23–24 May 1943. It was also the first time that more than 500 Lancasters and more than 300 Halifaxes were despatched, dropping a record quantity of 2,642 tons of bombs.

Mosquitos made a spoof attack on Berlin with TIs, bombs and flares and on Frankfurt-an-Oder but failed to draw any fighters away from the main force as the German night fighter controllers were able to plot the bomber stream soon after it crossed the English coast and over the North Sea. As they turned north to Denmark, it was too distant for any of the German fighters but as the stream left Denmark's east coast they made contact and harried the tail end of the stream, bringing down more than twenty aircraft. German fighters were ordered not to fly over Berlin in order to keep the target area free for flak defences, but in reality many fighters ignored this and proceeded to fly over the city to hunt for bombers.

Berlin was completely covered in cloud for most of the raid but DZ477 bombed at 2111hrs from 25,000ft and Nelles could see fires under the clouds when they left the target area. Ground markers were laid down but were not visible through the clouds so most bombed on H2S or sky markers, which fell in strong concentrations mainly over the central part of the city. The main force carried out their attacks from 19,000 to 21,000ft between 2111hrs and 2129hrs. Heavy bombing fell on central and south-western districts, with many places in the countryside yet again recording many bombs and fifty-nine people being killed. Damage to Berlin was extensive, with nearly 1,000 large and medium fires and a similar number of houses and temporary barracks destroyed. The reports of returning crews stated it was a scattered but effective attack, which was confirmed by the Mosquito crews. A huge pall of black smoke was seen to be rising over the city to 20,000ft and a pear-shaped area of fire in the north and east, tapering towards the south.

Some of Berlin's most important war industries were hit, including the large Siemensstadt area on the western fringe, where 320 people were killed. Nine air raid wardens, eighty foreign workers and one prisoner of war lost their lives but the diminishing proportion of civilian casualties reflected the large-scale evacuation that had taken place. Some 260 civilians were recorded as being buried alive but it is not known how many survived. Forty-three aircraft failed to return from what turned out to be the penultimate main force raid on the capital and unusually there were more Lancaster than Halifax casualties.

Saturday, 19 February
Target: Leipzig
Crew: P/O P. Yarema RCAF J18944 and Flying Officer A. F. Dodds RCAF J15674
Time: Up: 0110hrs, down: 0553hrs
Bomb Load: 4 × 500lb GPLD bombs

After three nights of rest, 561 Lancasters, 255 Halifaxes and seven Mosquitos from 627 Squadron set off for Leipzig with its aircraft factories, a priority target under the 'Point Blank Directive'. Bomber Command headed into its greatest disaster so far. Four H2S Halifaxes and forty-five Stirlings carried out a diversionary minelaying raid in Kiel Bay and fifteen Mosquitos went to Berlin. However, the Germans only partially took the bait, so when the bomber force used the familiar route across the Dutch coast, they were met by part of the German fighter force, which were joined a little later by the fighters sent north to Kiel. The two groups of fighters attacked the bomber stream in a battle that ensued all the way to the target.

The pre-operation briefing by the meteorological officer forecast good weather with some winds but there turned out to be very strong winds blowing from the west, so as the bomber stream reached the Leipzig area too early they had to orbit and wait the Pathfinders. Some experienced navigators persuaded their pilots to dog-leg several times in order to ensure they arrived over Leipzig after the Pathfinders but less-experienced crews did not correct the broadcast wind reports, causing their part of the bomber stream to become extended and broken. In an attempt to slow the advance to allow the Pathfinders to illuminate the target, some skippers started to zigzag across the bomber stream, which increased the risk of collisions. One rear gunner reported later that a Lancaster flew about 30 yards from his turret, so his pilot promptly turned the aircraft back into the bomber stream. When the Pathfinders arrived, the target was covered in cloud, so they had to use sky marking. The sight of falling bombers may well have prompted some crews to bomb early as the main force attack began at 0345hrs from 17,000 to 21,000ft, eleven minutes ahead of the first red sky markers and target indicators. The target indicators disappeared into ten-tenths cloud but a degree of concentrated sky marking was achieved and this seemed to be maintained throughout the attack.

DZ477 followed dead reckoning and arrived over the target at 0354hrs at 25,000ft, nine minutes after the first bombs fell, and reported a good concentration of red flares in the vicinity of their

Arthur T. Harris, Commander in Chief of Bomber Command 1942–45, later Marshal of the Royal Air Force, Sir Arthur Harris, Bt, GCB, OBE, AFC. (*Public domain*)

Acting Air Vice-Marshal Donald Bennett, the leader of the Pathfinder Force, later Air Vice-Marshal Donald Clifford Tyndall Bennett, CB, CBE, DSO. (*Public domain*)

Air Vice-Marshal Ralph Cochrane, Commanding Officer of 5 Group Bomber Command, later Air Chief Marshal Sir Ralph Cochrane, GBE, KCB, AFC. (*Public domain*)

Wing Commander Leonard Cheshire, commanding officer of 617 Squadron and pioneer of low-level target marking. Later, Group Captain Lord Cheshire of Woodhall, VC, OM, DSO and two bars and DFC. Post-war he started the Leonard Cheshire Foundation. (*Public domain*)

The only photograph known to be of DZ477. No. 627 Squadron commanding Officer Wing Commander George Curry poses with two ground crew members. The letter 'K' is the individual aircraft identification letter when used with the 627 Squadron AZ code (AZ:K). The letter is surrounded by bombs, each indicating one operational sortie. The nose art is of a pair of old-fashioned ladies bloomers with a bomb falling from each leg and the motto 'They Come Down at Night'. (*W. W. M. De Boos*)

Oil painting by John Carter commissioned by Ken Oatley depicting AZ:K, likely to be DZ477, which now hangs at the 627 Squadron Thorpe Camp Visitor Centre and kindly reproduced with permission from Rodger Oatley.

Above: Flying Officer J. R. Goodman and Flying Officer A. J. L. Hickcox with Mosquito DZ484, AZ:G 'an incomparable aircraft'. B Flight 627 Squadron RAF Oakington December 1943. (*Group Captain J. R. 'Benny' Goodman*)

Below: Jim Marshallsay and Nick Ranshaw with a rigger and fitter stand in front of Mosquito DK313 AZ:A at Oakington in December 1943. (*Jim Marshallsay*)

Above: 627 Squadron navigation Officer Squadron Leader Bill De Boos 'whistling' dressed in the dark blue RAAF uniform with Sheila Adamson (later De Boos) on his left arm. (*W. W. M. De Boos*)

Below: Bill and Sheila De Boos in their garden in Ballina, NSW, 1990. (*W. W. M. De Boos*)

Above: Wing Commander George Curry dancing with WAAF Sheila Adamson (later De Boos). (*W. W. M. De Boos*)

Below: Black colour scheme 627 Squadron Mosquito DZ484 AZ:G at the dispersal 1944. (*Group Captain J. R. 'Benny' Goodman*)

Above left: Battle of Britain Spitfire Ace Harry Steere photographed in 1940 when serving with 19 Squadron. (*Dilip Sarkar Archive*)

Above right: Flying Officer James Saint-Smith DFM RAAF, 627 Squadron. He was killed on his seventy-third operation as he and his navigator, Flying Officer Geoffrey Heath, headed for home. It is likely that they were killed owing to the premature detonation of a V-1 flying bomb near their Mosquito. (*Copyright expired – public domain via Australian War Memorial*)

Flight Lieutenant Ian Hanlon RNZAF, 627 Squadron. Having been posted from 627, Hanlon was severely injured in an air accident on 10 February 1945 when flying Hurricanes. (*Personnel Archives and Medals HRSC, New Zealand Defence Force*)

Above left: Pilot Officer Sid (Chip) Parlato RNZAF. A veteran of more than fifty Mosquito operations with 139 and 627 Squadron, he was killed in an avoidable accident on 11 March 1945 in similar circumstances to his former colleague, Ian Hanlon; the same exercise criteria with the same unit, flying a Hurricane. (*Personnel Archives and Medals HRSC, New Zealand Defence Force*)

Above right: *Hereford Times* request, 1990. (*Author*)

Form 78 recording an individual aircraft movement during its operational service. (*RAF Museum/Author*)

EXTRACT FROM RAF FORM 1180 (ACCIDENT RECORD CARD)

Date : 15/8/44		Unit :	1655 MTU
Aircraft : Mosquito IV		Group :	8
Serial : DZ477		Command :	B
Engine : Merlin 22		Duty :	Op. Training
Serial : —		Accident Time :	00.50 Hrs
: —		Flight Duration :	3 hr 20 m.
:		Pilot :	W/O Cooke (NZ#41
:			
Location : Hereford Ross Rd.		Casualties :	1 (S)

Pilot baled out. Fancied a/c inverted, rolled a/c several times then baled out. Nav. baled out also. Pilot and Nav. injured.

Pilot had baled out on a previous occasion. suspect he had a brainstorm.

Above: Extracts from Form 1180 RAF Crash Report. (*RAF Museum/Author*)

Left: Claude Evered Cook, the pilot of DZ477 on the night of the crash on 15 August 1944. (*Personnel Archives and Medals HRSC, New Zealand Defence Force*)

Above: DZ477 passed between the pine trees and the farmhouse to the right of photograph centre and continued its descent until striking the tree in the foreground, causing the aircraft to dive into the ground and explode. The house was renovated in the 1960s but the first-floor window from which Jim Morgan saw DZ477 remains. (*Author*)

Below: Crash site excavation, August 1990; Claire and James Crump looking for aircraft pieces. (*Author*)

Above: Excavation licence. (*Author*)

Left: Excavation findings and transfer of ownership. (*Author*)

Above, below and overleaf pages: A selection of parts found during the excavation of Mosquito DZ477. (*Author*)

139 – Squadron emblem.
(*Ministry of Defence © Crown Copyright 2025*)

627 – Squadron emblem.
(*Ministry of Defence © Crown Copyright 2025*)

aiming point. However, one 627 Squadron aircraft, Flying Officer H. Steere and Flying Officer K. W. Gale in DZ353 AZ:B, had their only 500-pounder hang up due to icing.

Forty-four Lancasters were lost to collisions or were shot down by flak and the Halifax loss rate was thirty-four. In all it was a near 10 per cent loss rate to the main force, forcing the Halifax II and V to be permanently withdrawn from operations over Germany after this raid.

Wednesday, 23 February
Target: Düsseldorf
Crew: Squadron Leader E. F. Nelles and Flying Officer A. E. Richards
Bomb Load: 3 × 500lb GP bombs and 1 × 500lb GPLP bomb
Time: Up: 1856hrs, down: 2150hrs

Seventeen Mosquitos, eight from 627 Squadron, bombed the target, although despite fair visibility, no ground detail was seen and offered no results. DZ477 bombed at 2046hrs from 26,000ft with red target indicators in its bombsight. Searchlights in the target area with heavy flak bursting at 26,000ft were encountered. Three aircraft, including DZ477, landed at Coltishall. Three aircraft from 692 Squadron became the first Mosquitos to drop the 4,000lb cookie.

Friday, 25 February
Target: Augsburg
Crew: Flying Officer R. L. Bartley and Flying Officer J. D. Mitchell
Bomb Load: 4 × 500lb GP bombs
Time: Up: 2025hrs, down: 0045hrs

This was the first large raid against Augsburg, which became one of those rare operations when all parts of the operation came together in near perfect harmony.

Along with various diversions, 461 Lancasters, 123 Halifaxes and ten Mosquitos, six from 627 Squadron, were split into two waves. No. 627 Squadron Flying Officer M. D. Gribbin and Flying Officer Griffiths in DZ484 AZ:G were forced to abandon their mission after about an hour in the air when the starboard radiator burst.

Wing Commander Northrop of 83 Pathfinder Squadron, the senior pilot on duty, was acting as visual marker for the first phase of the operation and was able to identify the aiming point without difficulty. In fact, some 627 crews were able to identify the target by the local features such as the river and built-up areas. As Northrop's aircraft approached the target under clear skies he saw the green target indicators fall at 2239hrs a couple of miles west of the aiming point. DZ477 followed immediately and bombed on the cluster of green target indicators at 2240hrs from 24,000ft. The 627 Mosquito DZ442 AZ:D, crewed by Flight Sergeant J. Marshallsay and Flight Sergeant N. A. Ranshaw, had dropped Window along the route to the target and then bombed the target with four 500-pounders at 2300hrs. Part of the second wave bombing spread to the northern and eastern parts of Augsburg and damage was caused to an important aircraft component factory and to some former paper and cotton mills that had been taken over by the MAN engineering group.

This RAF night raid became controversial because of the outstanding accuracy and this 'virgin' target in clear conditions, weak flak defences and accurate Pathfinder ground marking was a recipe for disaster for Augsburg. Concentrated bombing by two waves of the main force dropped 2,000 tons of high explosives, which burned out the heart of this beautiful and historic city, destroying centuries of culture. Many crews could see many large fires on leaving the target area with the glow visible from 150 miles.

In addition, almost 3,000 houses were destroyed and 5,000 damaged, with between 85,000 and 90,000 people bombed out. Sixteen churches and eleven hospitals were destroyed; thankfully all the patients were evacuated safely except sadly for two women workers. There were 246 large or medium fires and just over 800 smaller ones, making life very difficult for fire-fighters as the cold air temperature of –18 degrees Celsius froze the water in the hoses fed from the River Lech. About 750 people were killed with approximately 2,500 injured. The Germans publicised it as an extreme example of 'terror bombing'.

A total of sixteen Lancasters and five Halifaxes were lost, nearly 4 per cent of the force. The lower casualty numbers helped to confirm the advantages of dividing the force and would become a regular feature of heavy raids. It is important to remember that this was a weak target.

Wednesday, 1 March
Target: Munich
Crew: Squadron Leader E. F. Nelles and Flying Officer A. E. Richards
Bomb Load: 3 × 500lb GP bombs, 1 × 500lb GPLP bomb and 1 green target indicator
Time: Up: 0050hrs, down: 0542hrs

Seven Mosquitos from 627 Squadron took off shortly after midnight in perfect weather conditions to carry out a spoof attack on Munich intended to divert the enemy defences from the main force attack on Stuttgart. The spoof was thought to be successful as only four heavy bombers fell on their return home. DZ477 navigated by dead reckoning and bombed at 0256hrs from 26,000ft. Several crews saw widespread fires and red glows within the target area as they set course for home.

Friday, 3 March
Target: Berlin
Crew: Flying Officer A. Hindshaw and Flying Officer J. F. Daly
Bomb Load: 3 × 500lb General Purpose bombs and 1 × 500lb GPLP bomb
Time: Up: 0202hrs, down: 0603hrs

Sixteen Mosquitos, including five from 627 Squadron, bombed Berlin using dead reckoning in the absence of the Pathfinder markers. The Mosquitos arrived at Zero Hour in eight to ten-tenths cloud cover but could see bomb flashes in the target area. Only one crew reported slight predicted heavy flak and one small cone of searchlight. DZ477 bombed at 0400hrs from 25,000ft. No red flares or the results of bombing were seen.

Saturday, 4 March
Target: Berlin
Crew: Flight Sergeant J. Marshallsay and Flight Sergeant N. A. Ranshaw
Bomb Load: 4 × 500lb GPLD bombs
Time: Up: 0146hrs, down: 0336hrs

Six Mosquitos from 627 Squadron were detailed to carry out an attack on Berlin, with three aircraft attacking the primary target between 0402hrs and 0413hrs in some cloud but no haze. Although one crew identified built-up areas, the red flares went down twelve minutes late in slight, predicted heavy flak and many searchlights but there were no enemy fighters.

One Mosquito, DZ462 AZ:N, developed generator and GEE set problems shortly after attacking the target at 0402hrs from 28,000ft and as they flew through the Ruhr defences the aircraft was holed by heavy flak at 0455hrs. The crew, Flying Officer D. W. Peck DSO, DFC and Flying Officer E. F. Davies DFC and bar, landed safely at 0631hrs at Barford St John, Oxfordshire. The navigator, Davies, suffered a slight injury to his left arm but not serious enough for him to be detained. Peck and Davies were lucky men as their experiences with DZ462 were at times a bit tense. On 4 February 1944 they took off at 1838hrs to attack Frankfurt but had to return at 2031hrs owing to technical problems and on 14 June they had another early return, this time from the raid on Aunay-Sur-Odon, when the port engine failed after the exhaust stud failed; the crew landed safely at Exeter.

DZ477 abandoned the Berlin mission owing to engine trouble so it attacked Texel aerodrome as an alternative, bombing the western boundary with no results seen.

Friday, 10 March
Target: Duisburg
Crew: Pilot Officer J. G. Platts and Flying Officer C. G. Thompson RCAF J16603
Bomb Load: 3 × 500lb MC bombs and 1 × 500lb GPLP bomb
Time: Up: 2141hrs, down: 0018hrs

Seven Mosquitos from 627 Squadron were dispatched to carry out an attack on Duisburg. All the aircraft took off and attacked between 2300hrs and 2305hrs from 24,000–26,000ft, dropping twenty-one 500lb MC bombs and seven 500lb GPLD bombs in ten-tenths cloud. The first target indicator was seen to fall at 2256hrs, on which four aircraft bombed. The remaining three aircraft bombed on dead reckoning, which appeared to be an estimated position where the target indicators were dropped. DZ477 bombed at 2302hrs from 24,000ft with target indicators in the bomb sight. No results were seen but slight flak and a few ineffective searchlights were encountered.

Saturday, 11 March
Target: Hamburg
Crew: Flying Officer N. B. Rutherford and Warrant Officer F. H. Stanbury
Bomb Load: 3 × 500lb MC bombs and 1 × 500lb GPLP bomb
Time: Up: 1918hrs, down: 2302hrs

Seven Mosquitos from 627 Squadron carried out the attack on the Blohm and Voss factory and dock area in Hamburg in clear conditions, so all crews were able to identify the target visually as the river and bridge was easily seen. Among the probing searchlights and slight, predicted, accurate flak, the first red target indicators were seen to fall at 2120hrs. DZ477 acquired visual target identification and bombed on target indicators at 2123hrs from 28,000ft, followed promptly by DZ344 AZ:E with Squadron Leader N. W. Mackenzie and Flight Sergeant A. Denholm. However, they were hit by heavy flak directly over the target during their bombing run. Fortunately they remained intact and made it home safely.

Together, the seven Mosquitos dropped twenty-one 500lb MC bombs and seven 500lb GPLD bombs between 2121hrs and 2129hrs from 26,000 to 28,000ft. No bomb bursts were seen.

Monday, 13 March
Target: Frankfurt
Crew: Pilot Officer J. G. Platts and Flying Officer C. G. Thompson RCAF J16603
Bomb Load: 3 × 500lb MC bombs and 1 × 500lb GPLP bomb
Time: up: 1939hrs, down: 2324hrs

Eight Mosquitos from 627 Squadron were detailed to bomb Frankfurt and encountered slight to moderate heavy flak with co-operating searchlights. No fighters were seen. DZ477 bombed on red target indicators at 2101hrs from 24,000ft in three-tenths to six-tenths clouds. A fair concentration of target indicators and a large explosion in the north-east of the town was seen at 2100hrs.

Tuesday, 14 March
Target: Düsseldorf
Crew: Flying Officer N. B. Rutherford and Warrant Officer F. H. Stanbury
Bomb Load: 3 × 500lb GP bombs and 1 × 500lb GPLP bomb
Time: Up: 1959hrs, down: 2259hrs

Six Mosquitos from 627 Squadron took off in five-tenths cloud to attack Düsseldorf. All aircraft bombed on green target indicators, which were dropped at 21.14hrs but were scattered as much as 10 miles apart and some disappeared rapidly into cloud. DZ477 bombed at 2115hrs from 28,000ft with green target indicators in the bomb sight and, like other crews, they saw large yellow explosions ten seconds before the bombs were released in the area of target indicators. Once again there was an absence of fighters and with searchlight batteries operating ineffectively the heavy flak was slight to moderate.

Wednesday, 15 March
Target: Stuttgart
Crew: Flight Sergeant J. Marshallsay and Flight Sergeant N. A. Ranshaw
Bomb Load: 4 × 500lb GPLD Delayed Action bombs
Time: Up: 2037hrs, down: 0046hrs

A total force of 617 Lancasters, 230 Halifaxes and sixteen Mosquitos flew over France to near the Swiss frontier before turning northeast to approach Stuttgart. The German fighter controllers split their forces into two parts, which delayed the fighters contacting the bomber stream. However, when they did arrive just before Stuttgart was reached the usual fierce combats ensued. As the bomber stream reached the target area they were fortunate to see that the searchlights were ineffective owing to the cloud cover.

Eight 627 Squadron aircraft attacked Stuttgart between 2300hrs and 2354hrs from 23,000 to 26,000ft, with five making runs on dead reckoning. DZ477 bombed at 2259hrs from 23,500ft and all the Mosquito crews observed that the heavy bomber attack had started late, with the Pathfinder green/red star flares seen at 2310hrs. The 'Heavies' were delayed by adverse winds, which scattered their flares, causing the Pathfinder marking to fall back well short of the target. Some of the bombing fell in the centre of snow-covered Stuttgart, damaging the Akademie in the centre of the city and destroying some housing in the south-western suburbs. This killed eighty-eight people with more than 200 injured. It was a wasted effort for Bomber Command and was not worth the loss of twenty-seven Lancasters and ten Halifaxes, just over 4 per cent of the force falling to night fighters. Two Lancasters force-landed in Switzerland.

Friday, 17 March
Target: Cologne
Crew: Warrant Officer R. G. Boyden RCAF 103840 and Flight Sergeant R. W. Fenwick
Bomb Load: 1 × 500lb GP bombs and 3 × 500lb MC bomb
Time: Up: 1928hrs, down: 2220hrs

No. 627 Squadron sent eight Mosquitos to revisit Cologne. For the first time, two aircraft were fitted with the modified bomb bay that carried the 4,000lb cookies. The target markers and subsequent bombing appeared well concentrated and the glow of a particularly large fire was reflected in the cloud base. DZ477 bombed using dead reckoning and on ETA at 2050hrs from 28,000ft. No results were seen but the crew could view the glow of fires 30 miles from the target after they turned for home. This was the sixth consecutive raid without a failure or early return.

Saturday, 18 March
Target: Frankfurt
Crew: Flight Sergeant J. Marshallsay and Flight Sergeant N. A. Ranshaw
Bomb Load: 4 × 500lb MC bomb
Time: up: 2008hrs, down: 2318hrs

This raid employed 620 Lancasters, 209 Halifaxes and seventeen Mosquitos; nine from 627 were sent to Frankfurt in conjunction with a mining operation over Heligoland. The Germans night fighter forces were split, with some being lured north but the second group waited inside Germany and met the bomber stream just before the target was reached. However, they were hampered by cloud cover and haze, which enabled the Pathfinders to lead the way for the main force. A massive blow was delivered with heavy damage caused across Frankfurt; more than 6,000 buildings were destroyed or seriously damaged.

The conditions made initial identification difficult for the Pathfinders but they marked with accurate target indicators using the visual marking technique called 'Newhaven' combined with the H2S-based ground-marking system Parramatta and some Wanganui sky markers. The Mosquitos of 627 navigated by dead reckoning and dropped Window towards the target. DZ477 went in first, bombing at 2150hrs from 25,000ft and together with the remaining 627 Mosquitos dropped twenty-eight 500lb MC bombs between 2150 and 2157hrs. The four 1,000-pounders went down at 2243hrs from 23,000ft and 2256hrs from 25,000ft respectively. Once again, the searchlights were ineffective, with slight heavy flak and no fighter opposition. The later phase of the bombing was scattered, which was almost inevitable with such a large force and new inexperienced crews allocated to the final wave. The general opinion of returning crews was that the operation had been successful with concentrated bombing on accurate markers. They reported a huge red explosion that lit up the sky for thirty seconds and large fires and glows running east and west in a radius of about 5 miles.

The heavy bombing to the eastern, central and western districts of Frankfurt caused extensive destruction, with cultural buildings, including the Opera House and the preserved Medieval Quarter being destroyed. It was reported that 3,494 houses, nearly 100 industrial companies, 400 small businesses and nearly sixty public buildings were destroyed or seriously damaged. Just over 400 civilians were killed and 55,000 people were bombed out. A military train was hit with twenty soldiers killed and eighty wounded but it is possible that this may have been a result of Fighter Command intruder aircraft as a Frankfurt report stated that it was shot up by cannon fire.

The loss of ten Lancasters and twelve Halifaxes represented nearly 3 per cent of the force, which could be considered as relatively low for such a deep-penetration raid.

Wednesday, 22 March
Target: Frankfurt
Crew: Squadron Leader E. F. Nelles and Flying Officer A. E. Richards
Bomb Load: 4 × 500lb MC bomb
Time: Up: 1920hrs, down: 2319hrs

A force of 620 Lancasters and 184 Halifaxes were sent on an indirect route across the Dutch coast north of the Zuider Zee and then almost due south to Frankfurt, which combined with the Kiel minelaying diversion confused the Germans for some time as they considered Hanover was to be the likely target. Therefore only a few night fighters found the bomber stream.

The briefed weather forecast prompted a ground-marking plan to be prepared but when clouds began to drift across the target as the Pathfinders arrived they were forced to find the target by H2S and then employ a combination of 'Newhaven' and 'Wanganui' flares. Some were able to identify the target visually and bombed on sky markers, carrying out their attacks from 16,500 to 19,000ft between 2146hrs and 2204hrs.

Ten Mosquitos from 627 Squadron split into two waves. The first of seven aircraft carried out early Window dropping, then proceeded to drop twenty-eight 500lb MC bombs between 2139hrs and mid-raid at 2155hrs from 24,000 and 26,000ft in good visibility of two to four-tenths cloud. DZ477 bombed at 2146hrs from 25,000ft and its crew observed large fires and rising smoke when leaving the target area. The second wave of the three remaining aircraft each dropped cookies between 2324hrs and 2331hrs from 25,000ft in clear weather. The attack by heavies was opposed by slight moderate heavy flak with many ineffective searchlights, and the bombers achieved widespread concentration north to south, thought to be mainly over the built-up area. Large glows and fires were seen with a huge column of smoke rising to over 20,000ft from a large area of fires estimated as three to 5 miles and 10 miles in diameter that spread over an area of about 15 miles north-west to south-east. The glow of these fires were visible from 200 miles away.

The accurate marking and bombing of Frankfurt delivered a heavier blow than the raid carried out four nights earlier as all parts of the city were hit, with the greatest weight of the attack falling on the western districts. Half the city was without gas, water and electricity for a long period, severe damage was inflicted on the industrial areas and twenty-six Nazi Party buildings were hit. Nearly 1,000 people were killed, and up to 400 seriously injured. Some 120,000 people were bombed out. Old Frankfurt, with its history and culture built over hundreds of years, ceased to exist.

A total of 162 B17 Flying Fortresses of the American 8th Air Force used Frankfurt as a secondary target when they could not reach Schweinfurt thirty-six hours after this RAF raid and caused further damage. The Frankfurt raids of 18, 22 and 23 March were carried out by a combined plan of the British and American Air Forces and their combined effort was to deal the worst and most fateful blow of the war to Frankfurt, simply ending the existence of the old city, which had been built up since the Middle Ages.

Twenty-six Lancasters and seven Halifaxes, about 4 per cent of the force, failed to return. The vast majority were almost certainly the victims of the flak defences within the target area. Airmen that were fortunate to survive the loss of their aircraft within the Frankfurt area had to be protected by their guards from the assaults of angry civilians when they passed through Frankfurt to the nearby Oberursel interrogation transit camps.

In a letter to the author, Jim Marshallsay, the pilot of DZ477, wrote about their post-raid interrogation:

> Frankfurt was a devastating attack, the city was ablaze from end to end and everything was glowing red and white except for the river and bridges; an awesome sight. When we were being interrogated by the Intelligence Officer, he said that he had been told there were 'beautiful fires'. My navigator, Nick Ranshaw, was a bit upset by the choice of adjective and had a bit of a barny with the Intelligence Officer.

Friday, 24 March
Target: Berlin
Crew: Squadron Leader E. F. Nelles and Flying Officer A. E. Richards
Bomb Load: 3 × white flares and 3 × 500lb MC bombs
Time: Up: 1933hrs, down: 0100hrs

This final assault on Berlin was hard for Harris because his prediction of wrecking the city from end to end was not to be and never again would he send his heavy bombers to the capital. The final raid became known as the night of the strong winds when powerful north winds carried the bombers south at every stage of their flight.

Some 577 Lancasters, 216 Halifaxes and eighteen Mosquitos were sent. The eight Mosquitos from 627 Squadron were split, with two going to Kiel, each to deliver a 4,000lb cookie. The weather briefing before the raid had forecast winds over the North Sea to vary from 21mph increasing to 44mph but later, as the aircraft progressed over the North Sea, the navigators began to pick up even stronger winds on their GEE equipment. As they progressed further their GEE became jammed by the enemy defences, leading to a delay of around thirty minutes to re-establish their positions. In the meantime they had to rely upon estimated wind forecasts they had received via England from the 'wind-finder' aircraft sent out earlier that evening. During this period the wind direction remained steady but the strength had increased.

The main force navigators expected to take an outward route over the neck of Denmark, making landfall on the German coast before veering south-east with another dog-leg 30 miles from the capital, then a final course change south-west for the final run-in to the target. The reality was that they were 30 miles south of where they should have been, having been blown by winds of 130mph. This led to much confusion in the air as the stream became widely dispersed. Many bombers flew north in an attempt to regain their original track, wasting a lot of time and causing further confusion. The dispersed bomber stream had been hampered by highly inaccurate and downgraded wind readings being broadcast back to the stream owing to the HQ meteorological officers and staff refusing to believe the high velocities being reported to them. This miscalculation resulted in accumulated errors. The bombers had expected to arrive over the north-eastern outskirts of the 'Big City' at 2335hrs. However, 700 aircraft were now approaching the capital spread over a front 70 miles across with each bomber following its own course, not their leader, and they were all flying at different altitudes, with some at 17,000 and others at 18,000ft.

Two master bombers were co-ordinating the raid with the deputy master bomber circling in a high-flying meteorological Mosquito. The strong winds caused difficulty in marking, with many markers being carried well out to the south-west of the city and as the bomb run was one of the most dangerous periods of the mission, some of the initial crews arriving over the area were blown across the city so they had to bomb any targets they could find. The others approaching later were able to bomb the aiming point of Pathfinder markers and passed over the city at a welcome high escape velocity. Some crews made the hazardous decision to turn around and make a second orbit, which was a twenty-minute trip over the most heavily defended city in the world against a headwind of 100 knots. The aircraft had to circle out from the target to the south-east, following a return course with three dog-leg course changes. It was during this period that the majority of the sixty of the raiders fell to the Luftwaffe's night fighter aces that were roaming the night sky over Berlin.

The six 627 Squadron aircraft dropped twelve white flares and twenty 500lb MC bombs between 2221hrs and 2240hrs from 24,300 and 26,000ft. Two aircraft reported bombing on green target indicators dropped at 2221hrs; two others bombed on dead reckoning after the attack had opened by the heavies, one being DZ477. Its crew had 'Windowed' on Gee and then bombed on red fires at 2238hrs from 26,000ft, the crew seeing many bombs burst south of the target and then seeing glows from a considerable distance from the target.

Around Berlin, moderate heavy flak with numerous searchlights was in operation but there were no sightings of fighter flares. The bomber stream became very scattered on the homeward flight and the radar-predicted flak batteries in many places were able to score successes.

Part of the force strayed over the Ruhr defences on the return flight and it is believed that seventy-two aircraft were lost to flak and night fighters. The winds were so strong that many aircraft were blown so far they actually flew near Sagan, Silesia, 100 miles south-east of the capital, where Stalag Luft III was located. By complete coincidence this was the night of the Great Escape and because the stream passed close by, the Germans switched off the camp's electricity supply and all the searchlights went out. This reduced the number of escaping

PoWs to seventy-six passing through the tunnel rather than the 200 they had hoped for. One can only speculate how history may have been changed if the winds to and over Berlin had not been so strong. Of the seventy-three recaptured men, twenty-three were sent to other Nazi prison camps but the other fifty were not as lucky as an enraged Hitler ordered their execution. The Gestapo killed the men along quiet country lanes and in secluded locations. It was to be yet another direct violation of the Geneva Conventions.

Many bombs fell on more than 100 small towns and villages outside Berlin but the majority of the damage was caused in the south-western districts, where 20,000 people were bombed out and approximately 150 killed. Several industrial areas were damaged and five military establishments were badly hit, including the depot of the 1st SS Panzer Division Leibstandarte SS Adolf Hitler in Lichterfelde.

The Berlin reports say fourteen bombers were shot down by fighters in the target area, with the German night fighters claiming eighty-three four-engine aircraft destroyed between 2100hrs and 0015hrs that night. These claims appear to be wildly exaggerated when compared to the RAF Operations Records Books reports and it is possible that different fighters claimed the same victim. However, forty-four Lancasters and twenty-eight Halifaxes were lost; nearly 400 airmen losing their lives and 131 becoming prisoners of war. Although this was the final attack on the capital during the Battle of Berlin, the city would be bombed many times in the coming months by small forces of Mosquitos.

Sunday, 26 March
Target: Essen
Crew: Flight Sergeant J. Marshallsay and Flight Sergeant N. A. Ranshaw
Bomb Load: 4 × 500lb MC bombs
Time: Up: 2039hrs, down: 2351hrs

A total of 467 Lancasters, 207 Halifaxes and twenty-two Mosquitos were detailed for the operation to Essen. Ten 627 Squadron aircraft were split into two groups with three sent to Hanover, each dropping a 4,000lb cookie on a rather scattered cluster of target indicators at 2155hrs to 2156hrs from 24,000–25,000ft. The remaining seven aircraft attacked Essen and the sudden switch by Bomber Command to a Ruhr target just across the German frontier caught the German fighter controllers by surprise. Essen was completely covered by cloud but was within the parameters of Oboe, allowing the Pathfinders to mark accurately from 16,500 to 20,000ft between 2159hrs and 2209hrs, although the target indicators disappeared into the clouds.

The Mosquitos were 'Windowing' as they went in and bombed before the heavies, with DZ477 bombing at 2156hrs on red target indicators from 22,000ft. The crew could see the contrails of the approaching heavy bombers at about 18,000 to 19,000ft.

Jim Marshallsay in DZ477 remembers Windowing for the heavies, then circling the target to watch the attack develop. A heavy bomber had been hit by a night fighter and was set on fire, so the crew bailed out. Tragically, one parachute caught fire and the unfortunate man fell into the fires below. Someone was heard to say over the radio transmission 'hard luck mate'.

Returning crews commented on spoof enemy Wanganui flares attempting to lure the main force away from the main target.

No results were seen but forty-eight industrial buildings were seriously damaged and nearly 1,800 houses were destroyed, killing 550 people with forty-nine missing. The Essen reports broke down the figures for killed or missing as: Germans: 374 men, women and children, six soldiers, four policemen and two Hitler Youth. Foreigners: seventy-four forced workers and one prisoner of war. The remaining 138 victims were mixed German and foreign concentration camp prisoners, large numbers of whom were now providing the labour forces in German factories.

Allied losses amounted to six Lancasters and three Halifaxes, just over 1 per cent of the force.

During this time an unusual Mosquito landed at Oakington; it was a standard Mk IV with a modified bomb bay in order to carry a 4,000lb cookie. 'Benny' Goodman and Nick Ranshaw were ordered to fly the cookie carrier, DZ646, on only one trip, to Duisburg on 27 March 1944. Benny noticed that take-off was not difficult but she was not the 'scalded cat' he was used to and as the tail left the ground, he pushed the throttles quickly forward to the gate with plus 9lb boost 3,000rpm and eased the throttles to the full open plus 12lb 3,000rpm. He compared this aircraft to his regular G-George, which would have resulted in a glorious acceleration and a hop, skip and jump into the air. It was not the case with this pregnant lady, who waddled along using most of the available runway before she decided to unstick and enter a sedate climb, taking much longer to reach 25,000ft than G-George. They took a long time to settle to a steady cruise but eventually headed for the Ruhr. Over the target area, Benny confessed to a feeling of distinct nervousness as they were flying with the bulging bomb doors open waiting for a German gunner to blow them to pieces as Bill called out his bomb run instructions of 'left, left ... right ... steady'. When the call came to release the bomb it was time to manually move the solid metal bar to release the massive catch holding the cookie and down the bomb would go. However, if the bomb door had not been opened it was hard luck; the cookie would still drop, taking the bomb doors with it. At the call of 'bomb gone' the Mosquito suddenly shot up like a lift without the customary delicate porpoising as the usual four 500-pounders left the bomb bay; the altimeter moved instantly through 500ft of altitude. This was a new experience for Benny as their fat little bird became an almost normal Mosquito and quickly accelerated to a fast cruising speed.

Thursday, 30 March
Target: Nuremberg
Crew: Squadron Leader E. F. Nelles and Flying Officer A. E. Richards
Bomb Load: 4 × 500lb MC bombs
Time: Up: 2256hrs, down: 0321hrs

The Nuremburg attack was seen as Harris's final opportunity of the winter offensive to prove the efficiency of his policies in the Battle of Berlin before changing to the commitment of operations to support the planning of D-Day. On what would normally have been a stand-down period for the heavies of the main force, a raid to the distant target of Nuremberg was planned based entirely on an early weather forecast. With a low-pressure area over Norway and a slow-moving high layer of cloud coming from Ireland, this could have provided the bombers with the cover they needed on the outward flight and these weather conditions led Harris to consider a target in the south of Germany. With the moon up and the protective high cloud on the outward route the target would be clear for ground-marked bombing. A meteorological flight Mosquito that returned to base at 1525hrs reported by radio that the protective cloud was unlikely to be present on the outward journey but could well be present over the target. Harris insisted on continuing with the raid by reasoning that if the crews were unable to bomb large targets like Berlin and Frankfurt successfully how could they hope to hit smaller industrial targets that required greater accuracy without losing more lives? This decision to go ahead was met with the bitter opposition of the Pathfinder leader Don Bennett, who predicted a disaster if he was overruled and so offered an alternative plan. Many thought that the operation was unlikely to go ahead but they were wrong and at 2223hrs the first contingent took to the air. In all, 572 Lancasters, 214 Halifaxes and four Mosquitos from 627 Squadron were despatched.

Historically, the Nazis considered Nuremburg to be a significant city as well as an important transportation centre and it was clear that the RAF made no attempt to disguise a change from the normal habit of employing dog-leg course changes to the target. The group commanders decided on a straight 350-mile 'long leg', which routed past Brussels, then east between Koblenz and Bonn and then south to Nuremberg to a point about 50 miles north of the target, where the final run-in would begin.

Jim Marshallsay and Nick Ranshaw in DZ462 AZ:N were on their thirty-eighth trip, which started quite normally after getting airborne at 2300hrs. As Window openers to confuse the radar defences, they had to be over the target before the first marker aircraft arrived. As Jim and Nick turned into the long run they realised that something was going badly wrong. The expected cloud cover was not there and exposed a moon that was much too bright, causing the heavies to leave more than 3,000 persistent condensation trails and forming a great silver road in the air leading into Germany. Ranshaw logged sixteen heavies shot down in flames in less than five minutes on the long leg. He gave up recording the gruesome details and opted for the task of searching for night fighters. Mor than forty heavies went down on the long leg but as they neared Nuremburg, the clouds began to form. Jim and Nick threw out their Window, dropped their bombs and circled to watch the attack develop but saw little other than a few Wanganui flares. Their job done, Nick suggested going straight home, so Jim turned the Mosquito's nose towards Oakington and left at a great pace. Having landed back at base at 0317hrs after just over four hours in the air, they were debriefed and then ate their operational eggs. Shortly afterwards, as they headed off to bed, the first of the 7 Squadron Lancasters that had left Oakington about thirty minutes before the Mosquitos were circling to land in the low cloud base and flurries of snow in the air.

The German controllers ignored all the diversions and assembled their fighters at the two night fighter beacons, which happened to be astride the 350-mile 'long leg' route. Without the protective clouds the first fighters appeared just before the bomber stream crossed the Belgian border and it was here that the struggle for survival in the sky began, with a fierce battle in the moonlight lasting for the next hour. The experienced Mosquito crews understood what was happening to the heavies as they witnessed long bursts of tracer from night fighters, then flames from the wings of a heavy followed by a massive explosion and fire on the ground. The battle continued all the way to the target as the massacre of the bomber stream continued with a track of the burning wreckage of Lancasters and Halifaxes on the ground.

Wind-finder squadron crews were to record the wind speed and direction, then broadcast it back to group, who would collate the data and rebroadcast back to the main force. They did not immediately appreciate the presence of a Jetstream wind similar to the one that had compromised the Berlin operation a week earlier. Once again the wind finders did not believe the results they were witnessing and adjusted the data before sending it to group, who also disbelieved it and adjusted it further before broadcasting it back. Subsequently, many crews were unaware of the inaccurate navigation and as the aircraft turned on to the final leg from a false position it led to more than 100 bombers attacking Schweinfurt in error. The final approach to the target caused many of the Pathfinder aircraft to mark too far to the east, and with high losses before the target was reached, it substantially reduced the numbers available to attack Nuremberg. The crew of DZ477 saw route markers at Aachen at 0010hrs, then bombed on red flares with yellow stars at 0108hrs from 23,000ft. Pathfinders and the main force aircraft were under heavy fighter attack throughout the raid and a 10-mile long creep back developed into the countryside north of Nuremberg. Little damage was caused in Nuremberg, while sixty-nine people were killed in the city and surrounding villages.

The action was much reduced on the return flight as most of the German fighters had to land, but overall, sixty-four Lancasters and thirty-one Halifaxes were lost – nearly 12 per cent of the force. With no useful damage caused to the target, Bomber Command had suffered the biggest loss of the war, with additional bombers written off in landing crashes or left with battle damage too severe to repair. It was a bitter lesson.

Only one Victoria Cross was awarded to any Halifax pilot. On this night over Nuremberg a 578 Squadron Halifax LK797 LK:K piloted by Flying Officer Cyril J. Barton was attacked by a night fighter and suffered heavy damage. In the immediate confusion three crew members bailed out but Barton, displaying extraordinary courage and dedication, continued to fly the Halifax and gave the other crew members time to bail out. The actions of this brave man saved the life of his crew and now with Barton on the run for home and his aircraft low on fuel and failing engines, he brought the aircraft down near Ryhope Colliery, County Durham, with an impact so severe that the young pilot was killed together with a local miner on his way to work.

Thursday, 6 April
Target: Hamburg
Crew: Flying Officer N. B. Rutherford and Warrant Officer F. H. Stanbury
Bomb Load: 3 × 500lb MC bombs and 1 × 500lb GPLD bombs
Time: Up: 2043hrs, down: 0033hrs

Thirty-five Mosquitos detailed for the raid. Twelve were from 627 Squadron, with four each carrying a 4,000lb cookie.

DZ477 bombed on green target indicators at 2230hrs from 24,000ft in clear weather with some haze but all crews visually identified the target and dropped their bombs on green target indicators. Ex-Battle of Britain pilot Flying Officer Harry Steere and his navigator, Flying Officer K. W. Gale (RAAF), in DZ353 AZ:B, saw no results after bombing owing to being coned by searchlights and being hit by flak over the target but they returned safely. Sadly, one Mosquito DZ370, flown by Flying Officer A. M. Howden and Flying Officer F. Stevens, from 139 Squadron was lost without trace.

Thirty-nine people were killed and 161 were injured. Seven fires were reported, with 322 people bombed out.

Saturday. 8 April
Target: Essen
Crew: Flying Officer N. B. Rutherford and Warrant Officer F. H. Stanbury
Bomb Load: 1 × 500lb MC bomb and 1 × 500lb GPLD bomb
Time: Up: 2137hrs, down: 0007hrs

Forty Mosquitos, including twelve from 627 Squadron, were dispatched to Hamburg. Four 627 aircraft carried one 4,000lb cookie. All 627 aircraft Windowed as ordered and saw the first target indicators at 22.29hrs, which were backed up by further TIs from 2230hrs to 2236hrs that appeared well concentrated.

DZ477 bombed by dead reckoning through seven to ten-tenths cloud on three well-concentrated green target indicators at 2231hrs from 25,000ft. One large explosion was seen at 2233hrs immediately followed by the start of a massive fire that was burning well on leaving the target. One aircraft, DZ484 AZ:G crewed by Flying Officer M. D. Gribben and Flying Officer R. W. Griffiths (RCAF), did not see target indicators on arrival so made an orbit and bombed later on target indicators with a run on dead reckoning at 2242hrs. Flying

Officer I. H. Hanlon (RNZAF) and F/S J. Upton in DZ418 AZ:L were lining up and about to release their bombs when one engine developed trouble and they suspect that their bombs fell slightly short. Slight to moderate accurate flak was encountered and searchlights operating with one cone of five lights held one aircraft for three minutes, but they were mostly ineffective due to cloud.

Sunday, 9 April
Target: Mannheim
Crew: Squadron Leader E. F. Nelles and Flying Officer A. E. Richards
Bomb Load: 1 × 500lb GP bombs and 3 × 500lb MC bomb
Time: up: 2119hrs, down: 0040hrs

Thirty-six Mosquitos, of which twelve were from 627 Squadron, were dispatched to Mannheim. Four 627 Mosquitos carried 4,000lb cookies. DZ477 bombed on green target indicators at 2313hrs from 25,000ft in eight to ten-tenths cloud. The flash of bombs hitting the ground along with the glow of two fires was seen through the clouds and all crews agreed that numerous 4,000lb bursts were seen well positioned in relation to the markers. Slight to moderate flak was encountered but no searchlights and no fighter activity.

Monday, 10 April
Target: Hanover
Crew: Flying Officer I. H. Hanlon (RNZAF) and Flight Sergeant J. Upton
Bomb Load: 3 × 500lb Medium Capacity Instantaneous Burst bombs and 1 × 500 GPLD
Time: Up: 2126hrs, down: 0031hrs

Thirty-six Mosquitos, including twelve from 627 Squadron were despatched. Four carried 4,000lb cookies. All aircraft took off in two to six-tenths thin cloud cover with poor downward visibility but the route markers were seen by all aircraft crews. The crews dropped their cookies and twenty-four 500lb Instantaneous Burst bombs and eight 500lb LD bombs between 2259hrs and 2303hrs from 24,000 to 25,000ft. All drops were on green target indicators, the first of which was seen at 2257hrs, followed by two others between 2259hrs and 2303hrs.

DZ477 bombed at 2300hrs from 25,000ft on green target indicators in the bomb sight. Big fires were seen within 2 miles of the target at 2307hrs but this was believed to be a dummy. Some crew reported seeing the flash of a bursting 4,000lb bomb in the immediate vicinity just prior to the attack. Bomb bursts were also seen and also a large fire twelve minutes after leaving the target. Defences were slight to moderate heavy flak predicted with about sixty searchlights, one cone with others operating independently, but all were ineffective. No Allied losses.

Tuesday, 11 April
Target: Hanover
Crew: Flying Officer N. B. Rutherford and Warrant Officer F. H. Stanbury
Bomb Load: 3 × 500lb MC and 1 × 500 GPLD
Time: Up: 2115hrs, down: 0059hrs

Twelve Mosquitos from 627 Squadron were despatched, with four carrying 4,000lb cookies, to attack Hanover as a diversion raid for the attack on Aachen. Four cookies, twenty-four 500lb Medium Capacity Instantaneous Burst bombs and eight 500lb LD bombs were dropped between 2255hrs and 2300hrs from 23,000 to 26,000ft. The attack opened with well-placed yellow target indicators at 2250hrs and bombing was generally well concentrated, however a stick of 500-pounders was reported to fall 15 miles west of the target. DZ477 bombed with yellow target indicators in the bombsight at 2254hrs from 25,000ft but no results were seen. One explosion was reported in the target area at 2259hrs. No searchlights were in operation, there was slight to moderate heavy flak but no aircraft were lost.

Wednesday, 12 April
Target: Osnabrück
Crew: Squadron Leader E. F. Nelles and Flying Officer A. E. Richards
Bomb Load: 3 × 500 Medium Capacity Instantaneous Burst bombs and 1 × 500lb GPLD bomb
Time: up: 2113hrs, down: 0013hrs

Thirty-nine Mosquitos, including twelve from 627 Squadron, bombed Osnabrück as a harassing raid without loss. Four 627 Mosquitos carried the 4,000lb cookie. DZ477 bombed with red target indicators in the bombsight at 2246hrs from 22,000ft. Target marking was accurate and the bombing was well concentrated, with some crews seeing bomb flashes and explosions near the markers and more flashes were seen on leaving the target area.

Thursday, 13 April
Target: Berlin
Crew: Flying Officer N. B. Rutherford and Warrant Officer F. H. Stanbury
Bomb Load: 3 × 500lb Medium Capacity Instantaneous Burst bombs and 1 × 500lb GPLD bomb
Time: up: 2125hrs, down: 0136hrs

Twenty-nine Mosquitos, which included eight from 627 Squadron, were dispatched to attack Berlin. Six aircraft attacked the primary target, dropping Window on the run-in to the target, but one aircraft, DZ525 AZ:S with Flying Officer I. H. Hanlon (RNZAF) and Flight Sergeant J. Upton, was forced to attack the 'last resort' target of Osnabrück owing to adverse weather and a high engine temperature on the starboard engine. They dropped three 500lb Medium Capacity Instantaneous Burst bombs and one 500lb GPLD bomb at 2258hrs from 25,000ft, with a considerable number of searchlights operating under the clouds. The remaining aircraft continued to Berlin but Wing Commander R. J. Boyden (RCAF) and Flight Sergeant R. W. Fenwick, in DZ484 AZ:G, had to return early as they were unable to maintain enough height to clear the cloud tops despite using maximum engine power.

In cloudless conditions but some ground haze, eighteen 500lb GPLD bombs were dropped between 2331hrs and 2335hrs from 22,000 to 26,000ft. Very intense searchlight activity was encountered with accurate moderate to intense heavy flak. The crew of DZ516 AZ:O, Flying Officer J. A. Saint-Smith (RAAF) and Flying Officer G. E. Heath (RAAF), were held in a cone of searchlights, so they could not identify any ground detail. DZ415 AZ:Q, with P/O S. F. Parlato (RNZAF) and P/O D. D. Thomas, was also held in a large searchlight cone and as they were about to release their bombs, one 500-pounder hung up. DZ477 bombed on dead reckoning and at the expected time of Zero Hour at 2331hrs from 25,000ft with unobserved results. The crew reported a heavy concentration of searchlights that prevented the observation of bombing results. No losses.

On 14 April 1944 there was no operational flying but during the late evening of 13 April the squadron received the news that they were to proceed on temporary attachment to RAF Woodhall Spa in Lincolnshire and that the move should be complete by 2359hrs on 15 April.

The flight crews were called to a meeting addressed by a somewhat emotional Don Bennett, who informed them that they were being taken from him and sent to 5 Group, where Leonard Cheshire had demonstrated a new technique of dive-bombing marking. He would also lose two of his best Lancaster squadrons, which were to go to Coningsby as back-ups. On 14 April the crews were sent to Woodhall Spa to join 617 Squadron to become a specialised target-marking, reconnaissance and bombing unit for 5 Group. It soon became apparent that they were very much the poor relations of the famous Dambusters, who 'lorded' it up in the Petwood Hotel.

The following morning an advanced party led by Flying Officer Rutherford AFC travelled to Woodhall Spa to prepare the new quarters for the squadron, which consisted of a village of Nissen huts made from half-cylindrical metal corrugated skins over concrete floors. On 15 April the main body of the squadron travelled by road to Woodhall Spa, with four of their aircraft flown to the station at 1600hrs. The remaining four 4,000lb 'cookie' carriers were flown to Upwood to be exchanged for conventional 2,000lb carriers. All the personnel were given sleeping accommodation on the dispersed site approximately a mile from the aerodrome. The officers were provided with meals at the luxury Petwood Hotel, which had been taken over by the RAF in Woodhall Spa about 4 miles away. The Blue Bell Inn at Tattersall Thorpe quickly became their local public house. Crew briefings were at RAF Coningsby, 2½ miles away. The following day, the 16th, was spent reorganising and generally settling down, and on the 17th the officers moved into Tattersall Thorpe officers' mess but still retained sleeping quarters at dispersed sites.

Two flights of conventional aircraft arrived from Upwood and commenced dive-bombing practice over the airfield using 11.5lb practice bombs, which would produce a puff of smoke on impact, allowing the range observers to record their position. From 18 April there were no operations for the next two days so more day and night dive-bombing practice flights were carried out at Wainfleet bombing range in The Wash, some 20 miles away. The squadron prepared for a Window-dropping sortie on the marshalling yards at La Chapelle near Paris on the 20 April and from the start of May, the Normandy landings planned for June saw the attacks on railway targets in France becoming a priority. It was important that the surrounding civilian population should not be affected, so 627's precision target-marking technique was of great importance.

No. 627 Squadron used the Mosquito Mk IV throughout its service but had a number of Mosquito Mk XXs from July 1944. Known to the heavy bomber crews as the 'Model Aeroplane Club', 627 took part in 166 operations, with 1,058 sorties. Most were marking duties but from time to time they conducted some mining, Window dropping and meteorological sorties. In all, fifteen aircraft were lost, just over 1 per cent of the squadron.

Chapter 18

RAF Woodhall Spa

Woodhall Spa in the flat countryside of south Lincolnshire was a perfect location for a heavy bomber station and was an ideal place to home one of the most famous of all bomber squadrons, 617, the Dambusters, and the elite target markers, 627 Squadron.

Intended as a satellite station for nearby RAF Coningsby, the farmland was requisitioned by the Air Ministry in 1940 and the future airfield was deliberately ploughed to render it unusable as a possible enemy landing ground. Work began in 1941 between the villages of Woodhall Spa and Tattershall Thorpe with the Ostlers Plantation on the northern perimeter retained as excellent natural cover for thirty-three bomb storage and arming areas. The standard pattern of three concrete runways were linked to a perimeter track for the armourers to transport bombs from the stores to fusing areas and then on to the aircraft dispersals. The main 6,000ft runway and the thirty-four 120ft aircraft hard standings enabled the aircraft to be parked well away from each other, reducing the risk from air attack and accidental explosions. The bombs, minus their fins, were stored on raised concrete platforms surrounded by earth banks that would help to contain and direct a blast upwards in an accidental explosion. Smaller munitions such as flare and target indicators were stored in huts around the airfield. To the south side of the aerodrome perimeter track were more than seventy buildings housing almost all of the support services found on every busy wartime bomber station.

When Woodhall Spa opened in February 1942 the Lancasters of 97 Squadron moved in from Coningsby a month later so that base could prepare for the construction of concrete runways. No. 97 Squadron stayed until April 1943 before they moved to Bourn in Cambridgeshire and were immediately replaced by 619 Squadron Lancasters.

Woodhall Spa was to suffer a tragic coincidence on 18 August 1943 when 619 Squadron provided twelve of the nearly 600 aircraft that attacked the Peenemünde rocket research works on the Baltic coast. Three aircraft were shot down with twenty-two men killed, including one of the squadron's flight commanders, Wing Commander I. J. McGhie. That very same night McGhie's wife and family, also living in Woodhall Spa, narrowly escaped injury when the town was bombed. Three people died and sixty-one other civilians were injured as parachute mines destroyed a hotel and badly damaged a block of flats and a number of other buildings.

When 619 Squadron moved to Coningsby during January 1944, 617 Squadron moved in and would remain there until the end of the war, with the airfield providing better security. There was just enough room to house a single squadron, with the nearby grand Petwood Hotel commandeered to become the officers' mess. The local population thought Woodhall Spa was just another bomber station as nothing was said or heard outside of the perimeter but these were very special crews that trained hard and gained a reputation for highly accurate low-level marking and bombing of specific targets. It was from Woodhall Spa that Wing Commander Leonard Cheshire, a vastly experienced pilot and commander, became one of Bomber Command's most outstanding officers. Cheshire eventually carried out 100 operations before being ordered to stop operational flying and became one of the few men in history to be awarded the Victoria Cross for a sustained period of the highest service and bravery, rather than a single act of courage. Cheshire almost became 617's first casualty on 13 January 1944 when during an air test his Lancaster hit a flock of plovers. One bird crashed through the windscreen, narrowly missing Cheshire but striking his flight engineer and slightly injuring him. Cheshire landed his damaged plane and, as 617 legend has it, twenty plovers were served for dinner later that night in the officers' mess at Petwood Hotel. Cheshire and Micky Martin continued to develop their target-making techniques and went on to be the elite of Bomber Command and a squadron that, although part of 5 Group, did things their way.

On 14 April 1944 627 moved from 8 Group to 5 Group to join 617 and became the only non-Lancaster squadron in the group. On arrival, the crews were summoned to nearby RAF Coningsby, where in a briefing room they were given a formal introduction to the new technique of low-level marking.

After landing they were told to form a single line and the station commander arrived with a bevy of brass including the Air Officer Commanding Ralph Cochrane, accompanied by his principal staff officers. He moved along the line with Wing Commander Roy Elliott, who introduced him to the flight crews. This was not a common occurrence, so the crews were filled with the uneasy feeling that 'something was up' and it promised to be bloody dangerous.

The next day the whole squadron journeyed by bus to Coningsby and filed into the station cinema to join the assembled crew members of 83 and 97 Lancaster Pathfinder squadrons. Air Officer Commanding Ralph Cochrane revealed that 617 Squadron had made a number of successful attacks on pinpoint targets and it was now intended to repeat it on a wider scale. Leonard Cheshire then explained carefully how the low-level marking business was done, suggesting it was a matter of simply: flying along, crossing a river and getting a pinpoint. Then you cross another river, get another pinpoint. Find the wind between the two and you had it made! The 627 Squadron crews felt that it was not quite as simple as that! The

Lancaster Pathfinders were to identify the target areas on H2S and were to lay a carpet of hooded flares over a given target, the light from which would be directed downwards on to the target, making it as bright a day. Under the intense light, four or six 627 Squadron Mosquitos would then orbit the target, locate it and then mark the precise aiming point in a shallow dive with 500lb spot fires. Marker leaders would then access the position of the spot fires in relation to the aiming point and would pass this information to the master bomber in one of the Pathfinder Lancasters. He would then take over and direct the main force Lancasters in their attack on the target so the 5 Group bombers could then destroy the target.

To conclude, the 627 Squadron crews were lectured by the 54 Base Commander, Air Commodore Bobby Sharp, who was an egotistical officer with no relevant operational experience. The 54 Base was formed in January 1944 at Coningsby in 5 Group as the HQ responsible for Coningsby units and those at Woodhall Spa and Metheringham undertaking precision-marking and bombing attacks. Sharp commenced a verbal assault on the crews, stating they should disregard their bad 8 Group habits and buckle down to becoming proficient in 5 Group techniques. He added that as 8 Group crews they were unlikely to have experienced anything as complex as they would at 5 Group. It was the worst possible introduction for these proud Pathfinders and it would leave a bad taste for a considerable time.

The crews returned to Woodhall Spa, where the commanding officer called the flight commanders to his office and they devised a plan for an intensive programme of dive-bombing practice at Wainfleet Bombing Range. Cheshire had said low flying would produce the best results, so they started by dropping smoke bombs from various levels with attempts at diving from 15,000ft but this failed. They tried progressively lower heights and established that

Cheshire was correct; to get the smoke marker close to the target in The Wash they had to come down to 2,000ft and then dive directly at the blob in the sea when it was held in the middle of the windscreen. The bomb release was now the responsibility of the pilot, who had a button on the control column that he pressed with the right thumb when he judged the correct moment had arrived. It was a matter of perfecting the process and within a very short time the crews of 627 could plop their markers right alongside the Wainfleet target. It was now a matter of whether they could do it at night and under the intense pressure of hostile ground defences.

Nos 617 and 627 Squadrons shared the Woodhall Spa airfield for the final year of the war and it was with some irony that a certain Victoria Cross holder lost his life flying from the airfield on the night of 19–20 September 1944. Guy Gibson, the Dams raid commander, who at the time was Base Operations Commander at Coningsby, decided to fly a 627 marker aircraft to act as master bomber in an attack on Mönchengladbach and Rheydt. The speculation continues into the circumstances why Gibson and his navigator Warwick lost their lives that night, but it is likely that Gibson was unfamiliar with the Mosquito fuel systems.

The airfield was closed to flying after the war but the site was retained for the missile programme, with 112 Squadron equipped with sixteen Bloodhound missiles base and it remained at Woodhall Spa until 1965. Interestingly, after the war the Petwood Hotel, the comfortable officers' mess with its panelled walls that saw so many wartime parties including the anniversary celebrations of the Dambuster raids, returned to its former use as a hotel. The building still holds a certain air about it, possibly helped by the small squadron bar, preserved just as it was in wartime with its original furnishings and a wide range of squadron artefacts and photographs. The centre of the village houses the stunning 617 Squadron memorials.

Thursday, 20 April 1944
Target: La Chapelle
Crew: Flying Officer N. B. Rutherford and Warrant Officer F. H. Stanbury
Bomb Load: Window dropping
Time: up: 2330hrs, down: 0304hrs

No. 5 Group was instructed to attack the railway marshalling yards at Le Chapelle north of Paris in a first major test for the new marking method employing 617 Squadron's low-level markers and the three recently transferred Pathfinder squadrons from 8 Group. A few regular 8 Group Mosquitos were also used to drop Oboe markers to provide a first indication of the target's location for the 5 Group marking force.

Two attacks on two separate aiming points were separated by a delay of one hour carried out by 83, 97, 617 and 627 Squadrons, marking the aiming points in each attack assisted by Oboe and cascading target indicators. A total of 247 Lancasters of 5 Group and twenty-two Mosquitos from 5 and 8 Group were dispatched along with 627 Squadron acting as Window droppers. The plan was a complicated system of marking and attack and made this an operation of significant importance as a test of the new tactics by releasing the target indicators, then allowing a first wave of Lancasters to release flares over the target one minute later to light the target for Wing Commander Leonard Cheshire and his deputy, Flying Officer Fawke, to mark the aiming point.

At the opening of the attack, the 8 Group aircraft arrived punctually at Zero Hour but their green target indicators failed to cascade at once and the Oboe Mosquitos markers arrived late. However, additional communication problems were soon overcome as provision had been made for such an event.

The six Mosquitos of 627 Squadron, flying at a considerably greater altitude than the following Lancasters, continuously dropped Window at a rapid rate from 0100hrs until 0123hrs from 16,000ft and this fell at about 500ft per minute as the main force bombers arrived over the target. The first wave of flare-carrying aircraft orbited the target area as instructed until ninety seconds later a second wave of four flare-carrying aircraft arrived. Two of these aircraft released flares blindly by Oboe, whereupon the first wave of flare-carrying aircraft and the remaining two aircraft of the second wave released their flares. The attack was then able to proceed but the delay caused many flares to be dropped at once so it did not provide the six minutes of maximum target illumination expected to locate and mark the precise aiming point. However, Wing Commander Cheshire did find the aiming point and without delay marked it with a red spot fire. He then ordered Fawke to back up his marking with more red spot firers to make an even clearer marker for the bombing force. Cheshire then ordered the controller, Wing Commander Dean, to instruct the main force to begin bombing. The marking force used VHF radio to communicate with the main force by wireless telegraphy using a very simple code to convey instructions. However, a failure of the VHF radio telephone between Cheshire and Dean was made more difficult as Fawke's communications equipment was entirely unserviceable. Consequently, Dean did not hear Cheshire's instructions until seventeen minutes after Zero Hour, two minutes after the main force had arrived over the target area. The main force was instructed to begin immediate bombing on the very clearly marked aiming point and bombed with extreme accuracy but soon the two red spot fires were obscured by smoke. Wing Commander Dean, the controller, dropped another stick of red spot fires within 50 yards of the original markers, still within the target area.

Six Lancasters were lost.

Saturday, 22 April
Target: Brunswick
Crew: Squadron Leader E. F. Nelles and Flying Officer A. E. Richards
Bomb Load: 2 × 500lb GP bomb and flares
Time: Up: 2352hrs, down: 0424hrs

Originally, Brunswick (Braunschweig) was little more than a large market town but had become an important industrial centre for light engineering, aircraft components and tinned foods that were supplied to the German armed forces. The town had been attacked on a number of occasions with little success owing to poor weather conditions but the Allies believed that the enemy had employed dummy markers to lure the bomber stream that was now thought to be ineffective if 5 Group used its new tactics. Brunswick would provide a test for the Pathfinder marking system against a heavily defended target beyond the range of Oboe.

The weather forecast carried out by the 54 Base reconnaissance flight had predicted moderately thick cloud extending eastwards to the Rhine but could not say to what extent despite the hopes of clear sky over Brunswick. A total of 328 Lancasters and seventeen Mosquitos of 5 Group and ten Lancasters of 1 Group were despatched. DZ477 and DZ353 AZ:B, the latter crewed by Flying Officer T. L. Hogg and Flying Officer R. Woodhouse, took off twenty minutes before their squadron colleagues to reach a point north of Brunswick to drop three flares for a meteorological reconnaissance. They sent their report by VHF to the leader of the force of twenty Lancasters of 83 and 97 Squadrons thirty minutes before the attack was due to begin. However, once again communication between the various aspects of the force proved to be problematic and threatened the success of the operation. It was impossible for Nelles and Hogg to transmit their weather report because of violent interference on the VHF radio telephone, which would continue during the entire attack. Later, it was discovered that a faulty control in one radio telephone set in a 617 Squadron Lancaster had not been fitted properly. The Lancasters were carrying sky flares to illuminate the target if it was obscured by cloud in order to provide a point of aim above cloud for the main force bombing.

Mosquitos began dropping Window before Zero Hour and, nine minutes before the attack began at a point some miles short of the target, three waves of flare force aircraft dropped special long-burning green target indicators at one-minute intervals, which would ensure that the target was lit for up to seven minutes. They also kept some flares in reserve to release if called to use by the marker aircraft. The flares acted as a beacon to guide the main force and assist the Mosquitos that were to mark the aiming point. At the same time, ten Mosquitos dropped Window during a six-minute flight from the position marked by the green target indicators towards the target, which they were to reach three minutes before Zero Hour. Before the attack started the enemy began laying down dummy red target indicators but fortunately they were used before the force reached the point where they expected green target indicators nearer to the target.

The advantage and flexibility of the new tactics were vindicated when Wing Commander Cheshire made a low-level pass by their light and knew the markers were misplaced by 5 miles. So, holding his markers back, he waited for a minute or so until more accurate flares went down closer to Brunswick. Under the newly laid flares, Flying Officer Fawke of 617 Squadron identified the aiming point and dropped four red spot fires at seven minutes after Zero Hour, which Cheshire assessed as being correctly placed and ordered another four to be laid in the same place; Cheshire then instructed the main force to begin bombing.

As bombing got under way, the two 627 weather recon Mosquitos flew into the bomber stream, with DZ477 dive bombing at the centre of the incendiary fires at 0213hrs from 18,000ft. The red spot fires were becoming difficult to see, so a crew dropped green target indicators that fell to the south-west of the town. Again, Cheshire immediately saw what was happening and gave the order to bomb red spot fires and not green target indicators. Fellow 617 Squadron pilot Squadron Leader Les Munro, who was in communication with the main force by wireless telegraphy, misheard the order owing to the continual interference on the VHF and retransmitted it as an instruction in simple code to bomb red spot fires backed up by green target indicator; as a result the crews continued to aim at the green target indicators. The red spot fires that Cheshire and Fawke had placed were difficult so see owing to haze at a height of up to 22,000ft and Cheshire reported that only half of the main force's high-explosive and incendiary bombs fell within the target area, the rest being dropped on or near the misplaced green target indicators.

Later photographs showed widely scattered bombing but considerable destruction was caused to the built-up areas south of the city centre, where some industrial objectives were hit including a railway equipment works and an artillery tractor plant.

Despite the penetration so far into Germany, very few night fighters were seen and the target area ground defences were light and ineffective, so only four Lancasters were lost. One 627 Mosquito, DZ422 AZ:D, crewed by Flying Officer R. L. Bartley DFC and Flying Officer J. D. Mitchell DFC (RCAF), abandoned the mission and jettisoned their bombs owing to the loss of an exhaust stud from the port engine.

'Benny' Goodman and Nick Ranshaw in DZ484 AZ:G had taken off at 0115hrs on a late reconnaissance trip and immediately climbed straight up to 25,000ft, navigated directly to Brunswick and bombed it, then hung about for half an hour or so on fire-watching duties to report on the results as the target burned. They returned to base before the main force, so all the hierarchy were waiting for them at debriefing, including Air Officer Commanding Cochrane and the base commander, 'Razor' Sharp, who asked how it had gone. The answer of 'excellent, massive fires everywhere' was not the answer Sharp had expected. He enquired as to the height Goodman brought the Mosquito down to. Again, the reply of '25,000ft' was the wrong answer. Sharpe almost blew his top and threatened forcing Goodman and Ranshaw to do the same trip again and not exceed an altitude of 1,000ft all the way there and back. Their next trip was to Munich, this time operating out of Wyton but they flew so low they were out of GEE signal and failed to establish an accurate wind. However, the experienced crew did not miss their target, on which they dropped their bombs and got away again without much trouble. On their way home they considered that maybe this low-level business wasn't so bad at all.

Wednesday, 26 April
Target: Schweinfurt
Crew: Squadron Leader E. F. Nelles and Flying Officer A. E. Richards
Bomb Load: 2 × red spot fires and 2 green spot fires
Time: Up: 0002hrs, down: 0415hrs

A target of great importance, Schweinfurt was the centre of Germany's ball-bearing industry and was heavily defended by flak and searchlights and used an effective smokescreen and decoys. Schweinfurt was beyond the range of Oboe and previous similar targets had proved to be extremely difficult to attack by the ordinary tactical methods used for the bombing of larger cities during 1943. Two weeks earlier the American 8th Air Force had caused considerable damage to the five main ball-bearing factories in the town but had failed to destroy them, so it was considered necessary to attack them again. This trip to Schweinfurt was one of three major operations taking place, with the main effort on Essen while the railway yards at Villeneuve-St-Georges were being attended to by a Halifax main force.

The main force of 206 Lancasters and eleven Mosquitos from 5 Group and nine Lancasters of 1 Group flew southwards across France, hoping that the German night fighter controllers would expect the target to be in Italy but this time the enemy had conserved his fighters in anticipation of an attack on southern Germany. The main force was under way when without warning the wind swung round 20 degrees and increased by 9 knots, which gave the night fighters their opportunity.

Having taken a direct route to the target, and helped by a favourable wind, the nine Mosquitos of 627 were to operate in the low-level marking role for the first time, so were split into two waves. Four Mosquitos were early Window droppers and the remaining five performed the target marking for the first time, without any dummy runs. The differences in wind and the route distances caused a long time delay between the arrival of the initial markers led by 627 Squadron's Wing Commander Elliott and the arrival of the main force markers. This would give the ground defences ample warning and time to generate an effective smokescreen, which led to many aircraft having to wait in an area infested with night fighters before releasing their bombs. The first to mark was Squadron Leader Nelles and Flying Officer Richards in DZ477, who made a steep diving attack from 5,000 to 400ft at 0209hrs and through an effective smokescreen saw a church steeple, which they judged to be the town centre and this was the only visible landmark. Markers were estimated at 500 yards from the town and were well backed up by more red spots, with the first incendiaries straddling these markers. Green target indicators fell near 627's red spots.

The raid controller, Wing Commander Carter, found that his H2S set was faulty but was able to reach the target at Zero Hour by changing from the planned route and flying by dead reckoning on a course that took him straight through a searchlight belt between Karlsruhe and Mannheim. As it transpired no fewer than six H2S sets were found to be unserviceable in the Pathfinder flare force aircraft before they reached the target, forcing the crews of these aircraft to only hope to identify the target visually. This caused the flares to be dropped six minutes late and these were scattered to the south-west of the target area.

No. 83 Squadron Pathfinders experienced clear skies over the target but failed to take advantage of it and their debut as target markers proved to be inaccurate but they reported the lack of illumination as they orbited at 19,000ft. The remaining two 627 Squadron crews, Flying Officer S. F. Parlato (RNZAF) and Flying Officer D. D. Thomas in DZ521 AZ:M and DZ644 AZ:R flown by Pilot Officer J. G. Platts and Flying Officer C. G Thompson, took off more than ninety minutes after the main squadron in order to bomb the target and to photograph the development of the attack. Both aircraft were attacked by night fighters on the outward flight but once over the target they could see how the fires had extended over the whole area of the town and were very concentrated, producing a column of smoke up to 15,000ft that was visible from over 140 miles. Thompson came down to 15,000ft and could see fire reflected in the river and columns of smoke. Both crews encountered heavy flak up to 25,000ft with numerous searchlights. They left the target area at 03.40hrs.

Given the circumstances, it is remarkable that so many bombs fell within the target area and caused new damage to all five ball-bearing factories in Schweinfurt. However, Bomber Command considered this raid to be a failure and the results were achieved at a heavy cost; twenty-three aircraft were missing out of the 226 sent, 10 per cent of the force.

When aircraft were subjected to night fighter attacks and flak, the men of Bomber Command demonstrated supreme acts of courage and heroism in order to save the lives of their crewmates. One such man on this night was Sergeant Norman Jackson, a flight engineer in Lancaster ME669 of 106 Squadron. Following a successful run over the target the pilot, Flying Officer M. Mifflin, climbed the

Lancaster out of the area but it was then attacked by a fighter at a height of about 20,000ft. Despite being wounded in several places by shell splinters, Jackson requested permission from his skipper to attempt to extinguish a fire that had developed in a wing fuel tank. Jackson picked up a hand fire extinguisher and pushed it into the top of his life-saver jacket attached his parachute pack. He then jettisoned the hatch above the pilot's head and proceeded to climb out of the cockpit. However, halfway through the hatch his parachute pack opened and emptied the entire canopy and rigging lines into the cockpit. The pilot, bomb aimer and navigator gathered the parachute together and, holding the rigging lines, started to pay them out as Jackson began to crawl back along the fuselage towards the starboard wing. The force of the 200mph slipstream caused Jackson to lose his hold and he slipped from the fuselage. Somehow he managed to grasp an air intake on the starboard wing leading edge but during his efforts he lost the fire extinguisher. The fire was spreading rapidly and Jackson, who had been severely burnt on his face and hands, was unable to hold on and was swept through the flames and over the trailing edge of the wing, dragging his parachute behind; the last his crewmates were to see of their brave friend was a partially inflated parachute burning in a number of places. With the fire now out of control, the skipper ordered his crew to abandon the aircraft, so four of the six remaining crew bailed out and were taken prisoner. Flying Officer Mifflin DFC and Flight Sergeant N. H. Johnson were killed. Sergeant Jackson survived an became a POW. When he was repatriated after the war it was found that his burning parachute remained inflated but with badly burned hands he was unable to control his decent and he landed heavily, breaking an ankle. With his sight impaired by a closed right eye, he crawled to the nearest village, where he was taken prisoner. He made two attempts to escape from captivity before the end of the war. Jackson was decorated with the Victoria Cross by King George VI at Buckingham Palace on 13 November 1945. Sergeant Norman Jackson VC passed away on 26 March 1994 in Middlesex aged 75.

Friday, 28 April
Target: Kjeller
Crew: Squadron Leader E. F. Nelles and Flying Officer A. E. Richards
Bomb Load: 2 × green and 2 × red spot fires
Time: Up: 2310hrs, down: 0350hrs

Four Mosquitos of 627 Squadron flew to Lossiemouth in Scotland and were then dispatched to mark and bomb an airframe factory and Kjeller aerodrome near Oslo, Norway. DZ477 dive bombed from low level in clear visibility and dropped its markers directly through the roof of one building. The factory was completely obliterated by fifty-one main force Lancasters; no aircraft were lost.

Saturday, 29 April
Target: Clermont-Ferrand
Crew: Squadron Leader E. F. Nelles and Flying Officer A. E. Richards
Bomb Load: 4 red spot fires
Time: Up: 2313hrs, down: 0351hrs

Fifty-four Lancaster and five Mosquitos from 627 Squadron were dispatched to attack the airfield at Clermont-Ferrand, which they bombed accurately and without loss. DZ422 AK:D, flown by Flying Officer J. R. Goodman and Flying Officer H. J. Hickox, abandoned the mission owning to severe vibration on climbing caused by the exhaust studs shearing, causing the exhaust to break away from the starboard engine. DZ477, as marker aircraft, dived from 3,000 to 150ft at 0114hrs on the visually identified target. Its markers fell through the roof of the workshops on the south-eastern edge of the aerodrome and no further marking was necessary. The main force followed with well-concentrated bombing.

Monday, 1 May
Target: Tours
Crew: Squadron Leader E. F. Nelles and Flying Officer A. E. Richards
Bomb Load: 4 red spot fires
Time: Up: 2257hrs, down: 0251hrs

The Germans were using four large buildings in two pairs set at right angles to each other with storage dumps dispersed around its perimeter for the repair and overhaul of tanks and aircraft engines at the Usine Lictard engineering works near Tours in northern France. The target had been bombed a few days earlier by US 8th Air Force B-17s but reconnaissance photos showed that their bombs had fallen in nearby surrounding fields.

Forty-six Lancasters and four 627 Squadron Mosquitos set off to attack the aiming point at the apex between the main buildings as they met at right angles. DZ477 identified the target visually and dive bombed at 0055hrs from 1,000 to 200ft. This was considered accurate enough at 70 yards to the east of the aiming point so no further marking was required.

Main force intelligence briefings prior to the raid forecast light flak in the area, which must have surprised crews arriving over the target as the flares from 'heavy' Pathfinders burst over them, lighting the sky to near daylight conditions that made it very easy for defences to see the circling aircraft going round above them. The heavies actually experienced flak coming from all directions.

No. 627 Squadron's 'Benny' Goodman, in DZ421 AZ:C, takes up the story:

The target was the Usine Lictard engineering works outside Tours, so we air tested our aircraft in the morning and studied the maps of the Tours area and photographs of the target. At this time the Americans were conducting high-level 'precision' day-light bombing in their B-17 and B-24 aircraft using their Norden bombsight. Their contention was that they could drop a pickle into a barrel from 30,000ft so they called it 'pickle-barrel bombing'. The target had been bombed a few days earlier by US 8th Air Force B-17 Flying Fortress but reconnaissance photographs showed that their bombs had fallen in the surrounding fields, leaving the factory intact; obviously, their pickles had jumped out of the barrel. To drop bombs a few hundred yards from the aiming point might be good enough on a large area but on a pinpoint target like a factory the bombs had to be on target. We took off in the late evening and headed for France, climbing rapidly to 25,000ft.

The Pathfinder Lancasters of 83 and 97 Squadrons had taken off about an hour before 627 Squadron crews and were to drop a yellow target indicator 10 miles from Tours from which the four low-level marker aircraft would set course accurately for the target area. Having dropped the yellow indicator for us, the Lancasters would head directly to the target, identify it on H2S and discharge hundreds of illuminating flares above it. As Bill and I approached the final turning point, losing height steadily, the yellow target indicators suddenly cascaded down ahead of us – so far, so good. We flew over the target indicators and headed for the target, and as we approached Tours a great carpet of light suddenly spread out in front of us, We lost more height and soon we were under the carpet at 1,500ft and it was as bright as day. If a fighter appeared now we would be dead ducks and if there was light flak in the area we would certainly have a very rough time but nothing happened. We circled around and suddenly with the factory close by I immediately pressed the transmit button on my VHF and called 'Pen-nib Three Seven, Tally-ho'. This was the agreed method informing the other marker pilots that the target had been identified so they could withdraw from the illuminated area to give me more room to manoeuvre and make my dive on to the factory. I circled around the works losing speed and positioning the Mosquito for the dive, then opened the bomb doors and pressed the control column gently forwards. Our speed increased and the target leapt up towards us, filling the windscreen. At about 500ft I pressed the bomb release and there was a slight jerk as the four spot fires left their slips so I continued in the dive for another couple of seconds, selected bomb doors closed and turned sharply to the left in order to check our results. There was a red glow among the factory buildings and in fact the spots had fallen through the glass roof of the machine shop, which was splendid from my point of view. However, I had marked the target accurately but as the spot fires were inside the machine shop they could not be seen clearly by the Main Force crews, now heading towards Tours.

This was an important lesson for us all; the object of our efforts was not to drop the markers on the target but near it in a position where the red blob could be clearly seen by the Main Force. Marker leader Roy Elliott flew over the works and called for the next marker to lay his red indicators in the yard alongside the machine shop, which was then done. Marker leader then called the controller and told him that the target had been marked successfully. He then broadcast to the Main Force on W/T and VHF to bomb the mass of red spots. The marking had taken less than five minutes and the target was flattened.

Having successfully marked the target, they turned for home.

The raid master bomber was to be Wing Commander Northrop of 83 Squadron and before take-off Air Commodore 'Razor' Sharp informed him that he would be flying with him and his crew. However, with the crew assembled by the aircraft, Sharp was nowhere to be seen and after the crew had completed external aircraft checks they boarded the aircraft. Soon after, a large American staff car turned up flying the station commander's pennant and Sharp, dressed in an American flying suit, demanded to have the crew lined up to be presented to him one by one. Cursing under his breath, the skipper obliged and dragged his crew back out of the Lancaster for the ceremony. Eventually they reboarded but were held up by Sharp as he made his way to the navigator's compartment. They took off from Coningsby, maintaining radio silence in accordance with standard procedure. Sharp decided to carry out a radio test on the controller's frequency but was greeted by a number of unidentified voices telling him to belt up and keep quiet. This offended his ego greatly.

Weather conditions in the target area were good, with clear skies under moonlight, and the only ground defences were from light flak every time Northrop passed low across the aiming point. They spent about thirty minutes circling the target within the flak range, which was sending small strings of tracer flashing past the wingtips but with little danger of scoring a hit. Sharp disliked being shot at, so Northrop decided to climb little higher to keep him quiet. No. 83 Squadron crews successfully carried out their part of the operation and all aircraft returned safely. Northrop's aircraft touched down at 0330hrs and as it came to a stop, Sharp was whisked away without a word of appreciation to the crew or even the offer of a lift to debrief. Apparently, the following day brought the immediate award to Sharp of the DSO.

Bombing was very accurate, completely destroying the main buildings and large fires were seen in the target area with smoke rising to 1,000ft. More damage would be inflicted later as some bombs were fitted with six-hour-delay fuses. Some crews were lucky to escape disaster; 627's DZ547 AZ:R, crewed by Squadron Leader N. W. Mackenzie and Pilot Officer A. Denholm, had a close encounter with ground fire and was holed three times by fire and light flak while in the target area. DZ516 AZ:O, crewed by Flying Officer J. A. Saint-Smith and Flying Officer G. E. Heath, had its nose punctured by light flak.

Wednesday, 3 May
Target: Mailly military camp
Crew: Flying Officer N. B. Rutherford and W/O H. F. Stanbury
Bomb Load: 4 yellow target indicators
Time: Up: 2233hrs, down: 0214hrs

A successful attack on Mailly military camp near Épernay, to the east of Paris, was vital as the camp housed up to a reported 10,000 Wehrmacht troops, a Panzer depot and training centre, all of which posed a potential threat to the Allied forces during the coming invasion of Europe.

A total of 346 Lancasters, 14 Mosquitos of 1 and 5 Group and two Pathfinder Mosquitos of 617 Squadron led by Wing Commander Cheshire, appointed marker leader, were sent. Wing Commander Dean of 83 Squadron was overall raid controller, with Squadron Leader Sparks as his deputy. Oddly and significantly, Dean and Cheshire attended separate briefings and neither seemed aware of the complete plan.

No. 627 Squadron sent ten Mosquitos to attack two aspects of the target. Three aircraft attacked the camp to act as datum point markers, with DZ477 marking the datum point and this remained marked until 0032hrs. The remaining six attacked and destroyed the flak defences around the camp. The Flak 30 20mm guns with quadruple barrels posed a big threat to the oncoming bombers but

Flying Officer N. B. Gray and Flying Officer F. W. Boyle in DZ418 AZ:L attacked the guns with four 500lb MC bombs and they were not seen to fire after the fourth attack.

One aircraft, DZ615 AZ:H crewed by Flying Officer M. D. Gribbin and Flying Officer R. W. Griffiths (RCAF), returned to base owing to a rise in oil temperature due to an exhaust stub on a starboard engine being blown out. DZ644 AZ:R, crewed by P/O P. K. Turner and W/O J. F. Hewson, arrived over the target and asked permission to attack the flak defences but was advised not to, so they bombed a railway station on the main Paris–Laon line, then set course for base.

The target area was under excellent bombing conditions of clear skies and moonlight, with Cheshire and Dave Shannon, also 617, in position before midnight when the first flares from 83 and 97 Squadron Lancasters went down to illuminate the target below. At the stroke of midnight, Cheshire released his two red spot fires on to the aiming point from 1,500ft, with Shannon backing them up from 400ft five and a half minutes later. As far as Cheshire was concerned, the operation was on schedule as the aiming point was consolidated by a Lancaster from 97 Squadron, which laid markers accurately. Observing this, Cheshire passed instructions to Deane, circling at 5,000ft over the burning buildings, to call the bombers in, which were stacked at various heights. It was at this point the operation started to fragment when the VHF frequency used by the main force crews suffered severe interference from an American Forces network commercial radio station and as Deane called in the 5 Group bombers nothing happened. His instructions were swamped by interference and the call to bomb was only carried out by a small number of crews that happened to hear him. This small number caused smoke to cover the entire camp, so Cheshire decide to call Deane to pause the bombing as he needed to send in Fawke and Kearns to mark the second aiming point. This should have been completed by 0016hrs, providing Fawke and Kearns had a clear run across the target.

Unknown to Cheshire, most of the 5 Group crews were on their bombing run and Deane, who did not respond, would have been confused as a second aiming point was not mentioned at his pre-operation briefing earlier. Deane's fellow 83 Squadron deputy controller, Squadron Leader Sparks, found an interference-free channel on both W/T and R/T and transmitted an instruction to halt the bombing, which was heard by some crews. Kearns and Fawke then dived down on to the second aiming point at the western edge of the camp at 0023hrs and 0025hrs respectively, with 4,000lb cookies falling all round them. At 2,000ft, they were lucky to survive the extreme shockwave created by the exploding 4,000-pounders as 4,000ft was considered to be the minimum safe height. Under the circumstances they were not happy with the accuracy, so Flying Officer Edwards of 97 Squadron accurately dropped a stick of markers precisely on target. No. 83 Squadron then carried out their illuminating and bombing runs from 3,500 to 8,000ft up to 0032hrs, followed by Squadron Leader Sparks in Lancaster JB402 calling for the 1 Group main force to start their bombing run.

The night fighters continued to cause havoc among the circling Lancaster force, sending burning aircraft falling from the sky, and in a rare demonstration of a breach in discipline some 1 Group crews vented their frustration at Deane by broadcasting comments that were not of a complimentary nature. Having heard the comments, Deane now became aware of the destruction being inflicted on the Lancasters and, as the last to leave the target area and being the most vulnerable, he decided to ignore the planned route home. Instead he took his aircraft very low down and headed west to a point south of Paris, where he turned north-west to reach the Channel east of Cherbourg. There they were greeted by flak from light-fingered British naval vessels taking part in an invasion exercise. On the homeward route Squadron Leader Neville Sparks and his crew in JB402 were shot down by night fighters at 0045hrs near Orbais in the Marne, 12 miles north-east of Montmiral. Their loss was a devastating blow to the squadron but the news eventually came through that Sparks and five of the men on board had landed safely. They evaded capture and were helped to return to England. The other two become prisoners of war.

Most of the fleeing Mosquitos of 627 Squadron were long gone but 'Benny' Goodman and his navigator 'Bill' Hickcox, in DZ412 AZ:C, having already attacked the light flak position south-east of the target, had to make an instant decision. Goodman:

> I made a grave tactical miscalculation which might easily have killed us – or alternatively might have set Bill Hickox on another long hike home from enemy territory with me in tow. The Mosquito force arrived over Mailly five minutes before zero hour. Although the target was marked accurately and Cheshire passed the order to bomb, confusion occurred when the first wave did not receive instructions and began to orbit the target. This was fatal and the German night fighters moved in and began to shoot down the Lancs. Eventually the situation was sorted out and bombs began to crash down on to the depot.
>
> From our worm's eye view Bill and I could see bomber after bomber coming down in flames towards us. We had a scary time as we dived on the light flak batteries, dropped our bombs singly on them, avoided light flak and burning Lancasters and contrived to keep ourselves out of harm's way. When our fourth bomb had gone I called marker leader and was told to go home. Bill gave me a course to steer for the French coast and I should have climbed to 25,000ft but because of the mayhem in the target area I stayed at low level. All went well for a few minutes and then a searchlight shone directly on us, followed immediately by two or three more. Light flak batteries opened

up and the pretty blue, red, green and white tracery associated with light anti-aircraft fire came shooting up the beams and exploded all around us. We were at 500ft and I did not dare to lose height, nor could I climb because this would have been a gift to the German gunners. With Bill telling me to watch my instruments, I turned steeply to port through thirty degrees, levelled out for a few seconds, then rolled into a steep turn to starboard and repeated the performance. Although we were in flak and searchlights for quite a long time we were not being held by any one light or being shot at by any one gun for very long and we zigzagged our way steadily to the coast. It was a very tense time for us and we did not speak. We could hear the explosions around us from light anti-aircraft shells but incredibly we were not hit. Deliverance came eventually as we crested a low hill and ahead of us lay the sea with the final group of searchlights shining through the trees on the top of the hill we had just passed and the beams were actually above and lighting us on our way. We roared along the river estuary, below the level of the lighthouse at Le Tréport and then we were over the 'drink' and climbing to safety, home and bed.

Despite the problems and the carnage, the raid was viewed as a major success, having destroyed 80 per cent of the camp's buildings and over 100 vehicles, of which thirty-seven were tanks. However, more than 200 men were killed and forty-two Lancasters failed to return, two thirds of them from 1 Group. An investigation made the following day revealed that Deane's wireless operator had been slightly off frequency, which allowed the interference to ruin the transmission of instructions. The Air Officer Commanding of 1 Group, Air Vice Marshal Rice, refused to allow his crews to participate in further operations organised by 5 Group, which was a bitter blow to Air

Vice Marshal Cochrane and 5 Group. No doubt it brought a feeling of delight and satisfaction to Air Vice Marshal Bennett.

The following is an extract from an account sent to me by Ron Eeles, the rear gunner of Lancaster ND647 (EA-N), I received in March 1993. It was beautifully written in longhand in fountain pen. Ron takes up the story:

> The morning of Wednesday, 3 May was like any normal day at RAF Fiskerton, the home of 49 Squadron (Lancaster) in 5 Group, Bomber Command. We were on operations that evening and the briefing stressed the importance of Mailly le Camp and the need to destroy it.
>
> We were apprehensive of the raid arrangements of the planned concentration of aircraft over the target in a short space of time, particularly as crews were given bombing heights with only 100ft variations in altitude, increasing the risk of collision. Our individual bombing height was to be 7,100ft and the target was to be marked by Wing Commander Cheshire in a Mosquito. Our bomb load was high-explosive bombs only.
>
> We took off at 2157hrs with the usual wave off by station personnel at the end of the runway and I had a sense that this time something was different as I did not have the usual exhilaration when taking off on full power. Due to this feeling of foreboding, I thought I would not be coming back and that something was going to happen. What had also struck me as strange was that when I entered my turret at dispersal, for the first time ever Sergeant Kernahan, the WOP/AG, closed the turret doors behind me as they were difficult to close oneself with full flying clothing due to the restricted space and I had thanked him – the last time I was ever to speak to any member of the crew.

The flight to the target was uneventful at the lower than usual operational height. My electrically operated suit was unnecessary and I kept switching it on and off to maintain a reasonable temperature. On arrival at Mailly we were directed to proceed to a point some 15 miles away and once there orbit a yellow marker. After a few minutes we did not like this at all and the crew were worried as visibility was clear and good and we knew from experience the dangers of hanging around enemy territory any longer that absolutely necessary. We circled this flare for approximately half an hour and became increasingly worried as it appeared impossible to receive any radio instruction due to the American Forces Network Broadcasting Station blasting away. I remember only too well the tune 'Deep in heart of Texas' followed by hand clapping and noise like a party going on. Other garbled talk was going on in the background but drowned out by the music and I was suddenly aware from my position that several Lancasters were going down in flames and I saw some of the planes impact on the ground with the usual dull red glow after the initial crash. My job was to keep my eyes open for enemy aircraft so I did not dwell for more than fleeting seconds on these shot down planes. At this stage I did not see any night fighter activity or anti-aircraft fire but with regard to the latter we were still orbiting 15 miles away from Mailly.

At about 0030 hours my pilot, Pilot Officer G. E. Ball, commenced his run-in to the target and I could see several planes burning on the ground but I do not remember hearing any instructions to the pilot from outside sources, but obviously he would have obtained clearance to proceed with the bombing. During the bombing run with the bomb aimer, Sergeant G. A. Rae (RCAF), directing the pilot there was a sudden, huge bang and a blinding pink-red flash along the port side of the aircraft followed immediately by the pilot saying (not shouting) 'Christ, put on 'chutes chaps'. Within a second of this the plane was hit again by anti-aircraft fire along the fuselage. There was a sizzling sound in the intercom system and then it went dead. The pink-red glow on the port side persisted and I assumed we were on fire.

I disconnecting my electric suit plug and left my flying helmet on the seat with intercom and oxygen connected when I came to the point which has always mystified me and to this day I still think of it at times. I had a vision of my mother outside my turret and she said 'jump son, jump'. I was at this stage about to vacate the turret anyway. This may not be believed and that is why I have never mentioned it to anyone before but I can assure you it is perfectly true and shortly after my arrival as a PoW at Stalag Luft 3, I wrote of this experience in a log book provided by the Red Cross but after including what I have just described I deleted it as I was convinced no one would ever believe it. But there it is, believe or disbelieve.

On leaving my turret and attaching my parachute, I saw the mid-upper gunner using an axe to open the fuselage door, which came as no surprise as this door had previously been difficult to open despite the ground crew checking it out more than once and finding nothing wrong with it.

By the time I reached the door, Sergeant Quick had left the plane and the fuselage was now full of smoke and the plane seemed to be out of control. I rolled out of the plane in the recommended way to avoid hitting the tail plane but my legs brushed along the underside. Fortunately, my flying boots remained on. I have no recollection of pulling the parachute D ring, although I had it in my grasp as I bailed out and being at low level the descent did not take long but it was quite a pleasant sensation whilst it lasted and I was unaware of any noise. I was some distance from Mailly, somewhere in the area of Reims, and looking down during the descent I thought I was heading towards a small lake surrounded by woodland but suddenly and unexpectedly I landed heavily in what turned out to be a clearing, not water.

Although I did not realise it, I was floating backwards and on hitting the ground my head was protected by the padded collar of my Taylor suit, otherwise I would probably have been injured about the head. On the ground I could hear bangs and shouts and dogs barking in the near vicinity. I freed my parachute harness and discarded my Taylor and inside electric suit and the 'chute drifted across open space and came to a rest against nearby trees. I tore off my brevet and sergeant's chevrons and placed them in my battle dress pocket and made no attempt to hide or bury the 'chute and left the area. I recall a Mosquito flying very fast and low in the direction of Mailly presumably, probably to take a last look at the target. For the remainder of the night I kept walking and at dawn heard voices in a nearby field by a large fire. As I was uncertain if this was a crashed aircraft with military or merely farm workers, I gave the area a wide berth. At this time an observation plane approached at low altitude and slow speed, very close to where I was, so I hid behind a tree and do not think I was noticed. Walking on, I came to the outskirts of a village and saw German troops and motor cycles and sidecars and cautiously approached a small cottage and I rushed through the front door. A very elderly Frenchman and his yapping dog were naturally surprised and he tried to push me out, shouting 'allemandes, allemandes'. In view of the noise and perhaps his fear, I immediately left and ran out of the village. All I wanted to know was where I was as I had my silk escape map with me. I next remember coming up to a large isolated house but remember nothing further. Although I was not injured in any way I must have passed out; it was probably about 9am. When I came to, I was on the ground and was surrounded by soldiers and was being kicked about the body and saw a German officer pointing a pistol at my head. I was walked back to the same village I had left, searched in some Army HQ and then taken to a cell. Whilst there I was told a rear gunner had been taken out of the turret of a crashed plane and was very badly injured. I asked if I could see him, but the request was refused.

After two days I was taken to another town, where I was placed in a cell with a navigator from 50 Squadron also downed on the Mailly raid but we were separated after a few hours. Thereafter I was taken under guard to Oberursel Interrogation Centre at Dulag Luft near Frankfurt, arriving in the late evening with a bombing raid in progress, so I was taken by my guard into a large air raid shelter. Local inhabitants did not seem concerned, although there would be no doubt I was a shot-down flyer.

After twelve days in solitary confinement and two interrogations, I was taken to the transit camp. Here I met 'Speedy' Quick, who had become attached to the small headquarters staff workers in the kitchens distributing clothing and Red Cross food etc. He had no news of any other members of the crew and we concluded that they must have all been killed. I was then moved to the RAF officers' camp at Stalag Luft 3, Sagan, in Silisin (East Compound), PoW No. 4912. In this compound of some 700–800 RAF officers about a dozen aircrew sergeants were attached to the kitchens to collect rations, distribute soup and generally be useful.

In January 1945 the camp was evacuated due to the Russian advance from the east and we were part walked, part entrained in cattle trucks in dreadful winter conditions to the

Kriegsmarine Camp between Hamburg and Bremen. Late March saw us on the march again in an easterly direction because of the Allied advance. We would walk during the day and be herded into fields at night. Many times our marching columns would be subject to attack from Typhoon fighters and casualties were sometimes incurred.

For about three days we were billeted at a larger farm, when we were liberated by Comet tanks of the British Army and taken by road to an airfield and flown home by RAF Lancasters. We were then transferred to the rehabilitation centre for aircrew PoWs at RAF Cosford, where I again met 'Speedy' Quick on the railway station steps. We last met in 1948/9 and have lost touch since.

I subsequently learned that my fellow crew of ND647, less the two gunners, managed to return to base in a severely damaged aircraft following an attack by a night fighter and anti-aircraft fire. The pilot was awarded an immediate DFC. The crew, with two other squadron gunners, continued to fly operationally but towards the end of their tour they were shot down on 7–8 July 1944 during an attack on a V-1 site at St-Leu-d'Esserent (Creil).

Saturday, 6 May
Target: Aubigné
Crew: Flying Officer H. Steere and Flying Officer K. W. Gale RAAF 404241
Bomb Load: 2 red spot fires and 2 × 500lb MC bombs
Time: up: 2141hrs, down: 0412hrs

Fifty-two Lancasters and four Mosquitos of 627 Squadron attacked the ammunitions dump with great success as the entire target was destroyed by enormous explosions. DZ477 bombed at 0300hrs from 8,000 to 4,000ft, with the crew seeing up to eight large fires burning and about a dozen large explosions.

One aircraft, Lancaster III ND783 from 576 Squadron, was shot down by night fighters and on this occasion there were eight crew members rather than the usual seven as Air Commodore R. Ivelaw-Chapman was flying as second pilot. Six of the crew were killed but Sergeant J. A. Ford RAAF evaded capture. Ivelaw-Chapman went on the run in a bid to evade capture, knowing that a man of his knowledge and experience would be in extreme danger if captured by the Germans, who would almost certainly like to extract information from him using their brutal techniques. He was suffering from a severely dislocated shoulder caused after he failed to secure his parachute correctly before he vacated the Lancaster. Winston Churchill asked the French resistance to do all they could to help him return to England and he lasted for over a month before the house in which he was hiding was surrounded by the Gestapo and he was captured on 8 June. Fortunately the Germans were not aware of his importance. He was interrogated without success, treated as an ordinary officer prisoner of war and sent to a camp. Ivelaw-Chapman was the most senior officer of Bomber Command to be taken prisoner during the Second World War and had recently taken up a staff officer post with 1 Group. He survived the war and on his return to England received numerous promotions and postings and a knighthood. He died on 28 April 1978 aged 79.

Sunday, 7 May
Target: Tours
Crew: Squadron Leader E. F. Nelles and Flying Officer A. E. Richards
Bomb Load: 2 red spot fires and 2 × 500lb MC bombs
Time: Up: 0102hrs, down: 0449hrs

Early in the afternoon the squadron lost Flying Officer T. L. Hogg DFC and Flying Officer B. Woodhouse when their aircraft, DZ422 AZ:D, dived into the ground on the outskirts of the airfield while coming in to land on a one-engine approach. The Mosquito crashed very close to the bomb dump and immediately burst into flames, killing the crew instantly. This aircraft had previously lost its port engine on 22 April 1944 on a night attack on Brunswick.

Fifty-three Lancasters and five Mosquitos from 627 Squadron bombed Tours airfield and its buildings, which they easily identified and caused considerable damage. Flight Sergeant J. Marshallsay and Flight Sergeant N. A. Renshaw in DZ415 AZ:Q dive bombed and silenced a flak gun position at 0257hrs. DZ477 followed by dive bombing the airfield flak pen in two attacks from 2,500ft at 0306hrs, although no results were seen. Bombing was very good, with direct hits seen by the crews of 627 and fires observed near all three aiming points and two hangars on fire. The red spot fires were not required.

One 627 Squadron Mosquito, DZ644 AZ:R, crewed by Pilot Officer P. K. Turner (RAAF) and Warrant Officer J. F. Hewson, was lost. Nothing was heard from them after take-off.

The crew of DZ525 AZ:S, flown by Flying Officer A. Hindshaw and Flying Officer J. F. Daly, were lucky to escape from their aircraft when it went into a steep dive for no apparent reason 15 miles south of Portsmouth. The 627 ORB states that Hindshaw 'abandoned the mission owing to the indisposition of pilot, who found himself going into a dive for no apparent reason and found great difficulty flying the aircraft. No defect in aircraft found.' Hindshaw was removed from flying duties on the assumption that the loss of Turner and Hewson earlier in the day may have unsettled him. Even experienced pilots sometimes became disorientated and that may have played some part in the incident. However, a more sinister option was often assumed by the wartime armed forces – the awful branding of someone being of

'Lack of Moral Fibre – LMF' and the dreadful stigma attached to it. In reality, Hindshaw was a man with experience of many operations, so it is impossible to believe he was lacking in any way and this was confirmed with his award of the DFC on 30 June 1944 in recognition of gallantry and devotion to duty in the execution of air operations.

Lack of Moral Fibre (LMF)

The limited life expectancy of the men and women of the armed forces would inevitably cause anxiety and pressures that most civilians could never fully understand. All conflicts would present these dramatic circumstances to varying degrees, which service personnel would deal with in their own way.

Most bomber crews would show few signs of the worries of 'getting the chop' and would go about their duties in a regular and often prescribed pattern, with some adopting mascots such as a rabbit's foot or teddy bear or carry a family photograph. Some airmen urinated on the tail wheel of the aircraft before take-off. Flying in an unfamiliar aircraft was unpopular, which sometimes happened as their usual one may have been unserviceable. Close-knit crews were often wary of having a 'spare bod' aboard as replacement for an absent crewmate, so some airmen would fly even if not fit to do so. Bombers had been lost when a replacement rookie fresh from training joined as a temporary replacement for a highly experienced crewman and had a moment of indecision when called into sudden action.

In early 1940 Bomber Command was manned by mostly volunteer aircrews and RAF commanders started to have serious concerns about the mounting psychological effects on these men, who might change their minds about flying operationally as they began to witness the almost nightly heavy casualty rates. Senior officers attempted to minimise such instances with a zero-tolerance attitude to what was known as 'LMF'. In April, squadron commanders were told to identify men who had lost confidence and separate medical cases from those 'lacking moral fibre'.

Some commanding officers were sympathetic to aircrew that had flown a significant number of operations and these men were quietly removed from their operational crew and reassigned to staff duties. However, officers considered to have LMF would lose their commissions and be refused ground jobs in the RAF, while non-commissioned officers would be reduced in rank and assigned menial tasks for at least three months. From 1944, men released as 'LMF' could be called to the coal mines or drafted into the army. Some commanders took a severe approach to outward displays of stress and such airmen had their personnel file stamped with 'LMF' and were left with no option but to return to flying, which was usually done discreetly. However, the stigma of 'LMF' was a method to control the numbers.

The legendary post-dams 617 Squadron leader, Wing Commander Leonard Cheshire, viewed such harsh action as justified in a desperate situation and that the RAF had to be ruthless with dealing with 'LMF'. He did have concern for any individual whose internal tensions meant that he could no longer go on and there was a worry that one really frightened man could affect others around him. Cheshire did try to take a sympathetic approach to crew members with confidence problems by taking them on board his own aircraft until they sorted things out. However, pilots were transferred out immediately.

At the time the process of dealing with 'LMF' was considered to be harsh and was deeply resented by the airmen, although it was less harsh than a court martial. Towards the end of the war 'LMF' became politically sensitive and was officially dropped in 1945, although the term remained in popular use in the RAF until the 1960s. Modern-day standards now view this in an entirely different way and servicemen and women are likely to receive the help they need. However, those war-torn and desperate days during the 1940s may have demanded a less tolerant approach; we may never know.

Monday, 8 May
Target: Brest
Crew: Flying Officer H. Steere and Flying Officer K. W. Gale (RAAF)
Bomb load: 4 red spot fires
Time: Up: 2211hrs, down: 0132hrs

Five 627 Squadron aircraft and fifty-eight heavies attacked the airfield and sea plane base at Lanvéoc-Poulmic with great accuracy. In good visibility, DZ477 made a dummy run at 200ft over the target and on identification dropped two red spot fires within 40 yards of the aiming point. The four remaining 627 aircraft backed up the markers from 2351hrs. The bombing was concentrated on the red spot fires and fairly large explosions were seen but the crews did encounter intense light flak.

Three 83 Squadron Pathfinder crews took off at 2115hrs for an expected round trip of five and a half hours, two hours longer than the Mosquito force. All crews found the target area and bombed at midnight from 7,000ft about ten minutes after the Mosquitos completed the target marking. One of the Pathfinders, Flying Officer A. Whitford (RAAF) DFC, was a highly experienced pilot and was believed to be on his fortieth operation, but his Lancaster, ND818, was hit by light flak and disintegrated, scattering wreckage over the target area. It is likely it was hit before the crew had the opportunity to deliver the bomb load. The Operational Record Book refers to an enemy 'scarecrow' shell exploding on the seaplane base hangars at the beginning of the attack together with photo-flashes that illuminated the target. It is believed that the Germans invented a myth concerning scarecrows to simulate the explosion of a fully-laden bomber in order to intimidate the bomber crews. There is no definitive evidence that such shells existed but Bomber Command was keen to discourage the idea of such a weapon. The truth of the matter is that a bomber exploded that night, killing seven brave men.

Tuesday, 9 May
Target: Annecy
Crew: Squadron Leader E. F. Nelles and Flying Officer A. E. Richards
Bomb Load: 2 red spot fires and 2 × 500lb MC bombs
Time: Up: 0353hrs, down: 0416hrs

Eight Mosquitos from 627 Squadron were detailed to attack two separate targets, the important Gnome and Rhône aircraft engine factory at Gennevilliers near Paris and a small ball-bearing factory at Annecy in south-eastern France.

Ten minutes before the Annecy marker aircraft took off, four Mosquitos of 627 Squadron went to mark the engine factory for an attack by fifty-six Lancasters and eight Mosquitos of 5 Group. The accurate marking by the 627 crews led to the complete destruction of the factory, knocking it out of the war.

There are many examples of the determination and courage demonstrated by the target markers and the sorts of unexpected events that cropped up from time to time. During the raid, DZ516 AZ:O, crewed by Flying Officer James Saint-Smith (RAAF) DFM and Flying Officer Geoffrey Heath (RAAF) DFM, dive bombed from 5,800 to 1,000ft to release their spot flares, which were assessed as 300 yards south of the aiming point. However, on the low-level run across the target area their starboard wing clipped the works chimney. Saint-Smith made a safe landing back at Woodhall Spa and when the propellers had stopped and the crew had left the cockpit the ground crew were dismayed to find bricks forced into what was left of the missing section of wingtip! The two Australian aviators were delighted and claimed the bricks as souvenirs, leaving the ground crew to replace the wingtip. A month later, on 29 June, Saint-Smith and Heath failed to return from the squadron's first daylight operation to Beauvoir in an unexpected and bizarre loss that was hard to accept. While flying over a V-1 site a newly launched V-1 exploded prematurely, destroying their Mosquito.

The Annecy force comprised thirty-nine Lancasters and four Mosquitos from 627 Squadron that suffered from poor weather on the outward route, which prevented two Mosquitos reaching the target. DZ525 AZ:S, crewed by Flying Officer I. H. Hanlon (RNZAF) and F/S R. W. Fenwick, abandoned the mission owing to severe icing and ten-tenths cloud cover. DZ462 AZ:N, crewed by Flying Officer D. W. Peck and Flying Officer R. F. Davies, failed to identify the target, so jettisoned their bombs at 02.07hrs northwest of the area and safely returned to base. Having reached the target as a marker, the crew of DZ477 visually identified the target at 0157hrs and dived from 1,500 to 400ft to release two red spot fires within 50 yards and at twelve o'clock of the aiming point. They then circled and dropped their two 500-pounders from 2,000 to 1,000ft on their own markers. Flying Officer L. C. E. Devigne and Flying Officer N. Lewis in DZ426 AZ:A immediately followed them in, however their target indicators failed to ignite so they went round again to drop their two 500lb bombs, diving from 4,500 to 1,000ft. Main force bombing started nine minutes after the pair of Mosquitos cleared the target area and, although bombing was rather scattered at first, it improved with accurate and concentrated fires over the whole target.

Thursday, 11 May
Target: Bourg-Leopold
Crew: Squadron Leader E. F. Nelles and Flying Officer A. E. Richards
Bomb Load: 4 red spot fires
Time: Up: 2250hrs, down: 0130hrs

Eight aircraft from 627 Squadron were despatched to act as target markers for an attack by 190 Lancasters on a former Belgian gendarmerie barracks at Bourg-Leopold that was being used to accommodate 20,000 SS Panzer troops, who were waiting and preparing for the Allied invasion forces.

Once again, they experienced low cloud and poor visibility, which was hampered by a serious error in the broadcast winds. The master bomber, Squadron Leader Mitchell, with Flying Officer McDonald as his deputy, led nine others from their squadron. These were divided into three waves of flare droppers but were late in arriving over the target area and the flares that were dropped were scattered and provided inadequate illumination.

No. 627 Squadron marker aircraft DZ477 arrived late over the target after an Oboe Mosquito of 109 Squadron had dropped a yellow flare that had burned out very quickly, so Squadron Leader Mitchell called for another Mosquito to drop a red spot fire on the aiming point. Squadron Leader Nelles and Flying Officer Richards, flying DZ477, were hampered by the haze but during their run-in, the master bomber instructed Nelles to abandon their marking attack as ninety-four main force Lancasters had begun bombing and they were in extreme danger of being hit by falling bombs. Shortly after this all remaining main force bombers were ordered to abandon the raid and return to base as the dangers of hitting nearby civilian housing could not be justified. Five Lancasters were lost.

Friday, 19 May
Target: Amiens
Crew: Flying Officer H. Steere and Flying Officer K. W. Gale
RAAF 404241
Bomb load: 1 × special flare and 3 × red spot fires
Time: Up: 2349hrs, down: 0247hrs

A period of unfavourable weather prevented the main force squadron from taking part in operations, although 627 Squadron filled the time with air tests and dive bombing practice. When the bombing campaign restarted, the railway installations at Amiens were the objectives. However, owing to the close proximity of residential districts, the crews were ordered to avoid causing collateral damage even if that meant circling the target area while the master bomber assessed the accuracy of the marking. A total of 112 Lancasters and four 627 Squadron Mosquitos were led by the main target marker DZ477, which visually identified the target of the railway marshalling yards in poor visibility by flares and yellow target indicators at 0110hrs. However, they had fallen on the wrong yard, about 50 yards to the east of the town.

When the correct aiming point was identified, two attacks were made without releasing the flares as they had hung up due to an electrical fault. The master bomber ordered all aircraft to cease marking to allow marker number two, DZ421 AZ:C, crewed by Flying Officer R. L. Hartley and Flying Officer J. R. Mitchell (RCAF), to attempt to identify and successfully mark the correct aiming point with a red TI but that hung up too. By the time the other two aircraft could identify the target, the time had expired so all aircraft were ordered to return to base. By this time thirty-seven Lancasters had bombed, one of which, ND689, was lost. Four crew members were killed, with three being taken prisoner.

Monday, 22 May
Target: Brunswick
Crew: Squadron Leader E. F. Nelles and Flying Officer J. F. Daly
Bomb Load: 1 Yellow, 2 red target indicators and 1 Wanganui Flare
Time: Up: 2322hrs, down: 0312hrs

Two days of bad weather grounded all aircraft but the night of the 22nd saw the last attack of this series against German industrial cities. The weather proved to be entirely different to the prediction, with mostly very thick, low-hanging unbroken cloud and heavy showers from the coast right to the target. A total of 225 Lancasters and eleven Mosquitos followed the Pathfinders, who dropped flares at 7 and then 3 miles to the south and south-east of the target. The flares burst in the clouds and provided no illumination, so it proved almost impossible for the markers of 627 to identify the aiming point. Having seen flares within 3 miles of the target, by some miracle the crew of DZ477 visually identified the target by the river but found it impossible to drop their spot fires. Some of the other marker aircraft identified the built-up area and river north of the town but the weather conditions made it impossible to mark. A blind bombing attack was called for at 0126hrs with Wanganui flares and Green TIs going down but this resulted in scattered bombing.

Communications were difficult throughout the attack owing to interference on the master bomber's radio and there was considerable fighter activity along the route; fourteen aircraft were lost. The 627 crews were ordered to return home but looked for targets of opportunity; Flying Officer J. R. Goodman and Flying Officer. A. J. L. Hickox, in DZ601 AZ:A, dropped Window over Brunswick and bombed a searchlight belt near Damme, 10 miles west of Dummer See Lake in Lower Saxony, Germany, with four 500-pounders, scoring direct hits. Pilot Officer S. F. Parlato (RNZAF) and Pilot Officer D. D. Thomas, in DZ482 AZ:P, also Windowed over Brunswick and took the opportunity of bombing the flare path of Vechta aerodrome in Germany. A photo reconnaissance aircraft flying through the area one hour later found Brunswick to be completely free of cloud.

Navigator Flying Officer J. F. Daly, flying with 'Rocky' Nelles, had not flown since the incident with his pilot, Alex Hindshaw, on 7 May but sadly, on such a squadron there was no room for a pilotless navigator but the incident did coincide with the completion of Daly's second tour.

Wednesday, 24 May
Target: Antwerp
Crew: Squadron Leader E. F. Nelles and Flying Officer A. E. Richards
Bomb Load: 1 yellow target indicators, 1 green/red star and 2 red spot fires
Time: Up: 2330hrs, down: 0150hrs

Forty-four Lancasters and four Mosquitos from 627 Squadron took off to attack the Philips Works at Eindhoven but the raid was cancelled owing to adverse weather conditions over the target, so instead they targeted the Ford Motor factory at Antwerp in good visibility with no cloud. The flares went down early at the same time as the Pathfinder Force proximity flares. Sid Parlato, in DZ482 AZ:P, identified the docks with ease and dropped the first red spots at 00.36hrs. These were assessed to be 60 yards east of the marking point but were burning so faintly they were backed up with red spots dropped by DZ421 AZ:C, crewed by Flying Officer R. L. Bartley and Flying Officer J. D. Mitchell (RCAF), which were more effective but were assessed as 200 yards west-north-west of the marking point. 'Rocky' Nelles, in DZ477, went in from 3,000 to 800ft as third marker, visually identified the target and dropped red spot fire 120 yards north of it. No further marking was called for and with the bombing starting at 0040hrs well within the target, the Mosquitos returned to base. No losses were reported.

Saturday, 27 May
Target: Morsalines
Crew: Squadron Leader E. F. Nelles and Flying Officer A. E. Richards
Bomb Load: 2 × red, 1 × green spot fire and 1 × Wanganui flare
Time: Up: 2334hrs, down: 0214hrs

A total of 272 Lancasters, forty-nine Halifaxes and fifteen Mosquitos were sent on five separate raids to bomb battery positions on the French coast. No. 627 Squadron split their contingent of ten Mosquitos into three groups; three attacked the gun battery at St Valery and four attacked the railway marshalling yards at Nantes. The remaining three Mosquitos attacked gun batteries on the Normandy coast at Morsalines, about 100 metres south-west of the village of Morsalines. Its construction began in 1941, making it one of the oldest batteries of the Normandy Atlantic Wall, and its position on the heights dominated the coastline, making an ideal vantage point to protect the strongholds from any beach-launched invasion. As such it presented a vital target to Bomber Command.

Having picked out the Morsalines marking point, DZ477 dived from 3,000 to 800ft to re-mark the target with a single red spot fire, which was assessed as being within 120–150 yards north of the aiming point. Flying Officer J. G. Grey (RNZAF and Flying Officer F. W. Boyle (RAAF), in DZ418 AZ:L, dived into the target and released red spot fires to re-mark the aiming point. One skipped and was assessed as 125–150 yards north of the marking point. Bombing had started at 0049hrs, causing large clouds of smoke that obscured the marker, so the controller paused the bombing run and asked for re-marking. 'Rocky' Nelles went in again to put down a green target indicator at 0101hrs 150–200 yards north of the aiming point. Flying Officer N. B. Sutherland and W/O H. F. Stanbury, in DZ415 AZ:Q, later reported that they had experienced partial VHF failure and were unable to receive instructions despite several requests. Instead they decided to observe the bombing, which they considered to be very successful.

Sadly, Flying Officer P. S. Foxcroft DFC and Flying Officer D. H. Acworth DFC, in DZ463 AZ:D, were attacking a gun battery at Saint-Valery-en-Caux just along the coast with two other aircraft but failed to return, having taken off at 0020hrs. The other crews heard them over the target area but they were seen going down into the sea off the French coast.

Wednesday, 31 May
Target: Maisy
Crew: Squadron Leader E. F. Nelles and Flying Officer A. E. Richards
Bomb Load: 2 × red spot fires, 1 × green target indicator and 1 × Wanganui flare
Time: Up: 2325hrs, down: 0159hrs

Sixty-eight Lancasters and four Mosquitos were dispatched to bomb a coastal gun battery between Omaha and Utah beaches but as the target was covered with cloud, the master bomber ordered all aircraft to return to base. Two proximity Oboe markers were seen, the second of which was in the target area. Some flares and target markers were dropped over the target, which had been identified.

Monday, 5 June
Target: Saint-Pierre-du-Mont
Crew: Wing Commander G. W. Curry and Squadron Leader W. W. M. De Boos (RAAF)
Bomb Load: 3 × green and 1 × yellow target indicator
Time: Up: 0330hrs, down: 0615hrs

Eight Mosquitos were detailed to mark targets for main force attack on gun batteries on the Normandy coast prior to and in support of the Allied landings. Four Mosquitos attacked the gun battery at Saint-Pierre-du-Mont, with the markers starting to go down at 0447hrs on the first of three red Oboe target indicators that were seen to cascade and fall slightly to the east of the gun position. The second red TI actually fell on the target and the third slightly overshot to the south. Immediately after the red markers, Marker number 4, DZ477, identified the target in good visibility and dive bombed from 4,000 to 500ft, releasing three green target indicators at 0449hrs that were well placed for bombing to start. Curry and De Boos were ordered to return to base at 0500hrs but, along with other crews, they reported seeing naval vessels engaging the enemy shore defences. In the English Channel many transport and invasion craft were seen heading towards the French coast.

Tuesday. 6 June – D-Day
Target: Argenton
Crew: Squadron Leader E. F. Nelles and Flying Officer A. E. Richards
Bomb Load: 3 × green target indicators and 1 × Wanganui flare was not used
Time: Up: 2359hrs, down: 0256hrs

In order for the invading Allies to establish a beachhead, Bomber Command committed twenty squadrons to attack targets at nine different locations. DZ477 was Marker Number 1 for the attack on railway yards at Argenton, placing one marker at 0121hrs in a diving attack from 24,000ft to 1,000ft, assessed as 50–75 yards and 110 degrees off the aiming point; bombing then commenced and was well concentrated, with explosions seen.

Thursday, 8 June
Target: Rennes
Crew: Wing Commander G. W. Curry and Squadron Leader W. W. M. De Boos (RAAF)
Bomb Load: 3 × red, 2 × green target indicators and 1 × Wanganui flare
Time: Up: 2350hrs, down: 0325hrs

DZ477 was Marker Number 2 for a main force attack on a railway junction at Rennes, which was a vital German supply route to the

Normandy area. The aircraft's GEE set failed on crossing the English coast so they identified the target visually, and with a partially unserviceable VHF radio the request to back up the marking was only just heard. Curry took the Mosquito straight in, diving from 4,000 to 400ft and could see the marking point but could not see any red spot fires owing to smoke. He dropped two red spot fires on the marking point but they were difficult to identify. Curry went round again, this time placing one green target indicator on his reds near the marking point. The bombing commenced, which was seen to be travelling along the line of the marking point.

The marker leaders were Flying Officer H. Steere and Flying Officer K. W. Gale in DZ353 AZ:B, taking off at 2347hrs. While at low level, Steere was heard to say that they had been hit by flak and that they were on fire over the target. Seconds later Steere was also heard to say, almost certainly to his navigator, 'get out of this as soon as possible', which in reality was almost impossible owing to their lack of altitude. Their aircraft struck some trees and crashed in flames, killing both men instantly. Harry Steere had previously flown Spitfires with 19 Squadron during the Battle of Britain and had been awarded the DFM. He was now awarded an immediate DFC. Both men are buried at Orgères, near Saint-Erblon, France.

Thursday, 15 June
Target: Châtellerault
Crew: Flying Officer I. H. Hanlon (RNZAF) and Flight Sergeant J. Upton
Bomb Load: 2 × red, 1 × green target indicators and 1 × Wanganui flare
Time: Up: 2308hrs, down: 0310hrs

DZ477 was Marker Number 2 for the attack on a fuel and ammunition dump. The first flares went down at 0044hrs and DZ477 followed next at 0045hrs in a dive from 1,000ft to 180ft, releasing one red and one green target indicator at 0049hrs that the master bomber assessed as accurate. Hanlon and Upton were on their way back to base when one engine cut out over Tours, so they had to land at Manston.

During a 627 Squadron operation on 8 January 1944, Flying Officer Hanlon crashed Mosquito W4072 AZ:Q into the sea off the Essex coast on the return from Frankfurt. Hanlon was saved but his navigator, Flying Officer Evans, was later found drowned on 10 January when his body was washed ashore at Bradwell Bay. Flying Officer Evans was buried at the RAF Regional Cemetery on 13 January. The squadron commander, officers, non-commissioned officers and airmen attended.

There followed five days of cancelled operations despite aircraft and targets being selected, so the crews took the opportunity to undertake practise bombing runs and general air tests. On the lighter side, but no less competitive, on 17 June, Coningsby held a sports day involving the personnel of 83 Squadron from the host airfield, 106 Squadron from Metheringham and 617 and 627 Squadrons from Woodhall Spa. No. 617 Squadron were the favourites to lift the trophy but in a closely contested affair in which every point was vital to the outcome, 83 Squadron gained a narrow victory.

Tuesday, 4 July
Target: Criel
Crew: Squadron Leader E. F. Nelles and Squadron Leader W. W. M. De Boos (RAAF)
Bomb Load: 4 × red target indicators
Time: Up: 0010hrs, down: 0238hrs

A total of 211 Lancasters, four Mosquitos (later increased to eleven), and one Mustang were sent to attack V-weapon storage caves at Criel, 3 miles north-east of Saint-Leu-d'Esserent and 30 miles north of Paris. The caves had originally been used for growing mushrooms and, despite being protected by a roof of clay and limestone 25ft deep, the Germans brought in substantial anti-aircraft defences.

The two aiming points were attacked between 0126hrs and 0143hrs, with the easterly aiming point targeted by 200 Lancasters and eleven Mosquitos, which dropped 1,119 tons of high explosives and forty-five 250lb marker bombs. The initial marking appeared to be reasonably accurate but as the attack progressed the large amount of smoke from the flares caused a tendency for bomb accuracy to creep north-north-east.

The westerly aiming point was attacked by Wing Commander Leonard Cheshire of 617 Squadron in Mustang HB837, but marker aircraft DZ477 visually identified the target and dropped four red target indicators in a dive from 2,000ft to 500ft at 0130hrs. The marking was assessed to be accurate, so bombing commenced at 0133hrs, with 617 Squadron dropping twelve 'Tallboy' bombs on target and well concentrated on the markers. Midway through the attack the target had been obliterated, so five Lancasters returned with their bombs as ordered. Although smaller than the later 22,000lb 'Grand Slam' bomb, the 'Tallboy' was a 12,000lb, 21ft long aerodynamic and ballistically perfect weapon. The brainchild of Barnes Wallis, when dropped from 18,000ft it would fall at 750mph for thirty-seven seconds. Its charge weight of 5,200lb of Torpex high explosive could penetrate the ground, displacing 1 million cu ft of earth and creating a crater requiring 5,000 tons of soil to back fill. The alternative was an instantaneous detonation that would produce a crater 25ft deep and more than 240ft across.

Moderate, heavy flak was encountered with considerable fighter activity throughout the whole route over enemy territory. One Bf 109 and one twin-engine enemy aircraft were claimed as destroyed. The raid was a success and collapsed the tunnel system and also cut railway lines with at least twenty-five craters. A bridge over the River Oise was also hit and partially destroyed. An estimated 2,000

V-weapons were buried, which immediately reduced the scale of the V-1 bombardment of London.

Pilot Officer S. F. Parlato RNZAF and Flying Officer D. D. Thomas, in DZ482 AZ:P, returned early owing to generator failure, and 627 navigator Flying Officer N. Lewis completed his 100th mission, acting as navigator for Flying Officer L. C. E. Devigne in Mosquito DZ367 AZ:D.

For Jim Marshallsay and Nick Ranshaw in DZ516 AZ:O it was to be their thirty-sixth trip with 627 Squadron, a squadron record, and their fiftieth and final operation. Marshallsay:

> We were marking on the Criel trip; normally Leo Devigne was primary marker and I backed up when he was satisfied with his efforts. Dimly, I recall a cliff face from very low level, a lot of smoke from the illuminating flares and the arrival of night fighters and quite a few combats. Mostly I remember it because it was the last trip of our tour and on return to Woodhall Spa the ground crew gave us a great reception. The Orderly Room had spotted that I had done over fifty ops so I was Screened (taken off ops), left the squadron and went to instruct on Wellingtons (which I had never flown!). When I left 627, I drew a new battledress from the stores. The wings came from my old battledress and I stuck them into my logbook, where they still are today. I notice I was Flight Sergeant on the crew state and P/O on the Criel trip so I must have been commissioned about June 4th.

When Cheshire returned to Woodhall Spa he was ordered by the commander of 5 Group to leave his squadron for a period of rest. Cheshire was a remarkable man both during and after the war. He had completed four tours and had flown more than 100 operations. Two months later, Cheshire was awarded the Victoria Cross for his four tours and for his courage and skill in developing low-level target marking; he did not fly on operations again. Cheshire was an extraordinary airman and leader; he borrowed a Mustang 'courtesy' of the US 8th Air Force on 25 June 1944 to mark the V-weapon site at Siracourt. The Mustang bore no squadron markings but did have black and white invasion stripes on its fuselage. This was his first flight in the high-performance, single-engine fighter, which he had to navigate himself to and from the target, then land it after dark. A man who set incredibly high standards of skill, leadership, bravery and achievement, Cheshire was a worthy recipient of the Victoria Cross.

Further crews were singled out when Squadron Leaders J. C. McCarthy, K. L. Munroe and D. J. Shannon, the three 617 Squadron flight commanders and survivors of the Dams raid, were also ordered to rest following this operation.

Friday, 7 July
Target: Saint-Leu-d'Esserent
Crew: Squadron Leader E. F. Nelles and Flying Officer K. G. Tice
Bomb Load: 2 × yellow spot fires and 9 × Wanganui flares
Time: Up: 2333hrs, down: 0218hrs

A total of 208 Lancaster and fifteen Mosquitos were detailed to attack the construction works and flying bomb storage area in the tunnels leading to and from the Creil site bombed two nights beforehand.

The first Oboe marker arrived two minutes early but some crews reported that they were dazzled by their Oboe screens, so the marking point could not be identified. The marker leader called for flare markers. These were able to identify the target by moonlight through patchy cloud at 9,000ft, with the markers falling some 500 yards south of the correct aiming point. Marker number 3 then dropped two red spot fires, assessed to be 100 yards south of the aiming point. Backing up was accurate except for two greens that fell about 200 to 300 yards south, so the marker leader told the controller that marking was accurate but the two Greens were to be disregarded. The main force Lancasters then bombed, the results of which were quite scattered but accurately directed on the mouth of the tunnels and the approach roads. The collapsed tunnels prevented the Germans moving the flying bombs via the series of railway lines leading away from the tunnel complex. One marker Mosquito KB195 AZ:B, crewed by Squadron Leader N. W. Mackenzie and Flying Officer P. N. G. Herbert, was unable to mark owing to yellow target indicator smoke causing a loss of visual reference. Instead the crew stooged around and carried out photographic reconnaissance. DZ477 dropped nine flares and two yellow target indicators at 0100hrs from 6,000ft some 2½ miles north-east of the target in a spoof attack.

German night fighters were active on outward and return routes and intercepted the bombing force on their way in, with twenty-nine Lancasters and two Mosquitos lost. No. 106 Squadron from Metheringham in Lincolnshire lost five of its sixteen Lancasters and 630 Squadron from East Kirkby lost its commanding officer, Wing Commander Dias, who was flying his sixty-ninth operation.

Wednesday, 12 July
Target: Culmont-Chalindrey
Crew: Wing Commander G. W. Curry and Squadron Leader W. W. M. De Boos (RAAF)
Bomb Load: 2 × red spot fires and 1 × Wanganui flare
Time: Up: 0002hrs, down: 0358hrs

DZ477, as marker leader, was the first of four marker aircraft for the attack on the railway yards at Culmont-Chalindrey. The crew identified the marking point and dropped two red spot fires at 0142hrs in a dive from 3,000ft to 350ft. They then circled the target and assessed that the marking accuracy was 50 yards at 135 degrees but Curry considered it necessary to back up the marking point as the reds were very faint. Marker number 2, Hanlon and Tice in DZ525 AZ:S, dropped two red target indicators but they overshot the first markers by 100 yards. There was a delay of six minutes between initial marking and backing because the Mosquitos had been ordered home by the deputy controller, but Hanlon and Tice had already been sent in. Main force bombing started at 0150hrs and was reported to be accurate.

Friday, 14 July
Target: Villeneuve-Saint-Georges
Crew: Wing Commander G. W. Curry and Squadron Leader W. W. M. De Boos (RAAF)
Bomb Load: 2 × red, 1 × yellow target indicators and 1 × Wanganui flare
Time: Up: 0002hrs, down: 0303hrs

DZ477 was marker leader but before it reached the target one Wanganui flare had dropped off the aircraft and De Boos found his Oboe screen was blinding him, making it impossible to identify the target. Curry dropped one yellow target indicator as a route marker for the controllers and then flew over a bridge and found the target by the light of flares dropped by Oboe at 0127hrs. Curry and De Boos assessed that Oboe was wrong, so they called for other crews to mark the target if they could see it. When no one came, Curry and De Boos decided to try again and at 0135hrs, in a dive from 3,000ft to 500ft, they dropped two red target indicators to within 100 yards at three o'clock. Unknown to Curry, DZ418 AZ:L, with Flying Officer J. G. Grey and Flying Officer F. W. Boyle, as Marker number 2, were going in to mark and had given the 'Tally-ho' at 0132hrs. With Curry on his run-in, Grey and Boyle pulled out of their dive and were immediately under fire from flak, so they circled, then backed up at 0145hrs again. However, in the middle of the dive the controller called off the markers, so they dropped and left the area.

It was recorded that some crews felt that the new 627 CO, Wing Commander Curry, was so desperate to assure Air Commodore 'Razor' Sharp he had marked first that to achieve his aim he had called the first marker out of its dive. After Johnny Grey had given the 'Tally-ho', they then waited for more than ten minutes for the markers to go down and a total of fourteen minutes elapsed before they could back up. This frustration must have spread through the main force.

Meanwhile, Marker 4, DZ611 AZ:G, crewed by Flying Officer W. W. Topper and V. W. Davies, had orbited several times and finally they responded to the call from the marker leader requesting for any crew available to back up. Topper took his aircraft into its descent towards the target when 'something happened' that put their aircraft into a spin at 4,000ft. Topper took immediate action and managed to regain control of the aircraft. He resumed his dive from 3,000ft to 650ft, backing up at 0143hrs with green target indicators that showed through the smoke. The railways were hit but much of the bombing fell east of the target.

Saturday, 15 July
Target: Nevers
Crew: Flying Officer N. B. Rutherford and Warrant Officer F. H. Stanbury
Bomb Load: 2 × red spot fires
Time: Up: 2357hrs, down: 0359hrs

Some 222 Lancasters and seven Mosquitos were split into two forces detailed to carry out simultaneous attacks on railway networks at Châlons-sur-Marne and Nevers. Four 627 Squadron Mosquitos and approximately 100 Lancasters attacked railway junctions at

Nevers, 150 miles south-east of Paris. At approximately 0300hrs on the 16th, two Lancasters collided, ME851 PO:B from 467 Squadron and ME807 EM:S from 207 Squadron. Both aircraft crashed and exploded at Marnay, with the loss of both crews who now lie together in Lignières de Touraine Communal Cemetery.

DZ477, as Marker number 3, released its markers in clear weather at 0153hrs in a dive from 2,000ft to 400ft, cancelling the spot fires of the lead marker. The lead marker, Flying Officer R. L. Bartley and Flying Officer J. F. Daly in DZ641 AZ:C, inadvertently released his markers at 01.47hrs in the early part of their marking dive from the north and they fell some 500 yards short.

Tuesday, 18 July
Target: Revigny
Crew: Squadron Leader R. G. Churcher and Pilot Officer J. H. Willis
Bomb Load: 4 × 500lb six-hour fused bombs
Time: Up: 2351hrs, down: 0324hrs

Four Mosquitos from 627 Squadron attacked the marshalling yards at Revigny. Flying Officer D. W. Peck and R. F. Davies, in DZ636 AZ:N, dropped a route yellow route marker at 01.00hrs on the way into the target area before initial flares were dropped at 0129hrs west of the town. The marking aircraft, DZ650 AZ:Q crewed by Flying Officer J. G. Grey (RNZAF) and Flying Officer F. W. Boyle (RAAF), identified the target at 0134hrs and dropped a 1,000lb red target indicator, which fell 500 yards and 50 degrees from the marking point; a large red explosion was seen.

At this point, H–Hour was delayed until 0145hrs to allow DZ477 to drop four 500lb bombs fitted with six-hour fuses at 01.42hrs in a dive from 1,500ft to 300ft. The weather was hazy but with no cloud cover, however, the target was difficult to locate. Marker number 3, Flying Officer M. D. Gribbin and Flying Officer R. W. Griffiths in

DZ534 AZ:H, identified the target. Large explosions were seen at 0144hrs.

Thursday, 20 July
Target: Alost
Crew: Flying Officer P. F. Mallender and Flight Sergeant W. S. Gaunt
Bomb Load: 2 × red and 2 × yellow spot fires
Time: Up: 2333hrs, down: 0202hrs

Five 627 Mosquitos carried out a 'spoof' raid at Alost, 45 miles east of Courtrai. The railway junctions were selected to act as a distraction to the main force raid on the railway yards at Courtrai involving 302 Lancasters and fifteen Mosquitos. Flying Officer M. D. Gribbin and Flying Officer R. W. Griffiths, in DZ636 AZ:N, set off about twenty minutes before the other crews to establish the weather conditions on a meteorological reconnaissance. Cloud cover broke soon after the crews crossed the English coast and remained clear until near the target. As they descended to 5,000ft, light could clearly be seen on the ground. Their weather report was passed to the raid controller at 0025hrs.

The 'spoof' was carried out in low cloud and slight haze lit by flares dropped at 00.45hrs. The target was identified and marked with two red and two yellow TIs by Flying Officer W. Topper and Pilot Officer V. Davies in KB195 AZ:B at 0049hrs. Next in was DZ477, which dropped markers at 0050hrs in a dive from 2,500ft to 500ft with a good concentration. Within two minutes, the three remaining Mosquitos had backed up the marking, again with a good concentration. On the ground, several trucks were destroyed.

The main force aircraft devastated the target.

This was DZ477's final operational sortie and it was now allocated to 1655 Mosquito Training Unit at RAF Warboys.

Chapter 19

Mosquito Crew Trainer

RAF Warboys, Cambridgeshire

Situated 7 miles north-east of Huntingdon and a short distance from RAF Upwood and RAF Wyton, Warboys was in 'Pathfinder Country' and, with an unusually long concrete runway of 6,290ft in 1940, served as a conventional bomber station. In 1942 it became deeply committed to the operational training of aircrew in the Pathfinder Navigational Training Unit, which saw only about 50 per cent of the selected crews satisfying the requirements to join a Pathfinder squadron.

In March 1944, 1655 Mosquito Training Unit was formed using Mosquitos and Oxford trainers and it remained at Warboys until the unit was disbanded in December 1944 to reform as 16 Operational Training Unit at RAF Upper Heyford. They left behind the H2S and Oboe training commitments, which were passed to the Pathfinder Force Navigation Training Unit, then flying some of the 1655 Mosquitos, and this continued until the end of the war.

Warboys closed as an airfield in January 1946 but was resurrected in 1960 to become a Bloodhound ground-to-air missiles base set in the middle of the old airfield. The missiles only stayed for four years before the airfield was sold, with the buildings being taken over by a transport firm and the airfield itself returned to agricultural use.

1655 Mosquito Training Unit

Originally 1655 Mosquito Conversion Unit at Horsham St Faith, the unit became 1655 Mosquito Training Unit following the move to its home at RAF Warboys in March 1944.

Commanded by Wing Commander J. R. G. 'Roy' Ralston DSO, DFC, who would later command 139 Squadron, 1655 Mosquito Training Unit was responsible for training new Mosquito crews selected or volunteering for conversion to the Mosquito bomber variant. The vast majority of aircrews were veterans of at least one tour or had demonstrated above average skills and aptitude, enabling fast tracking into the unit. A pilot and navigator simply didn't jump into a Mosquito and fly the high-performance machine. It could easily turn and bite even the most accomplished of pilots, so it was essential for the crews to become familiar with and learn how to fly it. A number of syllabus categories were practised, such as taxying the aircraft and take-off procedure. The flight dynamics such as stalling, single-engine flying, steep turns and landing were challenging skills to master with a powerful twin-engine aircraft when flying on a single engine. Aircraft emergencies were practised, including an overshoot procedure, flying in bad weather conditions and both dual and solo flight at night. With Mosquitos in short supply, Oxford trainers were used for bombing practice and navigational training as their handling qualities were close to those experienced on heavier aircraft, although they were easier to control.

Navigators did normal flight training, which included cross-country navigation flights during the day and at night, and they were instructed in Pathfinder navigation and marking techniques. After that they would be formed into crews with either a 'get to know you' session in the mess hall or some crews would pair up having known each other beforehand. Graduation from the unit would see crews posted to front-line Mosquito bombing units such as 139 and 627 Squadrons.

Chapter 20

The Men of Mosquito DZ477

The Mosquito crews of 139 and 627 Squadrons were similar to thousands of men across Bomber Command in terms of bravery and commitment to the fight against Nazi Germany. The number of airmen connected with DZ477 was limited and some would lose their lives in the closing stages of the war but the fortunate ones continued life either as a serviceman or left the RAF and blended back into everyday society.

The story of DZ477 would not be complete without some acknowledgment of the courageous men closely associated with the story, particularly Benny Goodman and Sid 'Chip' Parlato. 'Benny' flew DZ477 on two non-operational flights and was my inspiration by proving a source of wonderful anecdotes and first-hand accounts. There is no evidence to suggest that 'Chip' took DZ477 into the air on operations but he may have flown her on air tests; his log book may reveal the truth. 'Chip' carried out forty-eight sorties with 627 Squadron, an outstanding achievement.

Squadron Leader R. B. Bagguley and Flying Officer C. K. Hayden

Flying Officer R. B. Bagguley and Flying Officer C. K. Hayden were posted to 139 Squadron from 105 Squadron on 15 June 1942, with Bagguley appointed the rank of flight lieutenant. Their first operation was from RAF Horsham St Faith, Norwich, on the 25 June 1942 in Mosquito W4072, loaned from 105 Squadron to carry out a low-level (50ft) bombing attack on Stade Aerodrome near Dorum. Their aircraft developed a fault that prevented the flaps from operating, so their return landing approach at 0110hrs was too fast and they overran the flare path. A wheel was caught in the trench, collapsing the undercarriage but the crew were uninjured. This aircraft was to serve with 627 Squadron at RAF Oakington and would be lost in January 1944 when returning from a mission with Ian Hanlon and his navigator Francis Evans.

On 6 December 1942, at 139 Squadron, Hayden acted as navigator for Flying Officer M. Wayman in DZ373. During their attack on the Philips radio and valve factory at Eindhoven their aircraft was subjected to light flak, which required the pilot to take immediate evasive action at extremely low level. They returned safely.

On 6 March ten Mosquitos with a further six from 105 Squadron attacked aero engine sheds at Le Mans but Bagguley and Hayden in DZ469 were hit over the target and lost. Bagguley and Hayden had completed nine operations before this fateful night; they were awarded the DFC on 11 March.

Sergeant J. Massey DFM and Sergeant R. Fletcher DFM

Sergeant J. Massey DFM and Sergeant R. Fletcher DFM were posted to 139 Squadron from 17 Operational Training Unit on 7 August 1942 and along with other crews spent several weeks honing their skills in training flights and lectures. Whilst bombing the Amiens marshalling yards in DZ386 on 3 December 1942, they felt it was unsafe to release their bomb load under a cloud base of 800ft so elected to jettison their two 500lb bombs in the sea on the way back. On 1 February 1943, both men attended interviews at a press conference in London and both were awarded the DFM two days later. Massey and Fletcher completed fifteen operations with 139 Squadron before their posting to 618 Squadron at RAF Skitten on

3 March 1943. No. 618 Squadron was formed on 1 April with crews from 105 and 139 Squadron RAF to develop the use of Mosquitos carrying a variation of the Barnes Wallis-designed bouncing bomb code-named 'Highball'. For various reasons, the Highball was never used and the squadron disbanded at the end of the war.

Flying Officer Pereira DFC

Born in the Caribbean in 1913, Charles Vernon Pereira was posted to 139 Squadron from 17 Operational Training Unit on 30 September 1942. Flying Officer G. H. Gilbert was Pereira's regular navigator and their first trip was to Tours engine shed on 14 February 1943. Pereira and Gilbert, in DZ478, were intercepted by two Fw 190s 25 miles from their target, Aulnoye engine sheds on 3 April 1943, forcing Pereira to aim his bombs at a goods train as he took evasive action. A week later, in DZ470, they were attacked by Fw 190s on an aborted attack on Orleans. On 27 May 1943, as they attacked the Schott works at Jena, their Mosquito, DZ598, suffered a starboard engine failure just before they reached the target, which forced them to leave formation. They did, however, bomb a river bridge near Kassel and made the return journey at low level for over 450 miles, narrowly escaping the interest of six Fw 190s and making a good landing at base. Unsurprisingly, Pereira was assessed as having exceptional ability and had completed eleven operations with 139 before he was posted to 105 Squadron with Gilbert on 8 June 1943. Pereira flew eighty Mosquito operations with 105 and 139 Squadrons and the Pathfinder Force on both daylight low-level and night raids.

Squadron Leader E. F. Nelles

Flying Officer Edward Forbes 'Rocky' Nelles was posted to 139 Squadron from 1655 Mosquito Training Unit on 31 August 1943 and carried out his first raid to Cologne on 2 September 1943 in DZ355. Flying Officer Nelles and Sergeant A. N. Dykes went to Berlin in DZ518 on 17 October and were coned by searchlights for six minutes over the target. Nelles was promoted to flying officer on 9 October 1943 with effect from 25 September 1943. Nelles completed twenty-eight operational sorties with 139 Squadron before reporting for flying duties at 627 Squadron on 19 January 1944. He was awarded the DFC on 24 May 1944, followed by a bar in October. On the afternoon of 4 June 1944, Squadron Leader Nelles and his navigator, Wing Commander John Simpson DSO DFC, took off in their Mosquito, DZ525, for a training flight but as they landed back at Woodhall Spa the undercarriage collapsed, causing minor damage. Fortunately, they were uninjured. Nelles completed thirty-one operations with 627 Squadron.

Squadron Leader William Wentworth Meade De Boos DFC and Bar

Born in Wakefield, England, on 30 December 1917, Bill De Boos's flying career began with training in Canada followed by an OTU at Pershore, Worcestershire. His first tour was on Wellington bombers in the Middle East with 37 Squadron, after delivering a new aircraft via Gibraltar and Malta, where he spent a few days. During this period De Boos sought the cover of a 45-gallon drum during an air attack by two Bf 109s, which raked the runway and a nearby Beaufighter with cannon shells.

His posting in the Middle East consisted of bombing raids over Benghazi until his unit had to retreat prior to El-Alamein. Bill spent periods of leave in Palestine, as it was then called, and he considered the slogan 'Join the RAAF and see the world' to be true enough.

Bill came back to the UK on a 'civvy' passport via Khartoum in the Belgian Congo and Lagos on an Empire flying boat followed via

Gambia and Portugal in an American Clipper flying boat. Bill then spent a time at 27 Operational Training Unit as a navigation officer at Church Broughton in Derbyshire, tasked with supervising night flying training.

No. 27 Operational Training Unit had already lost eleven aircraft in 1943 and the alarming number of instructor losses prompted Bill to apply for a posting as he did not wish to add to the number. Bill went to 7 then 37 Squadrons before applying to join the Mosquito force in August 1943. Following his Mosquito training course at 1655 Mosquito Training Unit, he joined 139 Squadron on 28 September 1943. His first flight was to Cologne on 2 October 1943 in DZ423. De Boos was promoted to flying officer 8 October 1943. He became the 627 Squadron navigation leader on 15 November 1943 and was awarded the DFC the following May.

Just before 627 left Oakington, De Boos and Wing Commander Roy Elliott flew to Woodhall Spa for the first time on 14 April 1944 and De Boos met WAAF Section Officer Sheila Adamson, who was in charge of preparing the messing and accommodation facilities. Their relationship developed but De Boos was acutely aware of the dangers of mixing marriage at that time and delayed popping the question until his Mosquito tour ended. When the day came the answer was 'yes' and the couple were married in Boston.

Bill's flew as navigator with several pilots but his final 627 operation was a target-marking job for an incendiary attack on Bremerhaven on 18 September 1944 with his pilot, Wing Commander George Curry. Bill and George had completed fifteen operations together and De Boos had complete confidence in Curry's control of the aircraft and his leadership. That night a highly experienced crew was lost, Flying Officer Norman Rutherford AFC, a fellow Australian, and P/O Frederick Stanbury, in DZ635 AZ-N. It was a shattering blow to 627 Squadron. A day or two later, Wing Commander Curry called Bill into his office to announce that he was being taken off operations, having completed seventy-six. Bill stated that his feelings at this moment were indescribable and he felt like throwing his arms in the air and screaming, 'I'm going to live'. Following the death of George Curry during a Battle of Britain airshow, De Boos wrote a letter of sympathy to his widow, stating that George died doing what he enjoyed most of all – flying.

Bill's final posting was as Base Navigation Officer with 3 Training Station at Bottesford, where he remembered that the winter was so cold that he must have just about avoided becoming sterile. Bill was discharged from his RAF career on 1 September 1945.

In response to my letter to Bill in March 1990 from the comfort of his home in Ballina, New South Wales, Australia, he replied:

> Receiving your enquiry from so far away about events so long ago was a strange but pleasant experience. After reading accounts of the devastation and casualties resulting from attacks marked by us, one doesn't know whether to feel ashamed or proud of the part we played. I guess had I come from Rotterdam or Coventry I'd feel a little more certain.

Bill passed away in 2006.

Flying Officer H. Steere DFM, DFC and Flying Officer K. W. Gale (RAAF)

Harry Steere was born on 7 February 1914 in Wallasey, Cheshire. A former 'Halton Brat' RAF apprentice, Steere volunteered for RAF service in September 1930 as an aircraft apprentice on a twelve-year service and passed out as a metal rigger on 18 August 1933 with the rank of leading aircraftsman. Steere applied and was selected for pilot training and began a flying course on 25 November 1935, passing out as a sergeant pilot the following August. Steere married Joan Margaret Witter in April 1938 in his home town.

On 13 June 1939 Steere was promoted to flight sergeant and when war broke out he was flying Spitfires with 19 Squadron at Duxford. He shared the squadron's first victory of a Ju 88 on 11 May 1940 over the English Channel and claimed five victories over Dunkirk. Steere was particularly friendly with George Unwin and were both considered as 'older' men in 1940. Unwin, nicknamed 'Grumpy' by the legless ace Douglas Bader, went on to survive the war. His story can be found within publications by my good friend and renowned author and Battle of Britain historian Dilip Sarkar. Harry was the younger brother of Jack Steere, a pilot with 72 Squadron during the Battle of Britain.

In June 1940 Steere was awarded the DFM, with the citation saying that he destroyed three enemy aircraft and had assisted in the destruction of three others, displaying considerable coolness and gallantry in the face of the enemy. At all times, he set an example to his fellow pilots by his devotion to duty. Steere saw further action during the Battle of Britain and by late November he had been credited with shooting down a total of six German aircraft, with a further five shared destroyed and two probables.

After a posting as a flying instructor with 8 Flying Training School at Montrose, Steere was commissioned in 1941 and requested to resume single-seat flying. However, he was rejected so the only way he could fly operationally was to transfer to Mosquitos at 1655 Mosquito Training Unit. On completing the course, Steere and navigator Kenneth Gale were posted to 139 Squadron on 6 October 1943; Gale was promoted to flying officer two days later. Their first operation was on 16 October, when they took DZ597 to Dortmund and completed a further seven operations before being posted to 627 on 2 December 1943.

On 27 May 1944, Steere and his navigator, 'Windy' Gale, took Mosquito DZ353 AZ-B to attack gun emplacement sites on the French coast, where they encountered continuous heavy anti-aircraft fire. Steere spent considerable time and effort over the target area in order to accurately identify the precise target but their aircraft was struck by a shell that severely damaged the starboard elevator, which forced the Mosquito into an uncontrollable steep climb. Displaying great coolness, Steere promptly transmitted clear instructions to his deputy to assume control of the operation and then, regaining some control, he flew the damaged aircraft back to base.

On 9 June 1944 Steere and Gale took the repaired Mosquito to Rennes for an attack on a railway junction but during their attack Steere was heard to say that they had been hit and were on fire. He was then heard to say to Gale 'get out of this quickly'. Harry Steere and Kenneth Gale were killed when their aircraft came down near Orgères. This was Steere's thirty-ninth sortie with 627. Steere was awarded an immediate DFC. Gale was also awarded the DFC; the *London Gazette* citation said:

> Flying Officer Gale has accomplished numerous operations, the majority of which have been accomplished in the Middle East and the remainder from Great Britain. Throughout his operational career, this officer has maintained a fine reputation for determination in the face of the enemy. The aircraft in which he was navigator has, on several occasions been damaged by the enemy and has subsequently been forced to make crash landings, but these incidents have not arrested this officer's determination to bring every operational flight to a successful conclusion.

The loss of Steere and Gale was a massive blow to 627 Squadron and in particular to Johnny Grey DFC and Bar (RNZAF) and

Francis Boyle DFC and Bar, Croix de Guerre (RAAF), who were deeply affected by the loss as they had formed a close friendship. Grey, having completed ninety operations with 102, 139 and 627 Squadrons, returned to New Zealand soon after.

Harry Steere was thirty years old when he died and he is buried with his friend Kenneth Gale in Saint-Erblon Communal Cemetery, France; they are the only Commonwealth airmen to be buried there.

Flying Officer James Alexander 'Alec' Saint-Smith DFC, DFM

'Alec' Saint-Smith was born on 29 December 1917 in Singleton, New South Wales, Australia, and became a school teacher in that state before he enlisted in the Royal Australian Air Force in January 1941. He flew Tiger Moths at 4 Elementary Flying Training School, a Royal Australian Air Force pilot training unit established in January 1940 at Mascot, NSW. He was posted to Canada to attend pilot training, where he was presented with his wings. He continued his training in England before joining the RAAF's 460 Squadron at Breighton in Yorkshire, flying Wellingtons and later, Lancasters.

During the night of 18 June 1942, Wellingtons from 460 Squadron were tasked with minelaying so Saint-Smith and his crew, in Wellington Z1392, took off at 0030hrs. During the raid their aircraft was damaged by flak in the front turret and the port wing but they were able to make the return across the North Sea and land at Breighton at 0514hrs.

Saint-Smith's first operational sortie with a Lancaster bomber was as the captain of Lancaster W4783, G for George, to Mannheim in Germany on 6 December 1942. G-George became Saint-Smith's regular aircraft for another twelve operations, during which time he was commissioned in February 1943, with his tour ending in March. Flying Officer Saint-Smith was awarded a Distinguished Flying

Medal for gallantry in a mission over Berlin. The citation for the award of the DFM reads:

> This airman has displayed outstanding determination in pressing home his attacks on enemy targets during numerous operational sorties. Early in March, 1943, he participated in a raid on Berlin and obtained an excellent photograph after the bombs had been released. He has, at all times, taken great care to identify the target and has, as pilot, done all in his power to ensure accurate bombing. His high courage skill and initiative have set a magnificent example to his crew.
>
> Flight Sergeant Saint-Smith has completed a most successful tour of operations and always demonstrated a high degree of courage, skill and initiative, setting a magnificent example to his crew; he deserved his award of the DFM.

Alec Saint-Smith and Beryl Job from Goodword, New South Wales, had become engaged in October 1943 shortly before he completed his first tour with 460 Squadron and was posted to instructor positions and then for Mosquito training at 1655 Mosquito Training Unit. He was joined by his long-time friend and navigator Geoffrey Heath at 627 Squadron on Christmas Eve 1943; he was now on his second tour of operations as a commissioned flying officer. Saint-Smith and Heath took off at 1236hrs on 29 June 1944 in Mosquito Mk IV DZ516 AZ:O as one of four aircraft detailed to attack construction works near the V-1 site at Beauvoir in France. This was the first daylight operation carried out by the squadron, with DZ516 designated at Marker number 2, and it was seen to mark the target with target indicators concentrated in an area 500 to 100 yards from the actual marking point. The main force attack commenced and for about two minutes the bombs fell in the eastern half of the target but improved towards the end of the attack. With a large amount of smoke causing increased bombing errors, the effort was still considered to be good.

Saint-Smith and Heath and Mosquito DZ452 AZ:P, crewed by Flying Officer J. Platts and Flying Officer C. Thompson (RCAF), were not heard or seen after the attack was over and failed to return to base. It is believed that Saint-Smith and Heath were homebound when their aircraft was downed by a premature in-flight explosion of a V-1 flying bomb launched from a nearby site; they were killed instantly. It was established that the Mosquito crashed near the village of Vaulx, 3 miles south-east of Tournai in Belgium. Their Mosquito had been purchased by money raised in a Bournemouth Wings for Victory Week appeal.

Saint-Smith was posthumously awarded the DFC on 24 August 1944 for successfully completing numerous sorties over Germany and France. The citation for the award of the DFC reads:

> Flying Officer Saint-Smith has taken part in a number of major attacks on Germany and enemy-occupied territory. He has taken an important part in attacking an aircraft factory near Oslo and in several other operations against targets in Germany and France, exerting himself to the utmost to ensure their complete and final success. All these operations have had to be accomplished from a low level and have owed much of their effectiveness to his conspicuous gallantry and determination.

It is interesting to note that the Lancaster Mk I used by Saint-Smith and Heath is now preserved at the Australian War Memorial (AWM), Canberra, Australia. W4783 G-George used the 460 Squadron RAAF code AR-G and completed ninety operational sorties over occupied Europe. It is the second most prolific surviving Lancaster, behind R5868 S-Sugar of 83 Squadron RAF, 463 Squadron RAAF and 467 Squadron

RAAF, with a total of 136 operations. In a time when most operational Lancasters were fortunate to reach twenty sorties, of the 107,085 sorties by Lancasters despatched in bombing raids on Germany, 2,687 aircraft went missing. G-George has the added distinction of bringing home alive every crewman who flew aboard it. When G-George was retired from combat duty in 1944, it was flown to Australia by an all-RAAF crew of Bomber Command veterans and contributed to raising war bonds during a round-Australia publicity trip. G-George deteriorated when it was left in the open air at RAAF Base Fairbairn before being moved to the Air War Museum in the early 1950s. A five-year restoration programme at the Treloar Technology Centre restored the aircraft as faithfully as possible to its wartime configuration. In 2003 G-George was put on display at the new ANZAC Hall along with a sight and sound show to help convey the atmosphere of a Bomber Command raid, and it continued to serve as a memorial to all Australians who flew with Bomber Command and to the 1,018 dead of 460 Squadron.

Flying Officer G. E. Heath DFC DFM

Geoffrey Heath was born in Croydon, New South Wales, Australia, on 27 December 1917 and enlisted in Richmond, NSW, on 30 October 1939. He was awarded his air observers' badge on 18 August 1941. On arrival in the UK on 14 October 1941, he was posted to 14 Operational Training Unit, then 12 Squadron on 7 March 1942. There he met James Saint-Smith and became his regular navigator. They shared postings to 460 Squadron on 11 May 1942 and together they converted to the four-engine heavies, where they completed a tour and were awarded the DFM for services to 460 Squadron. Heath was commissioned to the rank of pilot officer on 15 January 1943 and was promoted to flying officer on 15 July 1943.

It was during his posting at Breighton that Geoffrey Heath met and married Elizabeth Waring from North Duffield, Yorkshire.

Heath was posted to 27 Operational Training Unit on 19 April 1943 as a navigation instructor but on 6 July 1943, Wellington BJ713 crashed soon after taking off from Church Broughton airfield. Heath injured his left leg and was admitted to Derby hospital. He and Saint-Smith were Gazetted on 14 May 1943. The citation for Heath reads:

> This airman has taken part in many successful sorties, including a raid on Milan, and three on Berlin. His last sorties against Berlin on the night of 1 March, 1943, Flt Sergeant Heath has displayed great skill, often in difficult circumstances, playing a large part in the successes obtained. Cool and resourceful in emergency, this airman has proved himself to be a valuable member of aircrew.

Heath and Saint-Smith were reunited at 1655 Mosquito Training Unit and both joined 627 Squadron on 24 December 1943, again with Heath as Saint-Smith's navigator. They completed forty-one sorties together. After his death, Heath was awarded the DFC for service with 627 Squadron, which was Gazetted on 15 August 1944, Heath's DFC citation reads:

> As navigator, Flying Officer Heath has flown on many long-distance sorties. The targets have been varied and in many cases difficult to locate but his navigational skill, together with his great determination, have invariably located the exact position. The success of many of these attacks can largely be attributed to this officer's initiative and co-operation.

Post-war, the war graves investigation unit exhumed both bodies and Alex Saint-Smith and Geoffrey Heath were later re-buried in a joint grave in Abbeville Communal Cemetery, Picardie, France. Both men were twenty-six years old.

Flying Officer P. F. Denny

Born in 1922, Peter Frederick Denny became a pilot with 139 Squadron on 17 July 1943; his first mission was in DZ458 to Kiel on 24 July. After completing twenty-two operations and twelve operational sorties with 627 Squadron, he converted to Lancasters at the Pathfinder Navigation Training Unit. Denny was posted to 83 Pathfinder Squadron at Wyton.

On 11 April 1944 Denny flew one of the 341 Lancasters accompanied by eleven Mosquitoes from 1, 3, 5 and 8 Groups to attack Aachen. Denny and his crew took off at 2044hrs in Lancaster III ND395 OL-E, and successfully reached the target. At 2240hrs they were coned by searchlights and were hit by flak at 13,000ft over Aachen. They crashed near a post office in the Schützenstraße; only the navigator survived. The 83 Squadron Pathfinder Operation Records Book stated that:

> Aachen has already had a flattening so it did not matter if the bombs fell in the town area as it was a German city. The marshalling yards are of high strategic value. The success of the raid was marred for this squadron by the loss of two crews – Flying Officer Denny and P/O McConnell. Although only newcomers to the squadron they were well liked in their respective messes and were very promising crews.

Peter Denny had completed thirty-four Mosquito raids and at the age of twenty-two was killed on his second Lancaster sortie.

Pilot Officer P. Yarema RCAF

Born in Teulon, Manitoba, Canada, in 1921, Peter Yarema enlisted in the Royal Air Force the day war broke out and was destined to fly a wide variety of aircraft ranging from the Tiger Moth to the

Avro Lancaster in assignments including ferrying planes, equipment and troops, reconnaissance sorties and bombing operations. One bizarre story has been related concerning Yarema's co-pilot, who is not identified but they had flown many operations together. On completion of their last trip together, the co-pilot stormed off without saying goodbye because he felt Yarema had put their lives in danger too many times. Dangers were ever-present for all crews, particularly when encountering enemy defences, but from time to time the unexpected happened. On one occasion, a flare ignited in Yarema's cockpit but fortunately the navigator was able to throw it out of the aircraft before it caused too much damage.

Yarema and navigator Flying officer A. F. Dodds RCAF had been members of the Mosquito-equipped 571 Pathfinder Squadron based at RAF Downham Market in Norfolk, carrying out independent raids on German industrial targets using 4,000lb cookie bombs. Having completed more than fifty bombing and Pathfinder marking missions over Germany, they were well equipped to transfer to 627 Squadron on 1 January 1944. Demonstrating exceptional qualities, Yarema transferred to the RCAF for his third tour over Europe, which earned him a DFC on 19 September 1944 having flown fifty sorties between January and June with 627 Squadron, a total of 174 hours and 40 minutes. The citation from his squadron commander read:

> This officer has now completed fifty sorties in this Group on Mosquitos, including ten to Berlin, ten to the Ruhr, six to Cologne and five to Ludwigshafen. The remainder have all been on heavily defended German targets. He has shown great keenness, skill and courage at all times and is the type of pilot who will fly any aircraft to any target at any time. He has been subject to most intense operational flying during the period of the squadron's formation. I think most highly of his

airmanship and his courage and of the good example he has set to his fellow pilots.

In another, final bizarre story, apparently Yarema was not aware of his decoration for a year or so because when the medal and citation arrived at his family home in Manitoba, his mother, who spoke little English, decided to put the envelope in a drawer, possibly unaware of its significance.

Flying Officer John Francis Daly DFC DFM

Born in Hackney in 1918, John Daly went on to complete thirty-six operations, thirty-three of which were with 37 Squadron as a navigator and bomb aimer. His high standards gained him the complete confidence of his crew mates as Daly had on several occasions contributed to the safe return of his aircraft in bad weather conditions. The courage and devotion to duty shown by Daly always set a fine example to the squadron. While serving with 37 Squadron in 1942, he was awarded the DFM and was commissioned in October 1943.

Daly joined 627 Squadron 2 February 1944 as a navigator from 1655 Mosquito Training Unit and by the beginning of June he had completed sixty-five and one-third operations. With 627 as part of his second tour, he completed seventeen and one-third operations. Daly navigated Mosquito DZ630 AZ-N with pilot Flying Officer S. B. Fletcher to attack the Gestapo HQ in Oslo, Norway, on 31 December 1944. During his tour with 627 Squadron, Daly was awarded a DFC and was featured in the *London Gazette* of 13 April 1945; his citation read:

> Since the award of the Distinguished Flying Medal in 1942, Flight Lieutenant Daly has continued to operate with outstanding success. In June 1944, while engaged on attacking Flying Bomb sites, fierce and accurate anti-aircraft fire was encountered. He

continued with his allotted task calm and unperturbed. He has taken a responsible part in highly successful attacks against the most strongly defended targets in Germany, and against enemy transport systems both before and after D Day. He has now completed his second tour of operations, continually displaying courage and devotion to duty of the highest order.

John Daly was promoted to flying officer on 12 November 1944, which was effective from 8 October 1944, and posted to 16 Operational Training Unit for instructor duties.

Flight Sergeant J. Marshallsay DFC and Flight Sergeant N. A. Ranshaw

Jim Marshallsay was a lovely man. I enjoyed our chats and I think extracts from Jim's letters best describe some of his exploits:

> I trained in Southern Rhodesia on Tigers and Oxfords but I do not know a lot about my flying here because on the way back to the UK in the 'Oransay' we were torpedoed by an Italian submarine – 'Archimedes' off the African coast. We took to the lifeboats and after eight days we were sighted by a Sunderland flying boat and picked up by HMS Brilliant the next day. I lost all my kit and my first log book.
>
> Back in the UK, I flew Oxfords for a while to get used to wartime flying conditions; no lights on the ground, rain, fog and snow. I was then posted to Mossies at Marham, where 139 and 105 were doing daylight low level. We returned from a 139 op from Dortmund on 16 October 1943 with a hung-up 500-pounder in DZ612. However, this thing fell off after we landed and had the ground crew in a bit of a panic. Earlier in the op we were coned by searchlights for 4 minutes and sustained superficial flak damage.

Marshallsay met Sergeant Nick Ranshaw at 1655 Mosquito Training Unit and were posted together as a crew to 139 Squadron on 17 July 1943 and would remain together for their entire Mosquito career. Their first trip was to Hamburg on 25 July in DZ348 but their incendiary hung up. On 14 September a trip to Berlin was cut short when Mosquito DZ597 iced up in cloud and the dramas continued on 20 October, when as they were about to leave for Berlin their aircraft, DZ423, swung on take-off causing the undercarriage to collapse. On 24 November, having completed eighteen operations with 139 Squadron, both men were posted to 627 Squadron at RAF Oakington, where they were to complete a further thirty-nine missions! On 6 June 1944 Marshallsay was appointed to a commissioned rank with effect from 2 May, with Ranshaw's appointment issued on 26 July.

Jim Marshallsay was often involved with operations consisting in a handful of Mosquitos attacking the big German cities, usually during the 'moon period' when it was much too bright for the heavies to operate. On other occasions it was possible to take off, climb into cloud, travel to Germany, bomb the target on ETA and return to base having seen nothing but the runway lights at base on take-off and landing. On clear nights with moonlight and stars the crews could expect to receive a hot reception from predicted flak and the massive searchlight cones, especially at 'Whitebait', the code name for Berlin. If one of the attacking Mosquitos had been caught by a cone of searchlight beams, most of the other crews would take the opportunity to take their chance to slip in, bomb and then get out of the area. When the crews had returned to base, the unfortunate crew that had been dazzled and blasted received little sympathy from the others, just a lot of banter and thanks for taking the flak off them.

> After the Creil trip in July 1944, the Orderly Room had spotted that I had done over 50 ops, so I was Screened, left the squadron and went to instruct on Wellingtons, which I had

never flown! It might be of interest to you to know that when I finished my tour, I was still only twenty-one years of age. When I left 627 I drew a new battledress from the stores. The wings came from my old battledress and I stuck them into my logbook, where they still are today. I got fed up with Wimpies, which were terrible great wallowing things, so I got moved to Training Command on Harvards and finished my RAF service as a Flight Commander at Cranwell.

From the total number of ops, you can see what an experienced squadron 627 was; they were a splendid lot – a first-class squadron – and it was an honour to be able fly with them. I have a photograph of Nick and I in front of our aircraft, DK313 Mk IV AZ-A. In the photo, taken in December 1943 at Oakington, we are joined by our ground crew, LACs Harding, Wookey and Kingscote. All three were conscientious 'Erks' and true friends. DK313 started out as GB-M on 105 Squadron on daylight low-level attacks. In 1942 it was hit by two Fw 190s and flew home with petrol swilling around the floor and belly landed. On 25 September 1942 DK313 became GB-V and attacked the Gestapo HQ in Oslo. One of the pursuing 190s crashed. After becoming AZ-A on 627 Squadron, Benny Goodman flew his first Mosquito op in it. It became 'my' aircraft and remained in daylight colours but some aircraft were repainted to night colours. Our aircraft has the stub exhausts instead of the 'saxophones' of the black aircraft; some pilots did not like the stubs because they caused glare and flash at night, especially when throttling back on landing, but they gave about fifteen to twenty mph extra speed and with them AZ-A went like a witch and was the fastest on the squadron. It is interesting to note that the black-painted aircraft (DZ477 was one of them) were not a success because we found that at night a black aircraft was easily seen whereas a light grey aircraft was almost invisible. Flying Officer Peck used AZ-A one night and taxied it into a pile of gravel, which did not amuse me at the time; the props threw the gravel all over the aircraft. Then we went on leave and a letter arrived at my home in Weymouth telling me that she had swung on take-off and poor DK313 had lost its undercarriage and was written off but I can see from your letter that DK313 was not scrapped as I thought.

Most pilots had quite a few flak hits, I had six marked down in my log book. These were quite heavy but I remember a lot more just 'peppering'. In Mosquito DZ388 we were one of five 139 Squadron Mosquitos on Bomber Command's only effort on 9 October 1943, a foggy night when Berlin was raided. In the Operational Record Book and in a book by a well-known author, it is stated that my helmet was grazed by quite a large piece of flak.

On 18 April 1944 at Woodhall Spa, I was a passenger on a Lancaster trip with 617 Squadron to observe their dive bombing and marking method. Our Wing Commander said this was a typical 617 Operation – French target, no flak, no fighters!

Jim and Nick were awarded a non-immediate DFC on 3 October 1944. A non-immediate DFC or DFM was awarded to non-commissioned officers and men for acts of gallantry while flying on active operations and in particular for sustained devotion to duty over a period of time, rather than for a single, conspicuous act. Such awards were usually given after the completion of an operational tour or at any point during it.

In the 1990s Jim had thoughts about the men he served with so long ago:

Rutherford and Stanbury, Saint-Smith and Heath, Parlato, Steer and Gale all crashed or shot down. Leo Devigne's navigator, Lewis, did over a 100 trips and stayed in after the war and was killed in a flying accident. Parlato's navigator, Dai Thomas, finished his tour but he did not know Sid Parlato was dead until he saw his headstone in Cambridge War Cemetery. Dai was very lucky when Guy Gibson borrowed one of our aircraft, KB267 AZ-E. Dai was down to fly with him as navigator but caught flu, so Gibson took Squadron Leader Warwick.

I remember the Australian Bill De Boos very well; he was the squadron navigation leader and a very pleasant chap and did some very good water colours of Wanganui flares descending over a target city. One day I flew him down to a Wimpy OTU in the West Country as he was going on leave. We caused quite a stir when we taxied up to the flying control in our black Mossie. Soon surrounded by training crews converting to Wellingtons, I dropped Bill off and after take-off climbed to 5,000ft, tore across the airfield after diving to pick up speed then turned on to course with a 90 degree steep turn at full throttle – a terrible line shoot.

'Shooting a line' was a sin in the RAF; it was boasting or showing off, often unintentionally. Most squadrons had a 'Line Book' in the mess and 'Lines' were recorded and the perpetrator had to buy drinks all round.

Marshallsay explained.

Some examples:

'It must be an easy trip tonight; I'm not on the Battle Order.'

'My bombs always blow out the markers and make it difficult for the others.'

'We don't like bombing too high in case we hit a Halifax.'

'The compass was giving a false reading, probably because of the metal of all the flak that had hit us!'

'My helmet colour has faded in the searchlights over the Ruhr.'

'Not Essen again, I'm sick of the place.' (the speaker had just completed one op)

'We could have walked home on the amount of flak we flew through.'

My favourite – 'If you enjoy adventure stories, you should read my log book!'

James Marshallsay was born on 31 October 1922, in Weymouth, Dorset. Following the war, he became a mathematics teacher. He died peacefully on 8 March 2004, aged 81 years in Wimborne, Dorset.

Pilot Officer J. G. Platts

Pilot Officer J. G. de Bretton Platts and his navigator, Flying Officer C. G. Thompson RCAF, were posted to 627 Squadron from 1655 Mosquito Training Unit on 11 February 1944 and flew twenty-seven missions together.

Benny Goodman remembers:

My good friend 'Googie' Platts was accused by the Base Commander, Air Cdre 'Bobby' 'Razor' Sharp, of marking the right aiming point but in the wrong marshalling yard! George Platts could not be termed lucky as after this wrong marshalling yard incident his run of bad luck continued when he took part in an operation against the Philips works at Eindhoven, Holland. Searching for the target flying in and out of cloud, a searchlight suddenly shone directly in his face. Startled, he pulled back on the control column and the Mosquito immediately roared up and over on to its back. 'Googie' now found the searchlights above his head, so in his own words, 'I half-rolled out and came home'.

He was not so lucky on 29 June when one of four crews in 627's first daylight marking sortie against a V-1 weapons site at Beauvoir in France. Shortly after releasing the markers from Mosquito IV DZ482 AZ-P, the crew set course for home in a stepped-down formation with another Mosquito behind and below him. After a short distance a V-1 'doodle bug' was launched from a ramp behind them and as it accelerated towards London it exploded directly below the Mosquitos. The crew of the second Mosquito, Alex Saint-Smith and Geoffrey Heath, were killed but Platts was able to gain sufficient altitude to allow them to bail out at 3,000ft. Platts was captured and became a prisoner of war at Stalag Luft 3, but George Thompson evaded capture and returned to England on 11 September 1944.

Flying Officer N. B. Rutherford AFC and Warrant Officer F. H. Stanbury

Norman Rutherford and Frederick Stanbury were posted to 627 Squadron from 1655 Mosquito Training Unit on 4 March 1944 and by the end of the month Rutherford was awarded an AFC. They flew together on thirty operations. On Monday, 18 September 1944 they took off in Mosquito IV DZ635 AZ-N at 1903hrs from Woodhall Spa for an attack on Bremerhaven. At 2210hrs, as they were in the process of marking the target, they were hit by flak and crashed at Schiffdorf on the eastern outskirts of Bremerhaven, with both of them killed. Initially the crew were buried in Geestemünde Civil Cemetery but were reinterred in a joint grave at Becklingen War Cemetery, Germany, on 19 August 1947. W/O Stanbury was appointed to commissioned rank on 26 June 1944, with effect from 4 March 1944.

Warrant Officer R. G. Boyden RCAF

When flying Avro Ansons as a staff pilot at Uplands in Ottawa, Canada, in 1942 Bob Boyden first saw a Mosquito. In wet conditions, with a low overcast cloud of about 500ft, Geoffrey de Havilland brought his Mosquito across the airfield in a slow rolling pass and then came back again, this time in a slow roll on one engine with the other feathered; it was an impressive sight.

Boyden had a considerable amount of flying time on the Anson, which included a lot of night flying on navigational trips to train navigators, so on his posting to England he increased his experience on Oxford trainers and Wellingtons and thought he was destined to fly Halifaxes or Lancasters. Classified as a 'crewless pilot', Boyden was becoming frustrated at waiting to pick up a crew for posting to a bomber squadron and eventually he was posted to 30 Operational Training Unit at RAF Seighford in Staffordshire.

One afternoon during a telephone conversation, Boyden was asked if he had been spoken to about flying Mosquitos and his negative answer saw him posted the following morning to 1655 Mosquito Training Unit at RAF Marham. An interview with a well-decorated, high-ranking officer left Boyden in no doubt that he would be allowed only one failure or prang; one more would see his career on Mosquitos terminated. As a result of a conversation with a sergeant navigator who had just completed a tour on Lancasters, Boyden teamed up with Ralph Fenwick despite the fact that Boyden had not yet completed a tour.

Bob and Ralph were posted from 1655 Mosquito Training Unit to 627 Squadron on 2 March 1944 and on the 13th they took DZ462 AZ:N to Frankfurt, delivering four 500lb bombs from 28,000ft. Boyden was promoted to flying officer on 31 December effective from 2 November 1944. Bob Boyden was awarded an immediate DFC on 19 January 1945. Bob and Ralph went on to fly more than thirty operations together before Bob was posted to RCAF 'R' Dept. for repatriation on 16 February 1945.

Flight Lieutenant Ian Hanlon DFC RNZAF

Ian Hanlon was born in Hawkes Bay, Napier, New Zealand, on 8 January 1917. After six years as a cadet and a member of the Wellington West Coast Regiment, Hanlon was mobilised on 23 November 1940 and commenced duty at the Ground Training School at Levin in November 1940; he was promoted to LAC airman pilot two months later. Hanlon was spent three months at the Elementary Flying Training School at Harewood before embarking for Canada for a seven-month spell of pilot training courses. Hanlon was awarded his pilot flying badge on 9 September 1941 and was granted the temporary commission with rank of pilot officer the following day. Training completed, Hanlon left Canada on 20 June 1941 and reached England on 2 July 1941, where he attended more advanced courses, receiving promotions in the process.

Flying Officer Hanlon became an operational pilot with 51 Squadron in 4 Group from September 1941, flying Whitley bombers for six months before being posted to 24 Operational Training Unit at RAF Honeybourne as an instructor with the rank of squadron leader to train Whitley crews. During this time Hanlon and his fiancée, Dorothy Stokes, were married on 6 October 1943 at Weston Sub Edge Parish Church in Gloucestershire. They later had a son, Anthony Noel, born in January 1945.

In December 1943 Hanlon relinquished his rank and was posted to 1655 Mosquito Training Unit, followed by the elite 627 Squadron. Just over two weeks later, on 8 January 1944, his twenty-seventh birthday, Hanlon and his navigator Flying Officer Francis Evans DFM took off at 1821hrs in Mosquito W4072 AZ:Q bound for Frankfurt. W4072 was a special aircraft: it was one of only a handful of true Mk IV series one Mosquito bomber conversions ever built and it took part in the first Mosquito bombing raid to Germany on 31 May 1942. Hanlon and Evans were an experienced crew and having completed their mission on the return journey at 2045hrs the starboard engine lost power and they started to lose altitude. Hanlon tried to get to Bradwell but had to ditch the aircraft in the sea off East Mersea, Essex. Hanlon escaped with minor injuries but was admitted to the Military Hospital, Colchester, on 9 January, where he stayed until being discharged on the 24th. Sadly, Flying Officer Evans drowned, with his body washed ashore at Bradwell Bay two days later. The squadron commander, officers, non-commissioned officers and airmen attended Evans' funeral on the 10th at the RAF Regional Cemetery in Cambridge.

Hanlon was mentioned in despatches on 8 June 1944 'in recognition of distinguished service and devotion to duty with 627 Squadron'.

He was posted to 1690 Bomber Defence Training Flight in December 1944 flying Hurricanes on fighter affiliation exercises with new bomber crews. On 10 February 1945, Hanlon took off at 1016hrs from RAF Metheringham in Hurricane IIc PZ744 for an exercise with Lancaster PB146 from 189 Squadron.

At 1101hrs Hanlon formatted on the Lancaster to indicate the exercise had ended owing to unserviceable radio equipment. Believing that the Lancaster pilot was aware that the exercise was over, Hanlon passed beneath the bomber and started to bank to starboard. The Hurricane was struck by the Lancaster, which appears to have followed him in the turn. This forced Hanlon to vacate the aircraft over Seacroft and parachute to a safe but heavy landing. The bomber landed safely but sadly the navigator, Sergeant W. T. Gothard, was killed in the collision. Hanlon was injured and was admitted to RAF Hospital, Rauceby, where it was established that Hanlon had sustained a compression fractures of his vertebrae; Hanlon was in a body plaster for ten weeks. One month later, former 627 colleague Sid Parlato and the crew of another Lancaster suffered an almost identical incident, with disastrous consequences. The physical injuries to Hanlon prompted an investigation by a medical board on 13 September 1945. It concluded that Hanlon had recovered from his injuries and declared him fit for full flying and ground duties in New Zealand and overseas and for civil occupation.

On 23 March 1945, Ian Hanlon was awarded the DFC; the citation reading:

> This officer has completed numerous operations against the enemy, in the course of which he has invariably displayed the utmost fortitude, courage and devotion to duty. Served with 627 Squadron from December 1943 to December 1944, being injured on 8th January 1944 when his aircraft crashed at sea after an engine failure whilst returning from a raid on Frankfurt. He was a Member of the 'Caterpillar Club' [Airmen saved by using a parachute]. On 10th February 1945, whilst flying a Hurricane over England, he was involved in a collision. He landed heavily by parachute and suffered back injuries.

Hanlon, with thirty-three operations with 627 Squadron and over 1,300 hours of flying covering a service period of five years, was repatriated from the UK, arriving in New Zealand on 25 July 1945. He was transferred to reserve class in November that year. Hanlon died at home in Russell on 11 August 1980.

Wing Commander George William Curry DSO and Bar, DFC

George Curry worked for an insurance company before joining the RAF and became a pilot as the Second World War started. Curry served as a pilot officer with 75 Squadron RNZAF from January to July 1941, flying Wellingtons from RAF Feltwell, and was promoted to acting squadron leader flying Lancasters with 57 Squadron in May 1943, also at Feltwell. Curry received a DFC with 75 Squadron on 23 September 1941 and another (bar) with 57 Squadron on 14 May 1943, the citation stating:

> Squadron Leader Curry has taken part in numerous sorties. On February 1 1943 he became deputy flight commander, in which capacity he has been of the greatest assistance to his squadron commander. Squadron Leader Curry participated in the daylight raid on Milan and two raids on Berlin and always pressed home his attacks with the greatest determination and courage.

On 3 June 1944 Curry took command of 627 Squadron, after which the records indicate that his ranks changed from time to time – a squadron leader as of 3 September 1944, then acting wing commander but left at the lower rank of squadron leader. Curry took part and often led at least twenty-seven operations and received two awards during his service with 627 Squadron. His first DSO on 17 October 1944 stated:

> Since assuming command of his squadron, Wing Commander Curry has taken part in a number of operations against a variety of enemy targets. His great determination and capable leadership have resulted in many successful operations. On several occasions his aircraft has been damaged by anti-aircraft

fire. The exceptional energy and initiative which this officer has displayed, together with his outstanding keenness and cheerful personality, have had a most marked effect upon the morale and efficiency of his squadron. He has set a worthy example.

On 27 February 1945 Curry's bar to his DSO citation stated:

Wing Commander Curry has completed a second tour of operational duty during which he has completed many notable sorties. On one occasion he took part in an attack which resulted in the breaching of the Dortmund-Ems Canal. On another occasion, Wing Commander Curry led the squadron on a target far into enemy territory. Whilst over the target considerable anti-aircraft fire was encountered. Every aircraft was hit. Nevertheless, the operation was completed successfully. Munchen-Gladbach, Stuttgart, Brunswick and Bremerhaven have been among the various targets Wing Commander Curry has attacked. This gallant and resourceful squadron commander has set a splendid example to all.

Curry's second DSO was received as a bar on the ribbon of the first DSO.

After the war Curry remained in the RAF and flew Venom jets and would regularly take part in the Battle of Britain celebrations on 18 September. However, during the 1948 celebration build-up at RAF Coningsby, Curry crashed a 139 Squadron Mosquito T3 VA887 while attempting a low slow roll. The aircraft lost height when inverted and then flicked shortly before striking the ground, killing Curry and his colleague, Corporal Herbert Davies. A Board of Inquiry concluded that the pilot was responsible for the aircraft being involved in aerobatic manoeuvres below the briefed 'safe' height and noted this was the third fatal Mosquito crash to occur on that day. The entire squadron attended both funerals, Davies' at Boston on 22 September and Curry's at Coningsby on the 23rd.

Benny Goodman remembers:

> I met George at the Empire Flying School, RAF Hullavington in 1947 when we were both Squadron Leaders, he was a student on the All Weather Flying Course. We had several long chats about the good old days. George went off to a flying job in India and the next thing I heard about him was that he had killed himself while flying a Mosquito during the Battle of Britain celebrations at Coningsby in 1948. Apparently, he rolled the Mossie at low level while flying past the front of the crowd and crashed inverted; pilot error, of course. Many pilots have done exactly this before – and will do so again, I have no doubt.

Squadron Leader R. G. Churcher DSO, LVO (1954), DFC and Bar

Ronald George Churcher was born on 9 May 1922 in Worthing and attended the local high school. He left school in July 1938 to become a solicitor's clerk but joined the RAF in 1940 as a RAFVR pilot officer and started pilot training. The following year he joined 106 Squadron, which was still equipped with the pre-war Handley Page Hampden bomber, and conducted minelaying sorties over the Baltic and bombing missions in the Ruhr. The squadron was then re-equipped with the underperforming Avro Manchester when in the spring of 1942 Guy Gibson arrived to command the squadron, which continued to attack targets across Germany. On 30 May 1942 Churcher and his Manchester crew took part in the first 1,000-bomber raid on Cologne, followed two nights later by a second of the three such sorties, this time to Essen.

After thirty operations, including a daring daylight raid on Danzig, now Gdańsk, in Poland, in the newly supplied Lancaster, Churcher was rested, with Gibson recommending him for the DFC for his skill, great ability and dash.

After a period as a bombing instructor, in April 1943 Churcher became the flight commander of a new Lancaster squadron, 619, and joined the Battle of the Ruhr with two attacks against Hamburg, including the devastating 'firestorm' raids. With attention focused on the German capital, on 23 August 1943 he flew in the raid that began the long and bitter Battle of Berlin and would be the first of six visits he would make to the 'Big City'. After another twenty-one operations, he was again rested and awarded a bar to his DFC for his exceptional skill and fine courage.

Churcher had completed two operational tours and was not required to fly a third, so was posted to Group HQ Operations Staff at Morton Hall. However, the lure of the Mosquito was too much for him to resist, so in July 1944 he converted to the Mosquito and spent a short time in the air with Flying Officer Rutherford to become familiar with the aircraft. He joined 627 Squadron at Woodhall Spa as a flight commander, flying target-marking roles against objectives in northern France in support of the Normandy landings. From time to time Churcher was appointed deputy controller for key targets in Germany and on the night of 19 September 1944 Mönchengladbach and the city's borough of Rheydt were the targets. It came as a surprise to the crews of 627 Squadron to learn that Guy Gibson VC had been appointed controller with Churcher his deputy; it was known that Gibson was not in regular flying practice.

Churcher had identified the target and had started his dive but was forced to break off his attack when his night vision was destroyed by the sudden glare caused by parts breaking off his aircraft's port engine. Confusion followed, which was not helped by Gibson's lack of experience in this type of attack, and as Churcher regained control and was about to place his markers, Gibson countermanded his orders and changed his instructions again. However, the raid was tailing off, with only a small number of Lancasters bombing Churcher's markers, when Gibson was heard to tell the crews to beat it for home. Gibson and his navigator, Squadron Leader James Warwick, crashed in the Netherlands on their way back.

On 13 December 1944 Churcher flew his seventy-fifth and final mission as the leader of a force that attacked German cruisers in Oslo Fjord; he added a DSO to his two DFCs.

At only twenty-two, on 13 April 1945 Churcher was awarded a DSO after an unaided raid by 5 Group on 23 March that drew high praise from the chief of the Allied 21st Army Group, Field Marshal Montgomery. Monty's advancing troops were poised to cross the Rhine as Nazi Germany crumbled and the field marshal recorded that the bombing of Wesel the previous night had been a masterpiece and was a decisive factor in making possible his ground forces' entry into the town before midnight.

Following the war, Churcher remained in the RAF and was posted to RAF Filton for secondment to BOAC, flying long-range routes, before training as a flying instructor. In December 1950 he was appointed to the King's Flight, flying the Viking and for the next three years he was entrusted with the safekeeping of Winston Churchill and Princess Margaret. After the death of George VI in 1952, when the King's Flight became the Queen's, he piloted the Queen and the Duke of Edinburgh. He flew them in Vickers Vikings and received the Queen's personal honour, membership of the Royal Victorian Order. The Royals' names are recorded in one of his flying log books, underlined in red.

Churcher flew the first British jet-powered fighter, the Gloster Meteor, then served in Singapore commanding 216 Squadron. He flew the Comet on long-range transport routes to the Far East,

Middle East and the USA until he took charge of administration at RAF Abingdon, one of the service's largest transport bases, in 1966. He was promoted to group captain when he was appointed station commander of RAF Henlow, responsible for the RAF Officer Cadet Training Unit, from 1975 to 1977. Churcher then retired from the RAF and served as air attaché in Rome.

Churcher spent ten years fundraising for schools and completed a humanities degree with the Open University. He was, in addition to his flying skills, a superb woodworker. Churcher was reluctant to apply for his Bomber Command clasp, which to some was considered as less than a medal, but was persuaded to by his wife Lyn. When it failed to arrive, she appealed to the Prime Minister, David Cameron. Downing Street replied to her letter and the clasp arrived in July 2013. Ronnie Churcher died on 25 October 2013, aged 91.

Flight Sergeant Sidney Frederick Parlato DFC RNZAF

Sid Parlato was born on 30 January 1911 in Upper Hutt, New Zealand, and post education became a diesel excavator driver/mechanic with New Zealand Railways in Taumarunui. In April 1939 he became a pilot at Middle Districts Aero Club before applying to join the RNZAF in July 1941. The Medical Board considered Parlato to be in good general health with a strong physique and mentally bright, so it accepted him for the Levin Initial Training Wing as airman pilot on 19 October 1941. Parlato attended the Elementary Flying Training School in November 1941, making his first solo flight on 5 December.

Parlato had his fair share of visits to the medical centre during service with the RNZAF and the RAF, suffering conditions such as a congested throat and acute appendicitis that was at first attributed to an overindulgence in under-ripe fruit the day before. However, he had an appendectomy in January 1942 at Christchurch Hospital, which put him out of action for one month. Parlato suffered bouts of tonsillitis, measles, rubella and acute pharyngitis but he battled on.

In April 1942, Parlato joined 1 Service Flying Training School at Wigram, flying the twin-engine Oxford both in daylight and at night. It was with this unit that Parlato applied for permission to get married but had to wait five days before learning that permission had been granted for him to marry Phyllis May Wilson. He was awarded his pilot's badge in June and was given the rank of sergeant on 5 September 1942. Eleven days later, Parlato was attached to the RAF and embarked for the UK the following day. He arrived at 3 Personnel Reception Centre in Bournemouth on 19 November and waited until January for a posting to 9 Elementary Flying Training School in Ansty, Warwickshire. Further posts with 3 (Pilots) Advanced Flying Unit in February and 1531 Beam Approach Training Flight in March led him to 1655 Mosquito Conversion Unit in May 1943. His first flight there was on 7 July.

Training with 1655 Mosquito Training Unit completed, Parlato was posted to 139 Squadron on 30 August 1943 and had to attend a mandatory two-day navigation course at the NTU at Upwood before his first operation. This was a diversionary raid on Oldenburg on 22 September 1943 in DZ370 with his navigator, Sergeant D. D. Thomas. The squadron record says: 'Sergeant Parlato was not content with the small fires at Oldenburg and went on to bomb Hamburg with the main force. It was his first trip.' He landed about an hour after his colleagues!

Parlato, along with his usual navigator David Thomas, known to his colleagues as Dai, attacked Hamborn on 26 September 1943 in Mosquito DZ370 but they were hit by flak at 2330 hrs, two minutes before bombing. Parlato was hit by shrapnel just above the left knee and two minutes later the aircraft was hit again in the engine nacelle but the engine kept running and with a damaged compass they returned to base using the bombsite compass. Parlato was admitted to the station sick quarters with a jagged wound above the patella and the shrapnel still embedded but it required more specialised treatment, so he was transferred to the RAF hospital in Ely. An RAF surgeon, Wing Commander Morley, removed the ¾in shell fragment and closed the wound. Parlato was discharged 6 October and sent on seven days sick leave and one month of convalescence. Apparently, Parlato recorded the incident in his logbook: 'Moderate flak. Aircraft hit including self.' During this time Parlato was promoted to temporary F/S but he and Thomas did not fly on operations until 22 October. They then carried out eight operational flights, on targets including Hanover, Düsseldorf, Hamborn, Frankfurt, Berlin (twice), Cologne and Bonn in Germany.

Parlato and Thomas were posted to 627 Squadron at Oakington in November 1943 and carried out a further forty-eight operational flights over France, Belgium and Germany, bringing his total to fifty-six. Thomas described one of their raids where their marking was not accurate enough and they were told to withdraw by the controller as the heavies were coming in. Suddenly, Parlato pushed the Mosquito's nose down and dived between two factory chimneys and planted the target indicators on the roof, a perfect mark. It is believed that Thomas nearly had a heart attack there and then. Parlato was awarded a DFC and Thomas received a 'mention in despatches', which warranted the individual being included in an official account written by a superior officer that was then sent to the War Office. This completed Parlato's first operational tour and in September 1944 he was awarded the DFC. The citation reads:

> Flying Officer Parlato has completed many successful operations during which he has displayed high skill, fortitude and devotion to duty.

At the end of his tour Parlato was posted to fighter affiliation duties on Hurricanes with 1690 Bomber Training Flight based at RAF Metheringham, Lincolnshire. Having amassed 172 hours on Hurricanes, Parlato took off in Mk IIC PZ740 at about 20.43hrs on 11 March 1945 for a routine exercise with Lancaster I LM130 from 463 Squadron. The Lancaster, named 'Nick, the Nazi Neutralizer', was a veteran of more than sixty raids and featured a horned laughing devil painted on its nose with a clawed right index finger pointing to the letter 'N' and its mission tally symbols painted alongside. Approximately fifteen minutes later, Parlato's Hurricane collided with the Lancaster, flown by P/O H. Orchard, RAAF. Both aircraft crashed just south of the airfield at 'the Asholt Field' at Blankney Village, some 9 miles north of Sleaford in Lincolnshire. Parlato and the seven men on board the Lancaster perished in the crash.

How ironic it was that Parlato, an incredibly experienced combat aviator with 837 flying hours in his logbook, should fall victim to an accidental training exercise accident. As mentioned earlier, one month prior to Parlato's accident 627 Squadron colleague Ian Hanlon, also a New Zealander, was seriously injured in an identical incident when his Hurricane collided with a Lancaster in the same airspace. Possibly prompted by the two training incidents, the RNZAF HQ Air Department conducted a Court of Enquiry on 21 August 1945 with the following extracted conclusions:

A. 1. On 11 March 1945, Flying Officer Orchard in Lancaster LM130 and Flying Officer Parlato in Hurricane PZ740 were detailed to carry out a night fighter affiliation exercise. This consisted of making visual contact over Metheringham Airfield at a specific time and height using Transmitter/Receiver 1196. When communication had been established the aircraft were to change to VHF and set course on the first leg across country and when well clear of the Metheringham circuit the Lancaster was to fly straight and level whilst the fighter made attacks from below, astern and from the quarters. The Lancaster should have burned its navigation and downward identification lights and the fighter its navigation lights.

2. The Lancaster called up over Metheringham, whereupon the fighter took off to join it. Flying Officer Parlato was heard to call the Lancaster requesting it to switch on its lights or to switch them on and off. Evidence is conflicting as to the exact words of the pilot and moreover there is no written log to confirm exactly what he did say. Shortly afterwards Flying Officer Parlato said that he was changing from TR.1196 to VHF and this was acknowledged by the bomber. 22 minutes after the fighter took off the two aircraft collided in mid-air. There were no eye witnesses of the collision. The wreckage fell within 5 miles of Metheringham Airfield indicating that the two aircraft had not started the actual affiliation. Examination of the wreckage revealed that the Hurricane struck the Lancaster amidships on the starboard side having slid along the top of its starboard main plane.

3. At the time of the accident it was a dark starlit night with no cloud and at the height the two aircraft were flying visibility was good.

B. 1. The accident resulted from a mid-air collision at night and was evidently due to either (i) failure of Flying Officer Orchard to burn correct lights or (ii) the failure of the Lancaster crew and the pilot of the Hurricane to keep sufficiently good lookout whilst making visual contact prior to the commencement of the affiliation exercise.

C. 1. Following this and other mid-air collisions during fighter affiliation the standard instructions in 5 Group for day and night affiliation exercises were improved and in the view of the detail covered in their present form no recommendations are considered necessary.

During my correspondence and conversions with Parlato's fellow fliers it puzzled me why some of his contemporaries referred to him as 'Chip'. I received an answer in a letter on 5 March 1990. Benny Goodman provided the answer: 'You asked why "Chip" Parlato was so named and what happened to him. The name was particularly apt for him as it derived from the small sausage, the chipolata. Chip was a little man (standing 5ft 4in). "Built for Mosquito", as we used to say.'

Parlato, who died aged thirty-four, is buried at the RAF Regional Plot, Borough Cemetery, Cambridge, along with some of the Lancaster crew lost the same day.

Jack 'Benny' Goodman DFC and Bar AFC

Born in January 1921, Goodman began his flying career in 1939 at the age of eighteen when he was transferred from 5 (Founder) Squadron of the Air Defence cadet Corp in Northampton to the Royal Air Force Volunteer Reserve for pilot training. Goodman was the first Northampton squadron cadet to be transferred and it was to lead to a thirty-seven-year career with the RAF. When war broke out in September 1939 he had flown thirty-three hours in the Tiger Moth and thought himself to be a red-hot pilot, but looking back he realised he was in fact hopelessly inexperienced and probably downright dangerous.

Goodman attended 2 Training School on the Blackburn B2, a side-by-side trainer that looked like a pregnant Tiger Moth with a shape that produced considerable drag, resulting in inferior performance compared to the Tiger Moth.

At the beginning of March 1940, Goodman was sent to Hullavington near Chippenham in Wiltshire for further training and he had no doubt that he would be sent to a Hurricane of Spitfire squadron. He was confident that the interview with a small selection board was sympathetic to his plea for fighter pilot training. Having thought he had clinched the deal, the squadron leader presiding became hostile when Goodman said that he didn't like the idea of bombing women and children. The squadron leader bristled and told him in no uncertain terms that the RAF did not go into that sort of thing and promptly sent him to join the Anson Flight to find out what bomber training was all about.

After receiving the coveted flying badge, he converted to Wellingtons and was posted to 37 Squadron at Feltwell, beginning his seven-year journey with Bomber Command. His first operation was on 26 August 1940. In November he transferred to 99 Squadron at Newmarket, where he completed a total of twenty-eight sorties on Wellington Mk 1c aircraft. Six months later, as a veteran having attacked targets in Germany and France throughout the winter, he considered the weather as being as great a hazard as the enemy. The following January, Goodman and his crew flew a Wellington from Stradishall to Benghazi in Libya in a flight time of eleven hours thirty minutes. With 37 Squadron at Shallufa in Egypt, Benny took part in eight bombing raids and also flew sorties over the desert and in the battles of Greece and Crete. He remained in the Middle East until September 1941.

Towards the end of 1941, Goodman was sent on so-called 'rest' to 15 Operational Training Unit at Harwell, where he flew Wellingtons with new crews on cross-countries for the next two years. In May 1942 Goodman was commissioned a few days before he took part in the first 1,000 bomber raids to Cologne and Essen, flying training Wellingtons. He told me:

> From time to time Operational Training Unit crews were used to make up the weight of the attack, usually manned by instructors plus members of their student crews. My fortieth trip on Wimpys was to Essen, one of the most feared targets, but I knew the score pretty well. It was vital not to get caught in a searchlight cone and with the heavy flak being directed at the Lancasters and Halifaxes up at 18,000ft, I thought I was OK. We were at 10,000ft, the maximum altitude of which my clapped out Operational Training Unit Wimpy was capable of, when we were picked up by a searchlight and immediately about twenty more flashed on to us. I knew that if I did not react at once the Germans would plaster the apex of the cone with heavy flak and HD942 would be blown to pieces. We used to reckon this would happen after about seven seconds so there was only one thing to do, stand HD942 on her nose and dive like hell with flak bursting just behind us all the way down from 10,000ft to ground level, and we came out over the Rhine at rooftop level. Nothing vital was hit but the Wimpy had something like 100 holes of various sizes in her; we were bloody lucky. HD942 carried us gallantly to Essen and back that night and I have never forgotten her. Some idiot crashed her a few days later; I still have one of its exhaust stubs in my possession and I treasure it. According to statistics, I should have been killed five times!
>
> You ask if you received a direct hit it meant 'curtains', no matter what aircraft you were flying. A near miss could also be fatal, depending on what was hit. The Lancaster, Halifax and Wellington could take a lot of battle damage. The Wellington was immensely strong. One night a 627 Squadron Mosquito

inadvertently struck a balloon cable as he came home through the balloons at Harwich. The pilot was unaware of this, merely feeling 'a bit of a bump' as he crossed the coast as the aircraft became slightly one wing low. The cable had struck just outboard of the starboard prop and had sliced through the leading edge of the wing and had scraped along to the main spar, taking off the leading edge to the wingtip. Incredible? We thought so too, but the Mossie was like that.

By mid-1943 the instructors of 15 OTU who had completed tours of operations earlier in the war were to return to squadrons for a second tour of operational duty. Veteran pilots, navigators, wireless operators and air gunners left for Lancaster and Halifax squadrons but only a very small number of pilots and navigators went to Mosquito squadrons. Goodman:

> Two of my closest friends at 15 Operational Training Unit had responded to the splendid character Hamish Mahaddie, or the '8 Group Body Snatcher' as he was known, who toured around Bomber Command attracting the right type of aircrew members into the Pathfinder Force. I was still considering the possibilities until an abrupt signal arrived posting me to 1655 Mosquito Training Unit at Marham in Norfolk, so my mind was made up for me; I was to join that elite force whether I liked it or not.

Goodman arrived at Marham in mid-September 1943, with 1,300 pilot hours in his flying log book:

> At that time, Marham had three Mosquito units, 105 and 109 Squadrons and 1655 Mosquito Training Unit, and it was quickly made clear to all the new arrivals at 1655 Mosquito

Training Unit that they were not to interest themselves in what the two squadrons were doing. A wall of secrecy surrounded them. It is now generally known that 105 and 109 Squadrons were high-level precision markers equipped with a superb bombing aid Oboe. So secret was Oboe no one was allowed even to mention its name in the Officers' Mess.

Goodman remembers that his first flight in a dual-control Mosquito took place on 23 September with Flying Officer Herbert as the instructor:

We were in the air for about one hour doing local familiarisation, single-engine flying and circuits and landings. It was a flight I shall never forget. The Mosquito was small, powerful and incredibly fast and instantly responsive to the slightest movement of the controls. Flying the Wellington had been a push and pull affair; by contrast the Mosquito had to be tickled. As the Flight Commander said, 'Treat her like your best girlfriend – gently'. My flying log book (RAF Form 414 – all service documents have form numbers!) reveals that I did three hours of dual instruction before going solo in Mosquito Mk III HJ971 on 25 September 1943. My first solo trip lasted fifty minutes and was a sheer joy, all 1,200 horses in the Merlin on each side neighing with delight – or so it seemed to me. Could there be anything more perfect than this?

All pilots posted to 8 Group Mosquitos had to complete a laid-down syllabus of thirty hours' flying at 1655 Mosquito Training Unit, with ten in the dual and twenty in the bomber flight, the latter complete with a navigator. No pilot was allowed to touch the controls of a Mosquito until he had 1,000 hours as first pilot under his belt and he had to be selected to fly the type. Having completed their prescribed time in Dual Flight, the pilots reported to the Bomber Flight and joined the navigators for the system of crewing up. Goodman:

> We assembled in the Crew Room and were told to sort ourselves out, which we did this fairly quickly as I soon found myself talking to a tall, rather quiet Flying Officer named John Hickox. He told me that he had done his first tour of ops on Wimpys and that he had been shot down and walked back through the desert. He did not relish the thought of being shot down in a Mosquito and walking back from Germany. I assured him that his thoughts accorded closely with mine so we shook hands and became a Mosquito crew.

Goodman and Bill Hickox were instructed in the technique of baling out of a Mosquito:

> We gathered round a Mk IV Mosquito for a drill in abandoning the aircraft. Squadron Leader Cairns, the Chief Ground Instructor, explained that if we were hit at high level we had about forty-five seconds in which to get out. We had to disconnect our oxygen tubes and radio intercom plugs, release our seat belts, switch off our engines if time permitted, jettison the bottom hatch and bail out. This sounds straightforward and indeed it was; but the Mosquito was a very small aircraft and the pilot and navigator were meant to climb in, strap in and stay put. When Bill and I tried to do it the first time there was an unholy mix-up and after forty-five seconds the Chief Ground Instructor announced 'you're dead'. The difficulty about getting out of a Mosquito wearing parachutes was that the navigator had to clip on his chest parachute and then manoeuvre his way through the main hatch in the floor of the aircraft. This hatch was scarcely large enough to get through

without a 'chute. It was suggested that the pilot should 'assist' a struggling navigator with a 'boot in the back' but if the navigator got out safely, the pilot was supposed to follow him wearing the pilot-type parachute attached to his backside. Bill and I decided that bailing out was a dangerous business and we would stay with the aircraft if humanly possible. I resolved that if all failed and we had to get out in a hurry I would wait until Bill was clear and then go out through the top hatch, which was the standard drill for the pilot seated in the left hand seat of a dual Mosquito. Fortunately our agreed plan was never put to the test, but other crews had to jump out over Germany and did so successfully.

Their course ended during October 1943 after completing four cross-country exercises by day and two by night. Crews were now allocated to squadrons, a small number to 105 and 109 but the majority went to 139 Squadron at Wyton, which was large enough to have three flights. Benny and Bill were posted to 139 Squadron on 24 October, with their first operational sortie on 3 November 1943. The target, Cologne, was marked by the Oboe-equipped Mosquitos from 105 and 109 Squadrons. Goodman:

> Our first operational take-off in DK313 carrying four 500lb HE bombs was only marginally longer than our take-offs from Marham in Mosquitos without bombs. The acceleration was rapid and in next to no time we were at the unstick speed of around 100 knots and climbing smoothly away. We climbed rapidly to 28,000ft, levelled out and settled down to an economical cruising speed of around 250 knots (true air speed). As we neared Cologne the first of the Oboe-aimed target indicators began to cascade down ahead of us. Bill took

his place at the bombing panel and began the time-honoured verbal direction 'Left, left ... Steady ...' and ultimately, 'bombs gone'. We then turned for home for more bacon and eggs and bed. The post-flight interrogation was much the same as any operational Squadron in Bomber Command, with the important exception that 139's full title was 139 (Jamaica) Squadron and we were all offered a tot of rum on return from every operational sortie. When I was on 139 we had with us a Jamaican named Ulric Cross, a Flying Officer navigator, who was highly efficient and well liked. He later became the Lord Chief Justice of Jamaica.

During the third week of November it was suddenly announced in the crew room that a new Mosquito squadron was to be formed at Oakington, near Cambridge. 'C' Flight of 139 Squadron would become the nucleus of the new 627 Squadron, so Benny, Bill and DZ615 prepared to move to their new station and on 24 November 1943 it became operational with immediate effect. Their first trip that very night was to Berlin.

The following extracts describe this period on an extremely busy squadron and create the picture of the gruelling slog of operations, night after night. Benny:

> It is true to say that once German fighters had found the bomber stream they did not let go and on occasions Bill and I would have a grandstand view from 25,000ft of flares being dropped by Ju 88s over the Main Force and then lines of tracer bullets followed by fires and explosions in the sky as Lancasters and Halifaxes went down. We know only too well that we were engaged in a battle of attrition, as was the USAAF with its Flying Fortresses, and the outcome could be defeat for the bombers ...

During the Battle of Berlin we lost Squadron Leader 'Dinger' Bell, our flight commander, but his navigator Flying Officer Battle managed to bail out and became a prisoner of war at Stalag Luft 3, Sagan, near Leipzig. Bill and I wondered if our luck was running out as, when on the way home from the 'Big City', the oil pressure on the starboard engine suddenly began to drop and the oil and coolant temps increased. Eventually, the readings reached their permitted limits and I throttled back the engine and feathered the propeller. We were now in trouble as we had to lose height and were eventually flying along at the same height and a speed comparable to that of our heavy bombers but with no means of defending ourselves if attacked. Since the only generator on the Mosquito was on the starboard engine, we had to turn off all our internal lights, the GEE box and our VHF set. So on we went through the darkness with our fingers and toes firmly crossed and feeling very tense. Eventually, as we crossed the Dutch coast, Bill switched on the GEE set and quickly plotted a fix. So far so good, so we turned the GEE box off and called up the 'Guardian Angels' on Channel C, the distress frequency. At once a reassuring voice asked me to transmit a little longer until she gave us a course to steer and shortly afterwards she said 'friends are with you'. Bill and I took a good look round and spotted a Beaufighter, which stayed with us until we reached the English coast. We got down fairly expertly, which drew from the imperturbable Mr Hickox the comment 'good show'; praise indeed …

Shortly after this there was another indication that Lady Luck was still on our side as we were briefed for yet another trip to Berlin but during the afternoon the raid was cancelled and a short-range attack on a Ruhr target was substituted. This all-Mosquito affair was led by 105 and 109, so our Commanding

Officer, Wing Commander Roy Elliott, decided that this was a good opportunity for new crews to have a go, so Bill and I were stood down. We had air tested the aircraft that morning and were satisfied that it was serviceable in all respects, yet as the Mosquitos lifted off at night and entered the area of blackness just beyond the upwind end of the flare path both engines failed and there came the dreadful sound of a crash as the aircraft hit the ground. Both crew members were killed. Would this have happened if Bill and I were on board? We shall never know.

This aircraft was likely to have been DZ616 AZ:G, crewed by Flying Officer Fahey and Flying Officer Hicks, which was lost two minutes after taking off at 0128hrs on Wednesday, 5 January. Goodman and Hickox did not fly that night and at that time this aircraft was allocated the code AZ:G. DZ484 was taken on charge by 627 Squadron in December 1943 and was presumably allocated the AZ:G code following the loss of DZ616. Goodman continues:

After this tragedy I was allocated Mosquito DZ484 'G' George, which I flew most of the time until my tour ended in June 1944. I was then posted back to 1655 Mosquito Training Unit as a flying instructor and 'G' George came too, joining the bomber flight. Eventually 'G' was retired to a Maintenance Unit and after the war was broken up and struck off charge. From time to time I flew other Mosquitos, including the famous DZ353, photos of which have featured in every book written about Mosquitos. I flew it twice, each time to Berlin, on my fifty-ninth and sixtieth sorties as an operational pilot. This aircraft was eventually lost at Rennes marshalling yards on 8 June 1944, and our deputy flight commander and his navigator (Harry Steere and Ken Gale) were killed. The aircrews did not sit around waiting for the chop; nothing could be further from the truth. When stood down we often had an uproarious time. The station commander at Oakington, a fierce group captain, lived in a suite of rooms at one end of the officers' mess and would retire to his suite at night and took no further notice of the high jinks that took place in the bar. One night a group of inebriated 7 Squadron 'toughs' decided to make the station commander a present of an ancient Austin 7, which stood outside the mess. They picked it up and carried it carefully along the long corridor, negotiating two sharp turns, and deposited it outside the commanding officer's door, almost blocking the corridor. Next day all hell was let loose and a small army of airmen took a long time to remove the offending car. Nos 7 and 627 Squadron crews were paraded by their respective commanding officers and the riot act was read, but no real attempt was made to track down the culprits. This was a good thing and raised the station commander in our estimation.

The deep rips into Germany continued. Goodman:

The flexibility and superiority of the new marking system was clearly revealed and, speaking for myself, I found the business of marking a German target no worse than marking anywhere else. The enemy anti-aircraft defences in Germany were almost exclusively of the heavy variety used against higher-flying aircraft. There was not much light flak as this was concentrated in France and the Low Countries. Consequently, when the Mosquitos of 627 circled Brunswick on 22 April, there was not much opposition from the ground. The aiming point was a large car park and we plonked our four spot fires into it with the greatest of ease. Much has been written about the all-5 Group blows on German targets and so far as

Brunswick and Munich were concerned, considerable damage was done. In the case of Munich, 90 per cent of the bombs fell in the right place, doing more damage in one night than had been achieved by Bomber Command and USAAF in the preceding four years. During the week in which these early low-level-marking efforts against German targets were taking place, Bill and I were suddenly called into the commanding officer's office, so we were desperately trying to figure out what we could have done wrong. When we were ushered into Roy Elliott's presence he got up from his chair, grinned broadly and announced that we had each been awarded the DFC. This was a proud moment for us, particularly since these were the first DFCs awarded to members of 627 Squadron.

After these attacks the group turned exclusively to support the bombing campaign against interdiction targets for Operation *Overlord* and, with D-Day approaching, the offset marking technique became a standard 5 Group practice and proved to be enormously successful. Goodman:

> Success depended on accurate placing of a small number of red spot fires, so it was vital for the Mosquito pilots being able to see their target. To illustrate this point, on 28 May our target was the heavy German gun at Saint-Martin-de-Varreville, Cherbourg, which was just behind what was to be one of the American landing beaches, Utah, on 6 June. These guns were defended by light flak and a barrage of the latter would betray the gun position. However, on this particular night the German commander held his light anti-aircraft in check, causing us problems with identifying the marking point. Although it was a clear night, we found on crossing the coast that the terrain was uniform with a road running

parallel to the sea, while inland there was a patchwork of fields with occasional tree clumps. The gun itself was well camouflaged and we could not find it. We began searching at Zero-minus five minutes but at Zero hour we still hadn't found it, so the main force were instructed to orbit. Finally, one of the marker pilots (Flight Lieutenant R. L. Bartley and Flight Lieutenant J. D. Mitchell in DZ421 AZ:C) noticed a large empty space with tracks leading to it and reasoned that a space like that could not be as blank as it appeared. So the target was marked and the gun destroyed by 100 Lancasters, each carrying armour-piercing bombs; no aircraft was lost on this operation. Though I might add that as I dropped my spot fires on top of the gun, a light-fingered Lancaster crewman above decided to drop his load but the stick fell short and Bill and I heard the crump-crump of bombs coming up behind; we were not amused! This attack merely emphasised just how the best-laid schemes of men 'oft gang agley'...

The 1st June 1944 was the same as any other day at Woodhall Spa and Bill and I walked to the flight office after breakfast. We found that we were on the battle order and went to dispersal and tested G-George. We then strolled to the operations room and were told that the target was going to be marshalling yards at Saumur. We attended the usual detailed target briefing and closely examined the maps and photographs, and at the end of the afternoon we attended the Air Officer Commanding broadcast link-up with the commanding officers of all squadrons participating, and then made ready to go. The operation was a copybook 5 Group attack with no problems. After landing we switched everything off and climbed out as we had done so often before. G-George stood black and silent and the ground crew moved in to ask if all was well; it was a lovely summer night. After debriefing we ate the usual bacon and eggs and went to bed. The following morning we discovered that our tour was over; we had flown together thirty-eight times, including seven trips to Berlin. Soon we would be instructors and our work in 5 Group was recognised by the award of a bar to the DFC to each of us, but Bill and I would never fly together again.

In July 1944 Goodman was posted as pilot instructor at 1655 Mosquito Training Unit, which enabled him to pass on his vast combat experience to new crews. The unit moved to Upper Heyford in December 1944 and was renamed 16 OTU, with Goodman promoted to flight commander and then chief instructor. A Mosquito 'expert', Benny flew over 1,200 hours in the Mosquito and was awarded the AFC for his service in this appointment.

From 1953 to 1975 Goodman carried out several administrative and intelligence roles at various levels with Station Command and the Ministry of Defence. His final appointment was to a group captain organisation at HQ Support Command, Andover. On 10 January 1976, Goodman retired; his fifty-fifth birthday. When asked about his RAF career, he responded:

> Regarding the units on which I served, the most important were the Squadrons – 37 Squadron, Felton, and 99 Squadron, Newmarket, both Wellington Squadrons. 139 and 627 Squadrons, both Mosquito Squadrons. After the war in May 1950 I served for three years at the Central Flying School, Little Rissington, as a Chief Ground Instructor to train Flying Instructors. I was posted to HQ Flying Training Command at Shinfield Park in Reading as a Staff Officer at the Accident Investigation Branch. Between April 1947 and April 1948 I was at the Empire Flying School, Hullavington, as a Testing Officer with the Examining Wing. The task of the Examining Wing

was to check instructional categories at the flying training schools. This involved flying with the instructors concerned, listening to their instructional 'patter', testing their knowledge of sequence and their technical knowledge and finally either confirming their categories or upgrading them – or, horror of horrors, downgrading them or taking them away! The latter only occurred in exceptional circumstances; most instructors improved their categories and a few gained the coveted A1 (exceptional) category after years of hard work. I should add that for many years I 'flew desks' at various Headquarters and at the Ministry of Defence. I am sure you are not in the least interested in having an account from me of the joys of catching the 08.20 from Maidenhead to London each day or of how staff work is carried out in the Royal Air Force. What mattered was the flying; everything was done in support of the flying task.

Goodman remembers some of the characters associated with DZ477: 'Leo Devigne and I were on the same Mosquito conversion course at 1655 Mosquito Training Unit Marham in 1943. I knew Peck, Marshallsay, Boyden, Nelles and of course dear old Chip P.'

A veteran of more than fifty Mosquito missions, Devigne was a colourful character, an extrovert who possessed extraordinary physical strength but was a born flyer with feather-like touch on the controls. Occasionally, 627 Squadron ground crews would present short talks to the aircrews about aircraft issues and changes and found it difficult to get Devigne to understand that a gyro compass did not respond well when the aircraft was slow rolled all the way from the Wainfleet ranges back to Woodhall Spa, which was his favourite method of flying. Devigne would celebrate the return from a successful trip with a victory roll over base but during their attack on gun positions at Walcheren, south of Middelburg, on 30 October 1944, Devigne and his navigator, Frank Boyle, in DZ643 were hit by light flak, which knocked out the port engine. Devigne's physical strength was required to fly the Mosquito back to Woodhall Spa on one engine. The ground crew inspected the damage and concluded that the lightest of manoeuvres could easily haven broken off the wing from near the engine casing. This near miss cured Devigne of further victory rolls. Devigne's physical strength almost got him into trouble during a late-night 'sortie' in the mess kitchen. Another pilot, Dougie Peck, made a witty comment that so annoyed Devigne he picked up a large saucepan and threw it one-handed, nearly taking Peck's head off. It has been said that the person retrieving the pan had to use both hands to pick it up. Devigne went on to fly jets and become a helicopter test pilot.

Goodman flew DZ477 twice, the first time on 2 February 1944 in a short flight to and from Coltishall. The second time was on 18 February on a night flying test, which meant that Goodman and his navigator Bill Hickox would have flown it on ops that night. The trip was scrubbed due to bad weather. The following night they flew their own Mosquito, DZ484 G-George; 'an incomparable aircraft', as he put it to me.

Group Captain 'Benny' Goodman, a superlative airman and true 'Mosquito expert', died on 13 August 2007 aged 86.

Warrant Officer Claude Evered Cook RNZAF

Claude Evered Cook was born in Greymouth, New Zealand, on 24 June 1923. He enlisted in Auckland on 10 January 1940 for the 9th Heavy Regiment of the New Zealand Artillery and was sent to North Head Cook. However, he had a number of disciplinary issues, including on 27 April 1940 when he failed to obey orders and was fined five shillings. Later in September he was fined a further ten shillings for drunkenness and confined to barracks for seven days. Cook was transferred to FCP Devonport on 11 December 1940.

On 10 March 1941 he transferred to the air force at RNZAF Ohakea and following several postings finally embarked as an airman pilot for training in Canada on 17 December 1941 aboard the SS *Mariposa*. On arrival in Canada, Cook was posted to RCAF No. 1 Y Depot and training began at 3 Service Flying Training School Calgary, with further training courses and considerable time in the air. Cook was considered as average in all respects for flying aptitude such as airmanship and landing skills, cockpit drill, instrument flying, night flying and map reading. He did display above-average aptitude for persistence and enterprise, which indicated that he wanted to do things his way. He was, however, described as below average for his sense of responsibility as he was felt to be overconfident and certainly fell some distance short of the credentials required to be a flying instructor.

January 1942 saw Cook flying the Cessna Crane and Avro Anson in further training courses and, although he was considered to be an above average pilot, he finished almost at the bottom of the intake, forty-fourth out of forty-seven. The report concluded that Cook had good air sense but was overconfident, irresponsible and was inclined to be erratic. He was, however, considered to be definitely a fighter-pilot type. Cook was certified to have passed all tests required and was presented with his pilot's badge on 24 April 1942, but with no recommendation for commissioned rank.

Whilst at 4 Bombing and Gunnery School RCAF Fingal, Ontario, a school that trained bomb aimers and air gunners, Cook went absent without leave (AWOL) from 0730hrs to 0530hrs on 2 to 3 July, a total of twenty-one hours thirty minutes, so he was forced to forfeit one day's pay. Matters got worse on 13 August when Cook 'negligently damaged aircraft belonging to His Majesty in that he at approximately 1640hrs caused damage to Avro Anson 8412 by striking the flag pole on top of No. 3 Control Quadrant Tower at No 4 Bombing and Gunnery School, Fingal, with the resulting forced landing additional damage to said aircraft. He neglected to obey station standing orders in that he at approximately 1640hrs flew an aircraft outside the limits of Aylmer flying area contrary to section 35, paragraph 6 of station standing order.' He was court martialled and reduced to the rank of leading aircraftman. He was also sentenced to undergo sixty days' detention. By the end of October he resumed duties as a staff pilot.

It is odd that, given that recent history, Cook was assessed again two months later as being of superior trade proficiency and of good character. The June 1943 6 Service Flying Training School report stated: 'This NCO has been here only a short time but has proven to be an excellent staff pilot and a keen flyer. Has the necessary temperament to make a good flight pilot, thoroughly recommend overseas posting and advancement in rank to Sergeant.' However, within one week another report was generated, which stated: 'While Captain of Harvard FE507 he taxied in such a manner as to cause damage to said aircraft which was assessed as carelessness.'

Cook was granted pre-embarkation leave of ten days before leaving Canada on 16 July for the UK; he arrived six days later. His first posting was 12 PRC and he attended yet more training courses until 17 Advanced Flying Unit at Wrexham in November, where he was described as above average. Moving on from Wrexham, Cook, now a warrant officer pilot, was posted to RAF Kidlington, RAF Feltwell and then 11 Operational Training Unit at Westcott flying the Wellington X. In July 1944, Cook found himself at his final posting, the Mosquito unit 1655 Mosquito Training Unit.

On 25 July 1944 Cook and his navigator, Sergeant William Ashley RAFVR, took Mosquito DZ421 on a night navigation cross-country exercise. In cloudy skies, showers, moderate visibility and a light wind, they were flying at a height of about 25,000ft over Yorkshire when at 0130hrs the aircraft started to break up. Cook claims to have been 'blown' out of the aircraft. He survived but Ashley was killed.

At the time of the accident, the events were obscure and became the subject of Air Investigation Branch enquiry but it was apparent that the wreckage of the aircraft at that height would be spread over a considerable area. The majority of the aircraft came down on land near Woodhouse Farm, Acklam, south-west of Malton. Part of the aircraft impacted at Westow and this could also be the location that the pilot landed. Later, the investigation found that the starboard undercarriage door had suddenly opened, broken off and struck the starboard tail plane, causing a loss of control. The pilot was able to escape from the aircraft as it broke up and managed to deploy his parachute. The crash investigation blamed poor maintenance of the cables that operated the undercarriage doors as being the contributing factor for the accident. DZ421 had suffered damage from two previous incidents with 139 Squadron. The first, on 6 July 1943, saw it suffer hydraulic failure on a raid to Cologne and it was recorded as damaged beyond the repair of the unit's capacity, although it could be repaired on site by another unit or contractor. The second, on 30 January 1944, was flying accident damage on a Berlin diversionary raid on Brunswick. Again, there was a similar repair assessment as the previous occasion, although the Operational Record Book does not describe the problem in detail. The aircraft was transferred to 627 Squadron at Woodall Spa on 21 April 1944 and became the regular aircraft for Flying Officer R.L. Bartley and Flying Officer J.D. Mitchell RCAF. With this crew on 19 May 1944 it failed to release its target markers from its bomb bay over Amiens railway marshalling yards.

Approximately one month later, Claude Cook would be involved in the crash of the 'Hereford Mosquito', DZ477; the following extracts are from the appraisal and considerations of the RAF investigation departments.

A memo was sent by Headquarters No. 8 Pathfinder Force Group to 12 RNZAF Personnel Dispatch & Reception Centre on 26 October 1944. The following edited extracts highlight the main points:

NZ411616 W/O Cook, C.E. – Pilot – A notice has today been issued posting the above named pilot to 12 RNZAF PD &RC, Padgate, Warrington, for interview by the Aircrew re-Selection Board with effect from 24 October 1944. Warrant Officer Cook has been under training at 1655 Mosquito Training Unit and had an unfortunate accident on a night cross country, when the aircraft disintegrated, and his Navigator was killed. On another cross country he became obsessed with the idea that he was flying upside down and eventually abandoned the aircraft which was quite airworthy. Warrant Officer Cook was posted to 1655 Mosquito Training Unit from 11 Operational Training Unit with effect from 8 June 1944 and prior to that had been an instructor in Canada on Harvard aircraft but has had the experience of a full Advanced Flying Unit and Bomber Command Operational Training Unit course in this country. At a Medical Board held at RAF Station Wyton on 28 August 1944, Warrant Officer Cook was categorised A2HBh (daylight), indicating that Cook was fit for only non-operational home flying and recommended for single-seater fighters with the recommendation that he be permitted to retain his flying brevet.

A memo on 3 November 1944 from the re-Selection Board to RNZAF HQ London:

NZ411616 W/O Cook, C.E. – Pilot – was posted to this Unit for Re-Selection from 1655 Mosquito Training Unit, 8 Group after 'bailing out' of a serviceable Mosquito aircraft. It is understood that your Headquarters are fully aware of Cook's story from an interview with him. The writer had a lengthy interview with this Warrant Officer and he apparently had an aircraft disintegrate in mid-air and on landing by parachute was slightly injured. A short time after he returned to flying duties and while on a night cross country bailed out of a perfectly survivable aircraft. The main point of Cook's story which he has related at Headquarters sounds highly fantastic, but it could happen. The main point though is that even if it did happen he lost complete faith in his instruments. In fact, he must have definitely panicked and is liable to repeat this if given an in line posting on to another type of aircraft. In view of this and the fact that he has been in pilot category so long that it is doubtful if he would be suitable in any other aircrew category, it is recommended that he be repatriated for discharge to civilian occupation.

On 30 November 1944 a confidential memorandum from RNZAF Headquarters to Air Department, Wellington, NZ:

NZ411616 W/O Cook, C.E. – Pilot – has been withdrawn from operational training and is being repatriated to New Zealand. Cook had completed over 1,000 hours flying when he arrived in the United Kingdom in the middle of 1943. He was employed for a period of 13 months as a Staff Pilot in Canada. He subsequently completed Advanced Flying Unit and Operational Training Unit in the United Kingdom and was then posted to 1655 Mosquito Training Unit Group in June last. On the 25 July when Cook was carrying out an exercise, the aircraft (a Mosquito) disintegrated at 25,000ft. Cook made a successful parachute landing, although his Navigator was killed. He was in no way to blame and in fact was commended for his calmness. On the 15 August Cook was on another night exercise in a Mosquito when he became obsessed with the idea that he was flying upside down, and decided to abandon the aircraft with his navigator. The aircraft was in perfect condition and the reason suggested by the Unit for Cook's action was that he was 'suffering from a temporary brain storm', which was confirmed by his Navigator. A medical board was then arranged and as a result, Warrant Officer Cook was categorised A2hBh (daylight), with the recommendation for single seater fighters. He was posted to No. 12 Personnel Dispatch & Reception Centre for disposal action. Air Ministry policy these days, mainly on account of the large accumulation of pilots awaiting absorption, does not normally permit giving a pilot a second chance on other aircraft. The President of the New Zealand Re-Selection Board at No. 12 Personnel Dispatch & Reception Centre points out it is apparent that Cook lost complete faith in his instruments, and in fact, must have definitely panicked. It was considered that this was liable to be repeated, even if Cook was given another chance of single engine aircraft. Under the circumstances, the Selection Board recommended that Cook should be repatriated and in that recommendation this Headquarters concurred. He is therefore, embarking in his existing rank and aircrew category, with retention of his badge. You will probably consider it inadvisable to afford this Warrant Officer any further opportunity of flying.

Cook arrived in New Zealand on 18 February 1945 and was posted to RNZAF Reserve Class C but was demobilised on 3 June 1945 with the classification 'unlikely to be recalled for further service'.

Claude Evered Cook passed away on 30 August 2009 aged 86.

Chapter 21

Why Did DZ477 'Come Down at Night'?

Mosquito Mk IV DZ477 was built at the Hatfield factory in the winter of 1942 as one of 273 B Mk IVs produced. It was fitted with two Rolls-Royce Merlin engines, was 40ft long and had an overall maximum weight of approximately 22,380lb. Its fuel load of 539 gallons produced a still air range of 1,430 miles. The famous Mosquito 139 Squadron took delivery of DZ477 on 11 February 1943 but it would not remain in pristine condition for long as it was nearly written off after being hit by flak 16 March 1943 when it attacked Paderborn engine sheds and workshops. DZ477 was sent to 10 Maintenance Unit on 13 November 1943 and following repair was sent to 139 Squadron on 12 November, then 627 Squadron the following day; it would not fly operationally until 27 January.

No. 627 Squadron Mosquitos were painted in various camouflage schemes based on the standard RAF green and grey. However, this aircraft had irregular camouflage following fuselage repairs and repaints in the field. In the only known photograph of DZ477 AZ:K, it is apparent that an overall black colour scheme was used, although it was not popular with the crews as they considered it to be less effective. In this photograph, taken at Woodhall Spa, it is believed that Wing Commander Curry is seen standing in front of DZ477 accompanied by two of the ground crew. The letter 'K' is visible surrounded by fifty-seven bombs and nose art depicting a pair of old-fashioned ladies' bloomers with a bomb dropping from each leg. Under the cartoon is the caption 'They Come Down at Night'.

Why Did DZ477 'Come Down at Night'?

Just before the D-Day invasion of Europe on 6 June 1944, most Allied planes received black and white stripes around the wings and the fear fuselage just before the fin. A supply of dope, paint and brushes was issued to officers, NCOs and airmen in order to get the job done as quickly as possible.

The loss of DZ477 saw the end of a Mosquito that had undertaken nearly seventy operational missions with 139 and 627 Squadrons and had been a reliable and consistently serviceable aircraft despite its battle damage. DZ477 was delivered to 1655 Mosquito Training Unit in late July 1944, almost at the same time as Warrant Officer Cook arrived for training.

'Benny' Goodman was extremely interested in the loss of DZ477 and gave it considerable attention:

> I see from the Mosquito Crash Log that the pilot of DZ477 'fancied aircraft was inverted so rolled aircraft several times before baling out' on 15.8.44. He was not alone taking this action; we lost a number of Mossies in 1944 because their pilots experienced an overwhelming feeling that they were either on their sides or that they were upside down. They promptly mistrusted their instruments and rolled the aircraft (as they thought) right way up. In fact they were the right way up originally and now found themselves upside down, hanging on their straps. Sometimes they sorted themselves out and came back badly shaken; sometimes they bailed out. At 1655 Mosquito Training Unit we called this phenomenon 'Bottom Effect' and we set about finding why it happened. Let me say immediately that I never experienced it myself and it seemed to happen only to a few pilots.
>
> We had several of these 'Bottom Effect' accidents at turning points on cross-country flights. The aircraft concerned

were invariably flying in cloud in bad visibility. The pilot experienced the strange 'upside down' feeling after completing a turn and rolling the aircraft straight and level. Here was the clue. You must remember that the Mosquito concerned would be flying considerably faster than the pilots had flown before, i.e. at about 300mph. The aircraft had very powerful trimming tabs operated by the pilot and they enabled the pilot to trim the Mossie 'hands and feet off'. If the aircraft was properly trimmed and the pilot then applied a bit of rudder, the aircraft would skid slightly. If the skid was maintained this would upset the balance mechanism in the pilot's middle ear and wing-down feeling could develop. By reducing rudder pressure and resuming normal straight and level flight the sensations would cease. The answer to 'Bottom Effect' was to trim the aircraft 'hand and feet off' and not to mishandle the controls. As my first Flight Commander used to say of the Mosquito – 'Treat her like your best girl-friend – gently'.

At 1655 Mosquito Training Unit I flew with several pilots who had experienced 'Bottom Effect' and needed sorting out. I used to demonstrate the effect of skidding the aircraft and showed in particular that it was not necessary to use the rudder when turning, or if it was used, the pressure would be very slight. Pushing and pulling at the controls was 'out'. The secret of flying this superb aircraft was to use the ailerons, elevator and rudder trimmers with great care to ensure that she would fly hands and feet off with the artificial horizon dead level and the Reid Sigrist turn and slip indicator absolutely vertical. Then, if unusual manoeuvres had to be resorted to on operations, the aircraft would return to its normal straight and level attitude when allowed to do so.

To sum up – only a small number of pilots experienced 'Bottom Effect' on Mosquitos but it could be fatal. It was probably confined to those who were a bit 'ham fisted' and needed more experience on type. The answer was to trim the aircraft 'hands and feet off' and then trust the instruments. Any pilots who did not respond to the additional instructions given after an attack of this strange phenomenon were immediately removed from Mosquito flying and would go to Lancasters and Halifaxes.

Benny certainly explains what may have happened to Cook and his navigator as they were conducting high-speed dynamic manoeuvres during their exercise and it is certain that Cook had trimmed DZ477 for 'hands and feet off' flight, as eyewitness Jim Morgan saw the aircraft in flat, level flight as it passed his house. He also saw flames spouting from the Merlin engine exhaust stacks, no doubt caused by poor fuel mixture and boost control leading to the fuel passing through the engine cylinders and in the exhaust system.

Jim Marshallsay added:

The 'Bottom Effect' was more common than Benny Goodman suggests. It often felt that you were flying 'one wing down' when in cloud but when you came out into clear sky you were flying straight and level. The golden rule was 'always believe your instruments'.

Nick [Ranshaw] and I went to attack a powder factory in France at Saint-Médard-en-Jalles. We had to dive below the illuminating parachute flares from the Lancasters to hit the target and as I pulled up after bombing I felt a heavy blow to the control column and we did a roll without meaning to. I levelled out and set out for home then found that our aircraft was extremely heavy. I moved the trim forward but still had to press hard forward to keep the aircraft level. I did not tell Nick because I thought I could manage to get the Mossie home.

He looked at me once and said 'why are you sweating so much?', but I kept quiet and struggled all the way home. When making the approach to landing I added a few more mph for safety and made a fairish touch down. I taxied our aircraft to our dispersal feeling very pleased with myself for behaving so well, Errol Flynn could have done no more. We got out and I went round to the tail plane expecting to see the flare parachute tangled up with the elevators but there was nothing there! I told the rigger about the controls so he gave them a good inspection but again, nothing. It had all been my imagination. These things did happen and Mossies took flak very well and it generally went straight through leaving a neat hole.

Benny also had thoughts about Warrant Officer Cook's first accident:

Regarding the unfortunate pilot, I regret that I did not know him. You see, I arrived at 1655 Mosquito Training Unit in July 1944 and became an instructor in the Dual Flight which was located at Warboys. The bomber flight was located at Wyton, about 3 miles south of Warboys. I should think that Warrant Officer Cook was at Wyton when I got to Warboys. I did not know that he had been blown out of a Mossie before he had a touch of 'Bottom Effect' in DZ447 on 15 August 1944. To me, it seems very likely that the 'explosion' in Cook's first Mosquito accident was a piece of the aircraft tearing off after he had over-controlled it during an attack of 'Bottom Effect'. I cannot believe that he was allowed to continue flying Mosquitos after losing one. Mosquitos were like gold dust to Bomber Command.

Bibliography

Books

Birtles, P., *Mosquito, The illustrated History*, Sutton, 1988.
Bishop, E., *Mosquito*, Airlife, 1988.
Bishop, Edward, *The Wooden Wonder*, Shrewsbury, UK: Airlife Publishing Ltd, 3rd edition 1995.
Bowman, M., *Mosquito: Menacing The Reich*, Pen and Sword, 2008.
Bowman, M., *Mosquitopanik!*, Pen and Sword, 2004.
Bowman, M., *The Reich Intruders*, Pen and Sword, 2005.
Bowman, W., *The Men Who Flew The Mosquito*, PSL, 1995.
Bowyer, C., *Bomber Barons*, Book Club Associates.
Bowyer, C., *Bomber Group at War*, Book Club Associates, 1981.
Bowyer, C., *Mosquito at War*, Ian Allan, 1973.
Bowyer, C., *Mosquito Squadrons of the Royal Air Force*, Ian Allan, 1984.
Bowyer, C., *Pathfinders at War*, Ian Allan, 1977.
Bowyer, M., *The Stirling Bomber*, Faber and Faber, 1980.
Bowyer, M.J.F., *2 Group RAF*, Faber, 1979.
Cheshire, Leonard, *Bomber Pilot*, Hutchinson & Co., 1943.
Chorley, *Royal Air Force Bomber Command Losses of the Second World War 1943*, Midland Publications, 1996.
Chorley, *Royal Air Force Bomber Command Losses of the Second World War 1944*, Midland Publications, 1997.
Chorlton, M., *The RAF Pathfinders*, Countryside Books, 2012.
Copeman, G., *Bomber Squadrons At War*, Sutton, 1997.
Feast, S., *The Pathfinder Companion*, Grub Street, 2012.
Garbett, M. and Goulding, B., *Lancaster at War vol. 1–5*, Ian Allan, 1971–96.
Grehan, J. and Mace, M., *Bomber Harris – Despatch on War Operations 1942–1945*, Pen and Sword, 2014.

Halfpenny, B., *Action Stations 2. Military airfields of Lincolnshire and the East Midlands*, PSL, 1981.
Halley, J. J., *The Squadrons of the Royal Air Force*, Air Britain, 1980.
Holmes, H., *Lancaster, The Definitive Record*, Airlife, 1996.
Howe, S., *The De Havilland Mosquito, An Illustrated History*, Aston, 2006.
Iredale, W., *The Pathfinders*, W.H. Allen, 2021.
Jones, R. V., *Most Secret War*, Penguin, 1978.
Lawrence, W. J., *No. 5 Group RAF*, Portway, 1951.
Maschmann, Melita *Account Rendered*, 1954.
Mason, F., *The Avro Lancaster*, Aston, 1989.
Mason, F., *The British Bomber*, Putnam, 1994.
McKee, A., *The Mosquito Log*, Souvenir Press, 1988.
Merrick, K., *The Handley Page Halifax*, Aston, 1990.
Middlebrook, M., and Everitt, C., *The Bomber Command War Diaries*, Viking, 1987.
Middlebrook, M., *The Battle of Hamburg*, Penguin, 1988.
Middlebrook, M., *The Berlin Raids*, Penguin, 1990.
Middlebrook, M., *The Nuremberg Raid*, Penguin, 1986.
Moyes, P., *Bomber Squadrons of the RAF and their Aircraft*, MacDonald, 1965.
Otter, P., *Lincolnshire Airfields in The Second World War*, Countryside Books, 1996.
RAF Museum, *The Mosquito Manual*, Aston, 1997.
Sarkar, D., *Battle of Britain – The Gathering Storm*, Pen and Sword, 2034.
Sarkar, D., *Spitfire Squadron*, Air Research Publications, 1990.
Scott, S. R., *Mosquito Thunder, 105 Squadron at War*, Sutton, 1999.
Scutts, Jerry, *Mosquito in Action, Part 1*. Squadron/Signal Publications Inc., 1993.
Scutts, Jerry, *Mosquito in Action, Part 2*. Squadron/Signal Publications Inc., 1993.
Sharp, C. and Bowyer, M., *Mosquito*, Crecy, 1995.
Simons, G., *Mosquito, The Original Multi-Role Combat Aircraft*, Pen and Sword, 2011.
Simpson, A., *'Ops' Victory at All Costs*, Tattered Flag, 2012.
Smith, D., *The De Havilland Mosquito Crash Log*, Midland Counties, 1980.
Smith, G., *Cambridgeshire Airfields in The Second World War*, Countryside Books, 1997.

Smith, G., *Norfolk Airfields in The Second World War*, Countryside Books, 1994.
Thirsk, I., *The De Havilland Mosquito, An Illustrated History Volume 2*, Crecy, 2008.
Ward, C. and Smith, S., *3 Group Bomber Command. An Operational Record*, Pen and Sword, 2008.
Ward, C., *5 Group Bomber Command an Operational Record*, Pen and Sword, 2007.
Webb, A., *At First Sight*, Webb, St Albans, UK, 1991.
Williams, G., *Flying Through Fire – FIDO, The Fogbuster of World War Two*, 1995.
Woldridge, *Low Attack*, Crecy, 1993.
At Second Sight – 627 Squadron in Retirement Pt 1 and 2, private publication.

The National Archive

AIR 14/2719 – 1655 Mosquito Training Unit
AIR 29/613/2 – Mosquito Conversion Unit
AIR27/852 – 109 Squadron Operational Record Book
AIR27/960 – 139 Squadron Operational Record Book
AIR27/2128 – 617 Squadron Operational Record Book
AIR27/2148 – 627 Squadron Operational Record Book

Web Sources

https://asn.flightsafety.org
www.peoplesmosquito.org.uk
www.rafupwood.co.uk
www.awm.gov.au
www.raf-pathfinders.com
www.wingcotomjefferson.wordpress.com/1655-mtu-raf-warboys
www.aircrewremembered.com/AlliedLossesIncidents
www.rafcommands.com/database
www.nationalarchives.gov.uk
www.raf.mod.uk/what-we-do/our-history/air-historical-branch
www.groupcaptaingoodman.org.uk
www.internationalbcc.co.uk
www.nzdf.mil.nz/nzdf/medal-and-service-records
www.thegazette.co.uk

Index

1 Group, 8, 152, 156, 164, 166, 168, 175, 214
2 Group, 8, 86
3 Group, 8, 12, 28, 76, 214
4 Group, 8, 28, 34, 225
5 Group, 8, 31, 38, 89–90, 142–3, 147–8, 150, 152, 156, 164–6, 168–9, 180, 192, 214, 232, 238, 248–51
6 Group, 9, 28
7 Group, 9
8 Group, 9, 31, 35, 42–3, 45–6, 74, 90–1, 108, 147–8, 150, 214, 241–2, 257

7 Squadron, 40, 46, 87, 135, 248
10 Squadron, 35
12 Squadron, 212
17 Squadron, 86
19 Squadron, 189, 207
34 Squadron, 73
35 Squadron, 24, 108
37 Squadron, 204–205, 216, 239, 251
38 Squadron, 76
49 Squadron, 169

50 Squadron, 173
51 Squadron, 76, 225
57 Squadron, 50, 228
62 Squadron, 74
72 Squadron, 207
75 Squadron, 88, 228
77 Squadron, 34
83 Squadron, 31, 46, 88–9, 101, 150, 152, 157, 161, 163–6, 179, 190, 211, 214
97 Squadron, 31, 46, 101, 146, 150, 152, 161, 165–6
99 Squadron, 239, 251
102 Squadron, 209
105 Squadron, 41, 43, 53, 74, 77, 80, 82–4, 201–203, 219, 242
106 Squadron, 157, 190, 194, 230
107 Squadron, 73
109 Squadron, 41, 57, 74, 77, 182, 241–2, 244
112 Squadron, 149
115 Squadron, 76
139 Squadron, 31, 43–4, 53, 73–5, 77, 79–80, 82–3, 88, 91, 138, 200–205, 207, 209, 214, 218, 220, 229, 234, 244–5, 251, 256, 260–1

Index 269

156 Squadron, 46
189 Squadron, 226
207 Squadron, 196
218 Squadron, 86
460 Squadron, 209–12
463 Squadron, 211, 236
467 Squadron, 196, 211
571 Squadron, 215
576 Squadron, 175
578 Squadron, 137
216 Squadron, 232
617 Squadron, 22, 31–2, 38, 45,
    60–1, 78, 143, 145–7, 149–50,
    153–4, 164, 178, 191, 193, 220
618 Squadron, 202–203
619 Squadron, 146, 231
627 Squadron, 3–4, 31, 46, 55, 75,
    85–6, 88–105, 107, 109–15, 117–24,
    126, 128, 130, 132, 135, 137–41,
    144–5, 147–51, 156–7, 159–60,
    162, 164, 167, 174, 176, 179–83,
    185–6, 190, 192, 196–7, 200–202,
    204–205, 208–210, 213–16, 218–19,
    220, 223, 225–8, 231, 235–6, 240,
    245, 247–9, 251–2, 256, 260–1
630 Squadron, 194
692 Squadron, 117
630 Squadron, 50

1655 Mosquito Training Unit, 1,
    54, 74, 198–200, 203, 205, 207,
    210, 213, 216, 218, 222–6, 234,
    241–2, 247, 251–2, 255, 257–8,
    261–2, 264

1939 Air Training Agreement, 47

Acworth, Flying Officer D. H., 186
Amond, Sergeant K.A., 82
Australia, 47–8, 206, 209, 211–12

Bagguley, Squadron Leader R. B.,
    79–80, 83, 201–202
Baldwin, Air Vice Marshal
    'Jack', 12
Ball, Pilot Officer G. E., 170
Barbarossa, Operation, 18
Bartley, Flying Officer R. L., 117,
    154, 185, 197, 250, 256
Barton, Flying Officer Cyril J., 137
Beaverbrook, Lord, 52, 73
Bennett, Air Vice Marshal
    Donald, 34–38, 42–6, 88–90,
    134, 142, 169
Berggen, Wing Commander, 84
Berlin, 14, 16–18, 22, 26–30, 35,
    38, 43–4, 46, 53–4, 60, 66–8, 71,
    74–5, 77, 89–91, 100, 106–16,
    119–21, 128, 130–1, 134, 136,
    141–2, 204, 210, 213, 215, 218,
    220, 228, 231, 235, 245–7, 251,
    256
Bomber Command, 8–9, 11,
    13–23, 26–8, 30–1, 33, 35, 37,
    46–7, 51, 56, 59, 70, 76–7, 87–89,
    91–2, 95, 108, 116, 124, 132, 137,
    146–7, 157, 169, 175, 177, 179,
    186, 188, 201, 212, 220, 233, 239,
    241, 245, 249, 257, 264

Boyden, Warrant Officer R. G., 124, 224–5, 252
Boyden, Wing Commander R. J., 142
Boyle, Flying Officer F. W., 111, 165, 186, 195, 197, 208, 252
British Overseas Airways Corporation, 52
Brown, Flying Officer J. H., 81
Budden, Flight Sergeant F. A., 82
Bufton, Group Captain S., 39
Bulpitt, Flying Officer A. N., 82
Burma, 74

Cambridge, 86, 221, 226, 238, 245
Canada, 34, 47–8, 204, 209, 214, 224–5, 254–5, 257–8
Chastise, Operation, 22
Cheshire, Wing Commander Leonard, 31, 45, 90, 142, 146–51, 153–4, 164–7, 169, 178, 191–3, 206
Churcher, Squadron Leader R. G., 197, 230–3
Clear, Flying Officer O. 'Pops', 80
Cochrane, Air Vice Marshal Ralph, 31, 38, 45–6, 147, 154, 169
Cologne, 15–16, 57–8, 77, 91, 124, 204–205, 215, 230, 235, 240, 244, 256
Coltishall, 112, 117, 253
Cook, Warrant Officer Claud Evered, 1, 253–9, 261, 263–4

Credenhill, 1
Cummings, Sergeant G., 79, 84
Curry, Wing Commander George, 90, 187–9, 194–6, 205–206, 228–30, 260
Czechoslovakia, 22, 47

Daly, Flying Officer J. F., 119, 176, 183–4, 197, 216–17
Darling, Squadron Leader D., 53
Davies, Flying Officer R. F., 109, 181, 197
Davies Flying Officer E. F., 120
De Boos, Squadron Leader Bill, 3, 110, 187–8, 190, 194–5, 204–206, 221
de Havilland, Geoffrey Jr, 2, 52–3, 74, 76, 224
Dean, Flying Officer G. E., 81
Denholm, Flight Sergeant A., 112–13, 164
Denmark, 40, 69, 93, 108, 114, 129
Denny, Flying Officer P. F., 112–13, 214
Der-Stepanian, Sergeant J., 81
Devigne, Flying Officer L. C. E., 181, 192, 220, 252–3
Düsseldorf, 16, 65, 117, 122–3, 235

East Kirkby, 50, 194
Eastbourne, 34
Elementary Air Navigation School, 34
Ellamy, Operation, 78

Elliott, Wing Commander Roy, 88–90, 110, 147, 156, 162, 205, 247, 249
Embury. Flying Officer, 83
Evans, Flying Officer, 190, 202, 226

Fawke, Flying Officer, 150–1, 153–4, 165–6
Fenwick, Flight Sergeant R. W., 124, 142, 181, 224
Flensburg, 40
Fletcher, Sergeant R., 82–3, 202
Ford, Sergeant J. A., 175
Foxcroft, Flying Officer P. S., 186
France, 8, 14, 16, 25, 30, 32–3, 45, 47, 69, 73, 79, 81, 86, 123, 144, 156, 160–1, 180, 189, 202, 209–11, 213, 223, 231, 235, 239, 248, 263
Frankfurt, 15, 40, 71, 87, 93, 112, 114, 120, 122, 124–128, 134, 173, 190, 225–7, 235

Gale, Flying Officer K. W., 109, 117, 138, 174, 179, 182, 189, 206–209, 220, 247
Garton, Doug, 4, 91
Gaunt, Flight Sergeant W. S., 198
Gestapo, 77, 131, 175, 216, 219
Gibson, Guy, 3–4, 149, 221, 230–2
Gilbert, Flying Officer G. H., 80, 203
Gleed, Sergeant M., 84

Goebbels, Joseph, 26, 44–5, 53, 111
Gomorrah, Operation, 23
Goodman, Flying Officer J. R. Benny, 3, 55, 90–1, 112, 133, 154–5, 160, 167, 184, 201, 219, 222, 230, 238–9, 241–4, 247–9, 251–3, 261, 263
Göring, Hermann, 26, 53–4
Granby, Operation, 78
Gray, Flying Officer N. B., 165
Grey, Flying Officer J. G., 111, 186, 195–7, 208–209
Gribbin, Flying Officer M. D., 118, 165, 197–8
Griffiths, Flying Officer, 118, 138, 165, 197–8

Hamburg, 18, 22–27, 29, 60, 66, 70, 93, 121, 137–8, 174, 218, 231, 234
Hanlon, Flying Officer I. H., 139, 141, 181, 189–90, 195, 202, 225–7, 236
Harris, Sir Arthur, 11–12, 15, 17–19, 21, 26, 28–31, 35–40, 43–6, 71, 76, 92–3, 128, 134
Hartley, Sergeant John, 1
Hayden, Flight Lieutenant K., 79
Heath, Flying Officer G. E., 111, 142, 164, 180, 210–13, 220, 223
Herbert, Flying Officer P. N. G., 194, 242

Hewson, Wing Officer J. F., 165, 176
Hickox, Flying Officer S. T. L., 90–1, 112
High Wycombe, 11, 92
Hindshaw, Flying Officer A., 119, 176–7, 184
Hitler, Adolf, 14, 25–6, 30–1, 44, 66–7, 74, 131
Hogg, Flying Officer T. L., 152, 176
Holland, 84, 106, 108, 223
Horsman, Bill, 49
Howden, Flying Officer A. M., 138
Hughes, Flying Officer John, 109, 112

Jackson, Sergeant Norman, 157–9
Johnson, Flight Sergeant N. H., 158

Kemp, Sergeant B. C., 79, 84
Kimmel, Flying Officer S. G., 82
Kirkland, Flying Officer H. N., 82

Langley, airfield, 38
Leeming, RAF, 34, 87
Lewis, Flying Officer N., 181, 192, 220
Longfield, Wing Commander G. P., 82
Ludlow-Hewitt, Sir Edgar, 11

Mackenzie, Squadron Leader N. W., 122, 164, 194
Madley, RAF, 1
Mallender, Flying Officer P. F., 198
Marham, RAF, 76–8, 217, 224, 241, 244, 252
Marshallsay, Flight Sergeant Jim, 3, 90, 113, 118, 120, 123–4, 128, 131–2, 135, 176, 192, 217–18, 221–222, 251–2, 263
Maschmann, Melita, 71–2
Massey, Sergeant J., 82–3, 85, 202
Matta, Sergeant E. G., 80
McCarthy, Squadron Leader J. C., 193
McDonald, Flying Officer, 182
McGeehan, Flight Sergeant P. J. D., 85
McGhie, Wing Commander I. J., 146
McPherson, Flying Officer Andrew, 73
Meurer, Manfred, 44
Mifflin, Flying Officer M., 157–8
Millns, Flying Officer R. F., 82
Mitchell, Flying Officer J. D., 117, 154, 185, 250, 256
Mitchell, Flying Officer J. R., 183
Moe, Lieutenant T. D. D. C., 83
Morris, Sergeant F., 82
Morris, Flying Officer R. C., 85
Munroe, Squadron Leader K. L., 193

Narborough, RAF, 76
Nelles, Squadron Leader E. F.
    'Rocky', 106–107, 110, 113–14,
    117, 119, 126, 128, 134, 139, 141,
    152, 155–6, 159–60, 175, 180–8,
    190, 193, 203–204, 252
New Zealand, 42, 47, 209, 225,
    227, 233, 236, 253, 258–9
Norfolk, 76, 83, 95, 215, 241
Northrop, Wing Commander, 118,
    163
Norway, 74, 77, 134, 159, 216
Nuremburg, 64, 134–5

Oakington, RAF, 75, 86–8, 90,
    106, 133, 135, 202, 205, 218–19,
    235, 245, 248
Oslo, 77, 159, 211, 216, 219, 232
Overlord, Operation, 19, 30, 249

Parlato, Flight Sergeant S., 90,
    142, 157, 185, 201, 220–1, 227,
    233–8
Pas-de-Calais, 31
Pathfinder Force, 9, 16, 19, 21,
    35–7, 39–40, 42–3, 45–6, 74, 76,
    185, 199, 203, 241, 256
Peck, Flying Officer D. W., 109,
    120, 181, 197, 220, 252–3
Peirse, Air Marshal Sir
    Richard E. C., 11–12
Pereira, Flying Officer C. V.,
    80, 83, 203

Platts, Pilot Officer J. G., 121–2,
    157, 211, 222–3
Ploughman, Operation, 74
Pointblank, Operation, 19
Poland, 13, 47, 231
Portal, Air Marshal Sir Charles,
    11, 18, 20
Pounder, Flying Officer G., 81

Rae, Sergeant G. A., 170
RAF Volunteer Reserve, 34
Ralston, Wing Commander J. R.
    G. 'Roy', 200
Ranshaw, Sergeant N. F., 90,
    113, 118, 120, 123–4, 128, 131,
    133, 135, 154–5, 192, 217–18,
    263
Rennie, Flying Officer
    W. E., 79
Rice, Air Vice-Marshal, 168
Richards, Flying Officer A. E.,
    106–107, 110, 113–14, 117, 119,
    126, 128, 134, 139, 141, 152,
    155–6, 159–60, 175, 181–2, 185,
    187–8
Ridgewell, 82
Royal Australian Air Force, 34, 47,
    204, 209, 212
Royal Canadian Air Force, 9, 47
Royal New Zealand Air Force, 47
Rutherford, Flying Officer N. B.,
    121–2, 137–8, 140–1, 143, 150,
    164, 196, 205, 220, 223, 231

Saint-Smith, Flying Officer J. A., 111, 142, 164, 180, 209–13, 220, 223
Sarkar, Dilip, 207
Saundby, Air Marshal Robert 'Sandy', 93
Schreiber, Alfred, 44
Sculthorpe, RAF, 78
Second World War, 6, 8, 13, 22, 61, 175, 228
Shader, Operation, 78
Shand, Wing Commander Peter, 74, 79, 83
Shannon, Squadron Leader D. J., 165, 193
Sharp, Air Commodore Bobby, 148, 155, 163, 196, 222
Simpson, Wing Commander John, 204
Sleeman, Sergeant G. J., 80
Smedsaas, Second Lieutenant O., 83
South Africa, 48
South Rhodesia, 48
Sparks, Squadron Leader Neville, 164, 166–7
Stanbury, Warrant Officer F. H., 121–2, 137–8, 140–1, 150, 164, 186, 196, 205, 220, 223–4
Steere, Flying Officer H., 109, 117, 138, 174, 179, 182, 189, 206–209, 247
Swinderby, RAF, 50

Sutherland, Flying Officer W., 81, 186

Talbot, Flying Officer W., 81
Taxable, Operation, 32, 60
Thomas, Sergeant D. D., 90, 142, 157, 184, 192, 221, 234–5
Thompson, Flying Officer C. G., 121–2, 157, 211, 222
Tice, Flying Officer K. G., 193, 195
Tirpitz, 35
Tizard, Sir Henry, 39
Topper, Flying Officer W. W., 196, 198
Turner, Pilot Officer P. K., 165, 176

United Kingdom, 14, 47, 258
United States of America (USA), 48, 233
Unwin, George 'Grumpy', 207
Upper Heyford, RAF, 199, 251
Upton, Flight Sergeant J., 139, 142, 189–90
Upwood, RAF, 74, 143, 199, 234

Vienna, 66

Warboys, RAF, 1, 198–200, 264
Wayman, Flying Officer Mike, 80, 202

Wenger, Second Lieutenant
H., 84
Whitford, Flying Officer A., 179
Willis, Pilot Officer J. H., 197
Wilmott, Pilot Officer, 109
Winthorpe, RAF, 49–50
Wittering, RAF, 75
Woodhall Spa, RAF, 142–3,
145–6, 148–9, 180, 190, 192,
204–205, 220, 223, 231, 250,
252–3, 260
Woodhouse, Flying Officer
R., 152
Wyton, RAF, 73–4, 77, 155, 199,
214, 244, 257, 264

Yarema, Pilot Officer P., 115,
214–16